Community Control
and
the Urban School

—

Community Control
and
the Urban School

Mario Fantini
Marilyn Gittell
Richard Magat

Introduction by
KENNETH B. CLARK

PRAEGER PUBLISHERS
New York · Washington · London

PRAEGER PUBLISHERS
111 Fourth Avenue, New York, N.Y. 10003, U.S.A.
5, Cromwell Place, London S.W.7, England

Published in the United States of America in 1970
by Praeger Publishers, Inc.

Library of Congress Catalog Card Number: 69–12706

Printed in the United States of America

To

Steffan, Todd, Brianne, and Marc
Amy and Ross
Claudia and Gordon
. . . and to your children

Contents

Introduction

by Kenneth B. Clark

Community Control and the Urban School presents a knowledgeable and highly useful account of the turbulent currents in the world of urban education. For those confused by the enormous complexities of many of the recent controversies in public education—the New York City teachers' strike, the New York demonstration districts, compensatory education, the Coleman Report, testing, alternative school systems, "black identity," and so on—this book will help identify the central issues and the priorities.

The three authors—Mario Fantini, Marilyn Gittell, and Richard Magat—have the dual advantage of participant and observer experience. Each has been deeply involved in the struggle for change in the schools; each has the capacity to view this involvement with the rigorous perspective of skilled observation. They have combined the skills of observer and scholar with a social sensitivity and commitment to produce the type of rational change essential for increased effectiveness of the public schools.

The general theme that permeates the book is one of growing importance and it deserves thoughtful exploration.

Community control of schools is a given in many of the towns, smaller cities, and suburbs of the nation. If an epidemic of low academic achievement swept over these schools, drastic measures would be imposed. Administrators and school boards would topple, and teachers would be trained or dismissed. If students were regularly demeaned and dehumanized in those schools, cries of outrage in the PTA's would be heard—and listened to—and action to remove the offending personnel would be taken immediately. Accountability is so implicit a given that the term "community control" never is used by those who have it. "Community control," as this book makes clear, is to be understood rather as a demand for school accountability by parents to whom the schools have never accounted, particularly those parents of low-status groups in Northern cities. It is a demand that their children be respected as human beings with the potential all normal children have and that they be taught by those hired for the purpose of teaching. It is a demand that the schools cease finding scapegoats and stop making excuses for their failure by claiming that these children are uneducable or too "disruptive" or too "culturally deprived" to respond. It is a desperate response to the subtle and flagrant racism that afflicts so many of the institutions of American education.

Most of those individuals in the minority communities who are now fighting for community control have been consistent fighters for integration. Their support for decentralization is not, therefore, to be seen as a desire for separatism or a rejection of integration, but, as the authors show, it is a strategy of despair, a strategy determined by the broken promises of the white community. Negroes have watched white families move to the suburbs or bus their children to private or parochial schools to escape desegregated public schools. They have watched as new schools were constructed in segregated neighborhoods and as district boundaries were gerrymandered to perpetuate the racial *status quo*. The demand for community control is initially their attempt to protect their children in the schools they are required to attend. The authors point out that it can also serve as an avenue to new educational purpose and effectiveness, for *all* children.

It can, that is, if the concept is not corrupted. One cannot assume that the strategy of community control will be successful. It may be used and exploited by those who are concerned only with personal profit and power. It may be manipulated by established institutions of power in the larger communities for their own ends. It may further isolate the poor and the minority groups from the majority society and bring the customary consequences of racial and class isolation—eroded facilities, inadequate teaching and administrative staffs, and minimum resources. Isolation does not bequeath power to the powerless; as the South learned over generations, there is no such thing as "separate and equal" when the separation is a function and a manifestation of inferior status. As most of the community action projects of the antipoverty program demonstrated, unfamiliarity with power and status, lack of experience with organizational skills, and apathy, disunity, and cynicism associated with long repression often characterize the communities of the poor, weakening their capacity to compete effectively with reinforced power and rendering the community vulnerable to those who would exploit it for their own ends.

Community control, therefore, requires a commitment of the city as a whole, genuine delegation of power, and continued efforts to relate the community to the larger society. Perhaps paradoxically, the lower-status community will never have genuine power until its isolation is ended.

This book is, ultimately, about quality education. As the authors clearly acknowledge, they have a point of view favoring community control, but their examination is sober as well as informed. They do not advance community control as a panacea, nor do they blink the hazards to which this, as any bold concept, is subject. I join them in hoping the book will touch off a serious dialogue on the role of community control, along with other developments, in providing essential and humane education to children who are now being denied it.

Preface

The concept of community control of urban education was given almost no serious consideration until the late 1960's. Its translation into the real world of the public schools has barely begun. Yet, community control is already triggering an astonishing volume of comment, not only in the professional literature of education but in the mass media and in books for the general public as well.

The popular interest in the subject arises, in part, from the high drama that marked the opening struggle for community control in urban education: the longest school strike in the nation's history; the white and black racial animus that muffled the issues and generated a high potential for violence, though none appeared; and the near collapse of the political career of one of the nation's most popular mayors.

That all these events occurred in New York City, a center of the mass media, is, we believe, another reason for the unusual literary outpouring on the subject. The community-control issue offered a drama tantalizing to the literary imagination—pent-up anger and fear straining toward catharsis. The drama even had opposing protagonists who lent themselves to typecasting as hero or villain: teachers' union president Albert Shanker and black school administrator Rhody McCoy.

The brew was stirred further by ideological crosscurrents, of which at least two were especially close to the hearts of many articulate journalists and intellectual critics in New York: the labor movement, which was still honored in nostalgia, even if it was now, on occasion, business-oriented and conservative, and the civil rights movement, whose bitter struggles and glorious victories of the early 1960's were being dimmed by factionalism and by the intractability of bedrock problems like poverty, housing, and a cumulative heritage of deprivation.

While these circumstances account for much of the literary and mass-media attention given the issue, other factors underlie the extensive professional discussion. One is the intrinsic importance of the issue; partisans and detractors of community control alike recognize that it has raised fundamental questions. Another, quite simply, is the continuing failure of urban schools to provide most of their students with an adequate education.

Also, as we recount in detail, the issue arose at a critical juncture. The bloom was beginning to fade from the rose of compensatory education (the promise of integration had already been tarnished in the nation's large cities as well as in the South). A reaction against powerlessness and voicelessness in a complex, increasingly bureaucratic society was beginning to stir. To say that the issue of community control of the public schools stands at the center of these forces would exaggerate the case. But the issue was nourished by these other developments and, in turn, fed them.

For professional educators, in particular, it was a time of melancholy reappraisal. A painstakingly constructed theory of the relation between integration and quality education, sanctified by the Supreme Court, had collided with the reality of white resistance. Then, a developing theory of educational disadvantage won tangible recognition in unprecedented public expenditures aimed at compensating for "cultural and environmental deprivation," but this effort proved disappointing. Enthusiasm for a gleaming array of curricular and methodological innovations was dulled by overselling, inadequate replication, or both. Some authorities despaired altogether, concluding that educational improvement for the "disadvantaged" could come only through the success of broader efforts, ranging from economic and social innovation to better housing and slum clearance.

With the slate of hopes, misconceptions, and self-deceptions wiped cleaner than it had been for a long time, the issue of school governance, posed not merely from a theoretical perch but from the most disadvantaged rung of society—from the victims of miseducation themselves—was bound to excite interest and debate.

Yet, for all the popular and professional attention, this issue has been only slightly elucidated in terms of its modern urban context, of the political dimensions involved, and of the redefinition of educational quality that is emerging as the school environment is being examined more critically than before for its effect on human development. Books have already been published on the New York City school confrontation *per se,* but they tend to subordinate the issues to personalities and tactics. Scholarly papers on community control of urban education generally deal with the *community school* (which, as we shall note, is not synonymous with community control of the schools) and with participation in theory rather than in relation to its educational consequences, both curricular and institutional.

Our study seeks to trace the development of the theory of community participation, to describe and analyze its first major test, and to examine subsequent developments and their implications.

                    *   *   *

Positions on community control, as on most highly controversial issues, have tended to polarize, and much of the debate has descended into mere rhetoric and polemic. Therefore, we think it is necessary to indicate where we stand and how we got there. Our aim is to illuminate the subject, but we make no pretense to a detached neutrality. We believe in the principle of community control of urban education. This is not to say that the concept is a quick path to an educational millennium, or that every one of its partisans has been a model citizen or leader, or that it can be uniformly applied in every urban setting at any time. But we do not hold with the detractors who dismiss community control as a passing echo of black power or as a romantic participatory-democracy panacea for a problem-ridden educational process. Nor is it our purpose, though we understand them, to confront the cosmic analysts who charge proponents of community control with having overlooked (or, worse, suppressed) "other factors"—the home, the environment, racial history, exquisitely detailed data on *schools as they have been,* and, now, even genetics. The subject of this book is the governance of urban schools—the people in charge, the need to engage others in decision-making, and the forgotten participants, the children.

We do not believe that partisans are incapable of accuracy and fairness, and we have striven for both. We appreciate shades of meaning and, yet, are aware that, in discussions on this subject, nuances, quite as much as oversimplifications, tend to becloud essentials.

Because this is an early work on the subject, the reader will not find elaborate evidence for all that has been claimed. Evidence—in the sense of extensive experience in many cities, mountains of test scores, and armies of demonstrably transformed students—simply does not exist. Even much of the most encouraging support is anecdotal and subjective rather than statistical, although it accords with the clinical judgment of the two authors who are academic professionals.

The compulsion to consider the most powerful ideas tentative until "solid" evidence can be marshaled dies hard, and, although there is now more substance to the concept than there was two or three years ago, we do not expect the limited experience gained thus far to convince the deeply skeptical, much less the hostile.

New Yorkers do not need to go out of their city to find precedents for community control. In the book, we refer to Principal Leonard Covello's concept for Benjamin Franklin High School in

East Harlem, when that neighborhood was composed mainly of Italian-Americans. This experiment foundered, as did the Bronx Park Community Project in the late 1930's and early 1940's. A variety of reasons has been given for this, but we suspect that, as with many ideas, there is a right time for the idea of community control of urban public schools and that the time was not then. We believe that now is.

*   *   *

As for the multiple authorship: The community-control issue brought us together. Two of the authors—Fantini and Magat—had worked for the same institution, in the same building, for nearly three years, without much more than a nodding acquaintance. The third—Gittell—had not met the other two until 1967. She was already well known for having advanced the principle of decentralization of the New York City schools, along with community participation, in a report she prepared for Mayor Wagner's commission on finances. We became colleagues and friends. All of us served as advisers or staff members of the Mayor's (Lindsay) Advisory Panel on Decentralization of the New York City Schools.

Let it be noted that, though the three of us became acquainted at the Ford Foundation, the interpretations and viewpoints in this book are our own and should, in no sense, be construed as those of the Ford Foundation. This point needs quite special emphasis because the foundation played a role in the first phase of the events that brought decentralization and community control to prominence. Our judgment is that, in this role, the foundation was responsible, in the best tradition of modern philanthropy; that it was bold, in facing the urban-education crisis in contemporary terms; and that, though not faultless (as no one involved in the concept's unfolding was), it hardly deserved to be used as a scapegoat. In the preparation of this book, the relation between the foundation and the two authors who are members of its staff has been at arm's length and consistent with the principles of intellectual freedom. The foundation has made no contribution to the work; the two of us who are on its staff carried out our regular foundation duties and worked on the book in our spare time. We note this ruefully (though not regretfully), for had we had the luxury of leaves of absence or relaxation of regular work loads, the book would have appeared far sooner.

*   *   *

We hope this book will serve as one thread in the transition to the next phase of the concept. We hope that parents, teachers, decision-makers at the city and state levels, and urban citizens generally will examine it in the context of their own schools and communities.

We are especially anxious that teachers and school administrators appraise its implications. The notion of partnership in public education is viable. Community control does not imply, as some fear, an ever present horde of parents and other neighborhood residents serving as watchdogs in every school. Community control is, above all, a democratic concept, and education in a democracy cannot proceed in a climate of surveillance of one hostile group over another. The present mood, in most urban systems, of great hostility between the public schools and the community has been building up for years and is symptomatic of more general discontent. One of the goals of community control is to dispel such tension and mistrust. Most parents want nothing more than the assurance that their children's schools are being run by men and women who truly believe in the capacity of *all* children to learn. Ironically, the more accountable the school is to the community, the lower the degree of community control is likely to be. We believe it is the professional's duty to stimulate functional community participation, so that the tragic gulf does not again develop between those who serve professionally and those who are supposed to be served. Community control ought to usher in a new concept of professionalism in education, in which the ideal working environment for the professional is proximity to, and constructive interaction with, the public.

In the same spirit, we look forward to many future studies of community control in urban education, not only by educators, academic observers, and journalists but also by the new partners in public education—parents, community leaders, and students themselves.

In working on a subject that is still lively and in which innumerable men and women have played active roles, it is impossible to acknowledge the special insights generously provided one or another of us by scores of educators, observers, parents, and other citizens. We shall, therefore, confine ourselves here to expressing special appreciation to the following: Mark Geier, for his general research assistance; Ione Harris, Linda Knoepfle, Phyllis Treitler, and Emily Stasi, for the tedious job of typing several manuscript drafts; and Ronald Masters, an education librarian at Queens College, for his good grace and perseverence in sifting through an array of data and sources. We also extend a heartfelt expression of gratitude to Arnold Dolin, our editor, whose patience was matched only by his effective prodding. We attribute both qualities to his experience as an active parent of New York City school children. He is used to hopes deferred; that this book finally emerged at all will, we hope, refresh his belief that even basic reform in urban education is possible.

M. D. F.
M. G.
R. M.

New York City
February, 1970

Community Control
and
the Urban School

1

The Crisis in the Schools

Every new opinion, at its starting, is precisely
in a minority of one.—THOMAS CARLYLE ("He-
roes and Hero-Worship")

It was like a thousand and one meetings that parents in New
York City had held intermittently for more than ten years—meetings that began soon after the 1954 Supreme Court decision
against legalized school segregation. The court's historic decree
reverberated most clamorously, of course, in the South, where
law, as well as custom, separated black and white school children.
But the grim foundation for the Court's decision—a mass of data
on the damaging effect of school segregation on Negro children
—had been assembled by a psychology professor from one of
New York City's municipal colleges, Dr. Kenneth Clark. And in
the long and tangled web of subsequent events, New York City,
nearly fifteen years later, became the scene of a landmark in
American education fully as significant as the Court's decree in
Brown vs. *Topeka*. Events have only begun to unfold in this later
development, which is the movement to improve education by
giving parents a meaningful voice in the process of education—or,
by what has come to be known as "community control" of urban
public schools.

It was not long after the 1954 decision that the veneer of en-
lightenment was stripped away from Northern cities, revealing
systems that segregated their nonwhite school children nearly as

3

effectively as Southern cities did theirs.* The North moved with no more deliberate speed than the South to right the wrong, and New York, center of the nation's liberal thought, hardly moved faster than other cities.

So, that night—it was in 1966—the Harlem Parents Committee, an integration-minded group, was meeting with some representatives from a sympathetic white organization called EQUAL to discuss the latest in a long chain of setbacks in their attempts, going on for several years, to reverse continuing *de facto* segregation in the New York City public schools.

"It was a particularly poignant gathering," recalls one of the parents:

> Isaiah Robinson suggested, almost as a joke, that since white children would not be sent into Harlem schools and black children were not being invited downtown in any meaningful numbers, *maybe the blacks had better accept segregation and run their own schools.* A jolt of recognition stung all of us: Isaiah's joke was a prophecy. It is hard to get across the sudden sadness we all felt. We had worked together for a long time, blacks and whites. We were close, loving friends. Now we had to agree to separate because the society would not recognize our marriage and, one way or another, the black children had to be legitimized.

I.S. 201: The First Turning Point

The movement (some call it a revolution) toward an effective parental role in the public schools cannot be traced to that one meeting, or to Isaiah Robinson, a Negro minister (later to be appointed as the Manhattan representative to an Interim Board of Education established under a 1969 Decentralization Bill), or even to the single school building then at issue, Intermediate School (I.S.) 201, located in Harlem. However, if one chooses to compare the movement to a revolution, I.S. 201 is the Bunker Hill. Of course, I.S. 201 was not planned to become the site and symbol of a new revolution in the history of American education.

---

* Between 1954 and 1959, 145 laws were passed in Southern states to ensure maintenance of segregated schools.

Rather, the initial attention it received had more to do with architecture than with education, and still less with social reform. A $5 million low-lying brick structure, the school won a series of architectural prizes for its innovative design; it is a three-story, air-conditioned, windowless building whose upper two floors rest on a colonnade of concrete pylons. Yet, it was intended to be educationally, as well as structurally, *avant garde*. Plans called for a maximum class size of twenty-four (compared with an average of more than thirty in the city's junior high schools), for advanced studies that crossed grade lines, for such community features as after-school courses in Negro and Puerto Rican history and culture, teenage and adult centers, and recreation activities, and for full-time community-relations specialists to encourage closer parent and citizen involvement in the school program. The handpicked staff of fifty-five included twenty-six black teachers. There were to be two Puerto Rican assistant principals and a black assistant principal. All but three members of the instructional staff were to be experienced teachers. A spokesman for the board of education said I.S. 201 would be "one of the finest schools in the country."

But none of these features could overcome the hard fact that the school's students would all be nonwhite—a danger against which parents in the community had warned throughout the years since the school had been proposed. The school is situated where Puerto Rican East Harlem meets Negro Central Harlem, at 127th and 128th streets, between Madison and Park avenues. The site is, literally, in the shadow of the elevated tracks of the Penn Central Railroad, which daily carries commuters to and from the middle- and upper-income suburbs of Westchester County and Connecticut. When plans for the school were announced in 1958, some Negro groups and parents opposed the site on the ground that another school deep within Harlem would perpetuate *de facto* racially segregated education. To sense the impact on the community of the prospect that I.S. 201 would eventually open as an unintegrated school, one must recall, even briefly, the anguished, prolonged, and largely unsuccessful twelve-year struggle for integration in the New York City public schools.

After the 1954 Supreme Court decision on segregation, the New York City Board of Education had been among the first in the nation to announce a firm commitment to reduce racial imbalance. Only seven months after the Court ruled publicly sanctioned school segregation illegal, the board declared:

> . . . modern psychological knowledge indicates clearly that segregated, radically homogeneous schools damage the personality of minority group children. These schools decrease their motivations and thus impair their ability to learn. White children are also damaged. Public education in a racially homogeneous setting is socially unrealistic and blocks the attainment of the goals of democratic education. Whether this segregation occurs by law or by fact . . . it is now the clearly reiterated policy and program of the Board of Education to devise and put into operation a plan which will prevent the further development of such schools and would integrate the existing ones as quickly as practicable.

It was three years before the board took a tangible step to implement its policy. The step—preparation of a master zoning plan designed, along with teacher transfers and busing of pupils, to promote integration—was fiercely opposed and never carried out. Still, the board was ahead of most of the country merely by virtue of its attempt. It was also a full six years ahead of official policy at the state level. In 1963, the state commissioner of education, in a message to school boards throughout the state, declared:

> . . . the racial imbalance existing in a school in which the enrollment is wholly or predominantly Negro interferes with the achievement of equality of educational opportunity and must therefore be eliminated from the schools of New York State. . . . In keeping with the principle of local control, it is the responsibility of the local school authorities in such communities to develop and implement the necessary plans.

Despite the board of education's acknowledgment of *de facto* segregation in the New York City schools and despite its policy and the state's, all efforts failed—both to correct the situation and to prevent its deterioration. By 1966, the state commissioner concluded: "Nothing undertaken by the New York City Board of Education since 1954, and nothing proposed since 1963, has contributed or will contribute in any meaningful degree to desegregating the public schools of the city."

The board tried various strategies, since attempted in other cities—rezoning of school-attendance districts, voluntary transfers of Negro students in overcrowded schools to underutilized schools in mainly white neighborhoods, and school pairing, in which student bodies in two ethnically different schools are redistributed so that all the children in certain grades attend one school, while the remaining grades go to the other school. Altogether, these plans failed to stem *de facto* segregation; they succumbed either to white opposition or to the relentless polarization of residential housing patterns caused by the flight of whites from integrated neighborhoods and by the spread of the boundaries of nonwhite ghettos. In 1960, 15 per cent (or 118) of New York City's schools had black and Puerto Rican enrollments of over 85 per cent; by 1968, the proportion had risen to 28 per cent.

Another device announced to promote integration, this time through grade reorganization, was the establishment of intermediate schools (grades six through eight). These schools were developed under a new board of education policy, initiated in 1965, that began to shift the schools from the traditional 6-3-3 grade pattern (for the elementary, junior, and senior high schools) in the direction of a 4-4-4 pattern. Since the board's efforts to integrate the early grades had largely failed, it instituted the reorganization in an attempt to concentrate on the upper eight grades, where, it was hoped, mobility as well as opposition from white parents would be lesser problems. The idea was to advance the children from their local elementary (kindergarten through sixth grade) schools one year earlier, into schools that were supposed to draw their students from a wider community and, thus, to achieve and enforce a kind of integration. However, ethnic data suggested that little in the way of integration could be accomplished even under this plan.

Planned before this reorganization policy, I.S. 201 had been intended simply as a mid-Harlem junior high school, built to relieve overcrowding in two adjacent junior high schools. Then school officials, ostensibly in the interest of integration, decided to make the new school an intermediate school. But, at the same time, they refused to change the site to a borderline area between white and Negro neighborhoods, thus virtually assuring that it would be as segregated as any ghetto school could be and contradicting the stated purpose of the intermediate-school device.

When the board of education persisted in its selection of the I.S. 201 site, parents and community organizations in Harlem demanded that the board transport white pupils in from other neighborhoods to integrate the school. Early in 1966, Mayor John Lindsay, Superintendent of Schools Bernard Donovan, and several other officials attended a meeting to listen to the complaints of the community. They were told that, if the board of education did not live up to its promise of integration, I.S. 201 would be closed down in the fall. One version has it that Lindsay and Donovan expressed concern and let it be known that the community had made an impression on them. But, according to Preston R. Wilcox, a black educator then at Columbia University's Teachers College and a confidant of some Harlem parent groups, "The Mayor, in measured and somewhat professorial tones, gave them a lecture on the tax base of the city, and told them that school integration might stimulate an escalation of the white exodus." In any event, the board's response was an invitation to 10,000 white families in the neighboring boroughs of Queens and the Bronx, across the river from Harlem, to *voluntarily* enroll their children in the brand-new Harlem school. To hardly anyone's surprise, none responded.

Parents and community representatives in the I.S. 201 area had posed as an alternative to integration an experiment in community control, and now they demanded direct community control —a representative parent-community council with the power to hire and fire teachers and administrators, to play a role in deciding what would be taught, and to set educational standards and check on whether they were being met. The board declared that these demands would violate the state education law, and disaffected parents announced they would boycott the school when it opened in the fall. Thus, when more than a million New York City pupils returned to the more than 900 New York City public schools on September 12, 1966, the doors of I.S. 201 remained closed. Pickets ringed the school, and the board of education decided not to open it, pending further efforts to resolve the controversy.

There were disruptions elsewhere as well that fall. At another Harlem school, Junior High School (J.H.S.) 139, twelve members of a black nationalist group were arrested on the first day of school for allegedly attempting to prevent students from entering. In certain Queens and Brooklyn neighborhoods, white parents demonstrated against the breakup of the neighborhood school pattern to achieve racial integration, and the Congress of Racial Equality (CORE) protested against school conditions.

In the next ten days, the issue raged over parent and community demands for the resignation of the white principal who had been assigned to I.S. 201 and his replacement with a Negro. Meanwhile, militant national Negro leaders, including Stokely Carmichael of the Student Nonviolent Coordinating Committee (SNCC) and Floyd McKissick, national director of CORE, arrived on the scene. The United Federation of Teachers (UFT) and the Council of Supervisory Associations (CSA) joined to support the board-appointed principal. In scuffles with police, five demonstrators were arrested. Students began returning to the school on September 21, picketing dwindled, the white principal was transferred, and the school was placed in charge of a Negro assistant principal. But the conflict was unresolved and tensions ran high in the school and in the community. I.S. 201 was to disappear from public notice, then reappear intermittently over the ensuing two years, and finally emerge again as a focal point of controversy.

Toward the Community as Decision-Maker

Long before the U.S. Riot Commission Report dramatized "the exclusion of ghetto residents from the decision-making process that affects their lives and community," a movement for meaningful participation of the poor was under way. It became a tenet of the 1964 Economic Opportunity Act, which declared that community-action programs should be "developed, conducted and administered with the maximum feasible participation of residents of the area and members of the groups served."

Prior to this, the traditional posture of residents in disadvantaged communities had been low self-esteem and acceptance of attempts to remedy their condition. Despite occasional lip service given to the citizen's role, consultation with the poor, when undertaken at all, was a token affair. As seen by the real decision-makers, consultation was essentially a one-way process, designed to explain—and possibly offset potential criticism of—decisions that had been made for the clients (sometimes referred to as "residents of target areas") by others. The most aggravated example of this pattern was the postwar urban-renewal program, undertaken in the name of, but often inimical to the interests of, the slum dweller.

Several precursors of the social action elements of the federal "war on poverty" had, instead, sought to cast the poor into real decision-making roles. One of the earliest—and still surviving—was Saul Alinsky's formula for community action, born in Chicago's Woodlawn neighborhood (near the University of Chicago) and since adopted in ghettos in several other cities. Other pre-OEO efforts included Mobilization for Youth, on New York's Lower East Side, and community-development programs assisted by the Ford Foundation in Oakland, California, Philadelphia, New Haven, Boston, Pittsburgh, and Washington. The underlying strategy in these efforts was that the poor could best define their own needs and direct the policies of institutions established to serve them. Also involved was a concern with the need for some redistribution of power in American society. And it was this latter aspect of community participation that threatened vested-power interests.

The most publicized attack on the concept, however, came in the book *Maximum Feasible Misunderstanding,* published shortly after its author, Daniel Patrick Moynihan, entered the Nixon Administration as Assistant to the President on Urban Affairs. Maintaining that giving control over institutions to the poor would not solve the problems of poverty, Moynihan criticized the federal poverty program's emphasis on community action at the expense of efforts directed to the economic needs of the poor. To place poor people in control of schools, he argued, simply weighs them down with yet another burden with which they are not competent to deal. Further, he maintained that a community-controlled school system would be discriminatory by emphasizing the hiring of blacks and Puerto Ricans at the expense of whites; in the New York school system, this discrimination would be felt by Jewish educators, in particular.

Moynihan's thesis errs seriously in overlooking the fact that control over local institutions (schools, especially) *does* provide the community with power resources, through control of jobs and public funds. The poor can change and influence the institutions most relevant to their lives, if the framework allows for really representative and direct participation. Jobs and money are unquestionably vital. But employed people who are only slightly less poor than the jobless would not, thereby, be in a very much better position to influence institutions that affect their lives. The antipoverty and community-control efforts seek not only increases in "goods"—income and education—for the poor but also some redistribution of decision-making power.

Finally, one must ask, was participation of the poor an option or a necessity? Before the Economic Opportunity Act, a tide of protest was already swelling, both at the organized level of civil rights organizations and at the grass-roots level of ghetto resistance to urban renewal and other "improvements" designed by external forces in which the people played no part. Whether or not most political structures captured effective control of most antipoverty programs, the concept of functional participation was implanted. It established enough roots so that there is hardly any city where relations between the central political structure and poor areas will ever be the same again. Community participation in Head Start programs, for example, was real and effective though not strong enough to effect reform of the regular school system by Head Start–type programs that sought to follow through in the regular elementary grades. The community-action programs, moreover, helped create (and fund) indigenous organizations that became a training ground for a new generation of minority leaders. They also provided some of the mundane elements too often overlooked in elevated analyses of social movements—time and economic sustenance for poor men and women who work on community problems. Much of the organizational skill for the community-participation movement in the New York City public schools, for example, came from community residents employed by public and private antipoverty agencies. Moreover, the poor generally gained experience in documenting and voicing their complaints and in selecting their representatives for community bodies.

More recently, demands have been made for community control of agencies outside the antipoverty apparatus—the police, for example. In a few extreme cases, there are calls for political separation of black communities from other entities. In California, the Black Panther group, for example, has petitioned for a place on the ballot for a proposition to incorporate the Negro part of Contra Costa County. In other instances, ethnic identity and solidarity are manifesting themselves through means similar to those employed by European immigrant groups to maintain cohesiveness—through religious-ethnic organizations and through bloc voting in regular political elections. By 1970, there were some 1500 black elected officials in the United States. Some are in Congress and state legislatures, but the vast majority occupy positions in local government (including school boards), where bloc voting is most effective.

Coinciding with an awakening desire among the urban poor for power is a trend toward decentralization of services. This impetus, however, is more a matter of administrative efficiency than of responsiveness to community desire. It recognizes the difficulty of prescribing at the center uniform rules and procedures that can apply equally effectively across the whole of a large and diverse city. It acknowledges, furthermore, the deadening effect on the initiative and creativity of personnel, to say nothing of morale, in centralized decision-making on all matters. It is, in short, the counterpart, at the governmental level, of a practice long followed by many large corporations that have discovered that decentralization is more effective and profitable than a rein held tightly at the center. Administrative decentralization of government, however, should not be mistaken for community control or participation. It can facilitate community participation by locating the decision-making agencies closer to hand. But it is no guarantee in and of itself of community participation. In some instances, indeed, a decentralized agency of government, if it lacks sufficient decision-making authority, can frustrate community desires by deflecting them from the real seat of authority.

The murmurs for community control of the public schools in one corner of Harlem echoed a number of profound developments throughout the country—not only in ghettos but among the great middle class as well, not only in the schools but in the colleges and universities, and among the public at large. The themes expressed by hippies on the most vivid and garish level had deeper roots. The growing complexity of life in a modern technological society—increasingly interdependent, increasingly urbanized, and subject to controls by a vastly expanded centralized government—was straining the traditional fabric of American society. Anxiety had long been developing as a response to remote forces over which men and women felt they had no control—international conflicts and scientific forces, in particular. This anxiety was underscored by a developing crisis of impotence and voicelessness even in relation to a force that was closer to the individual's choice—his own government. The polling place was proving an insufficient, too infrequent channel for the public will. Other means were needed for government to appreciate the needs and concerns of the communities it served, to render an account of its activities to its constituents, and, quite as important, actively to engage the ideas and energies of the constituents.

Old and New Ideologies

One of the great ironies of the school–community-control movement is that it shatters traditionally clear lines between liberal and conservative thought. Certainly, since the New Deal, liberals had looked to Washington for progressive legislation and affirmative government action on behalf of the oppressed, the disfranchised, and the afflicted. Liberals regarded local and state government either as totally corrupt or too easily manipulable by economic and social elites. And, of course, the slogan "states' rights" was seen as a transparent euphemism for the preservation of racial segregation, to say nothing of antiunion and other conservative, if not reactionary, behavior. Reduced to simplified terms, liberal thought tended to sympathize with the underdog and distrusted local government to act in his best interests. But the underdog of the ghettos in the 1960's, in apparent contradiction of prevailing liberal ideas, began calling for an unprecedented degree of local autonomy.

And so, as former Presidential assistant Richard N. Goodwin wrote, early in 1969, Jeffersonian ideas (for example, "It is not by the consolidation or concentration of powers, but by their distribution, that good government is effected") have "a greater vitality than at any other time since they were written. If anything, their relevance has been increased by modern technology, for it has stripped us of the protections of distance and time, which once compelled a certain diffusion of power." Goodwin, referring mainly to the middle class, talks of "the most sensitive nerve in the American consciousness: the individual's desire for mastery over his own life and environment."

With a different, more quietly desperate variation on the same theme, a Negro educator described a New York City ghetto in which he works:

> . . . there are people groping in the dark, who for a long time have felt themselves outside the mainstream of public concern. The city takes no notice of them. In the midst of a crowd or wherever groups of people assemble or pass, these people are obscure, unnoticed, as though they do not exist. They are not censured or reproached; they simply are not seen. They are the invisible residents of a demoralized, poverty-ridden, inner city. To be ignored or overlooked is a denial of one's rights to dignity, respect and membership in the human race. These residents have been frustrated at every turn in their attempt to reverse the process.

The man—Rhody McCoy; the ghetto—Ocean Hill–Brownsville, in Brooklyn. Both were to become the focus of nationwide attention when events in the schools McCoy administered in Ocean Hill–Brownsville touched off a bitter citywide seven-week strike by the UFT in the fall of 1968.

The most forceful surge for a voice in their destiny arose from the people who had been most stifled and ignored—the American Negroes. Beginning with isolated actions in the South for actual achievement of some of the rights and privileges that had already been won in the courts, the civil rights movement in the 1960's took on national dimensions and a new militancy. It was no longer confined to nonviolent action or to legislative and judicial moves. These continued, but to them were added civil disobedience and, beginning in 1963 and culminating in 1967, mass disorders in cities throughout the country.

In the meantime, the vast majority of blacks, who had never participated in any public action for civil rights, were being transformed. They were beginning to feel their own power, and, in the place of passivity and sometimes self-hate, pride and a sense of self-worth were growing. Millions of American Negroes had felt anger at the injustice and indignity they had inherited at the day of birth. But there had been no effective outlets for their anger, just frustration. Now, hope arose—not so much hope for a change in the hearts and minds of the white majority, but hope in the Negroes' own power to improve their lives and win both dignity and opportunity.

In June, 1966, on a march from Memphis to Jackson, Mississippi, Stokely Carmichael's shout of "Black Power" was heard around the country. It was new to the nation at large, but, as the Report of the National Advisory Commission on Civil Disorders notes, "the slogan expressed tendencies that had been present for a long time and had been gaining strength in the Negro community." Three months later, Carmichael was outside the doors of I.S. 201 in Harlem. He had not started the movement for parent participation in the New York schools, and he soon left the scene. His presence for a fleeting moment was symbolic, but he was not needed, for Harlem parents and parents in other parts of the city and country were beginning to bestir themselves. They probably were not seeking so absolute a concept as power. What began to grow, rather, was a feeling that they had a legitimate role to play in the public schools, an institution vital to the lives of their children. Given the tradition of parental exclusion from the public schools, this was nearly as significant and revolutionary as the power concept.

The disruptions at I.S. 201 and other New York schools in the fall of 1966 were not the first in New York City, or even the largest. In 1965, two school boycotts by pupils were aimed at greater progress in desegregation. A counter boycott was staged by white parents protesting plans to move children from predominantly white to predominantly nonwhite neighborhoods and vice versa.

In the course of this struggle to desegregate the New York schools, parent leaders began to learn the intricacies of the school bureaucracy with which they were locked in struggle. They also began to document the failure of the public schools. It was not enough to rest on the Supreme Court finding that separate education was inherently damaging to the minority child. Integrationists accumulated the hard evidence of what individual parents and teachers had long known: that the majority of nonwhite pupils were failing. Under community pressure, the New York City Board of Education, in 1966, published for the first time reading scores on a school-by-school basis. The figures showed one-fifth of the pupils in the city's elementary and junior high schools to be two years or more behind in reading. A wide difference was found between schools in middle-class neighborhoods and those in predominantly black or Puerto Rican areas; the latter were from three to five years behind the former. A year later, the lag had increased further.

That the failure was nationwide had been confirmed in the Coleman Report (*Equality of Educational Opportunity*), the most exhaustive study of educational achievement in American public schools ever conducted. It showed, for example, that, in urban areas of the Northeast, Negro students, on the average, begin the first grade with somewhat lower scores on standard achievement tests than whites, are about 1.6 grades behind in the sixth grade, and have fallen 3.3 grades behind in the twelfth grade. (These figures are, of course, apart from the fact that less than one-third as many Negroes as whites even reach the twelfth grade.) This evidence is corroborated by any number of other measures, including performance in basic verbal skills on the Selective Service tests, and on apprenticeship and other employment tests. It is both remarkable and, in retrospect, appalling that, until the Coleman Report, so little measurement of—and concern for—the educational productivity of public education had been evidenced.

Sources of Resistance and Reform

The institution most immune to community action both before and during the early stages of the antipoverty program was the public school system. One of the notable achievements of the antipoverty program in education, Operation Head Start, did enjoy a great degree of parental involvement in the actual operation of classes. But its effects lasted only as long as the children had not entered the public system. Attempts to carry through to the public schools the principal elements of the Head Start approach, including a strong parental role, ran into considerable difficulty.*

In the early 1960's, Mobilization for Youth, a federal and privately financed project on the predominantly Negro and Puerto Rican Lower East Side of New York, sought to question the suspension of youngsters from schools. Mothers organized under MFY wanted observers to sit in on suspension hearings and, if necessary, to challenge the grounds on which pupils were suspended from school. The attempt was met with a strong protest by school principals in the area, who also enlisted the aid of local political leaders. MFY apparently held little hope for changing school patterns by cooperating with the established order. "The schools strongly resist [our] change objective of increasing their responsiveness and accountability to low-income people," wrote the project's director. "This, combined with the limitation upon the project's strategic maneuverability, clearly suggests the necessity of employing pressure methods."

This analysis was borne out by antipoverty efforts that did seek to work within and coax or bargain the established school framework into change. Writing of several programs funded by the President's Committee on Juvenile Delinquency and by the Ford Foundation, Peter Marris and Martin Rein concluded that the schools accepted only methods already widely endorsed in the teaching profession—remedial counseling, team teaching, and cultural enrichment. If the community-development agencies

---

* A top medical examiner consultant of the Head Start program was dismissed within hours of stating publicly, before a Congressional committee in March 1969, that children in the Head Start program lost all their gains once they entered regular public school because of faulty organization and philosophy in the public school system.

sought to introduce more challenging innovations, "the schools might not give them a fair test, and the trading of unwilling commitment to each other's aims only condemned all the programs to half-hearted and muddled implementation."

Proposals in the MFY neighborhood to have teachers visit pupils' homes were accepted grudgingly and only in return for Mobilization's support of a conventional guidance-counseling program. The trade was an uneasy one, as a Mobilization official concedes: "Settlement by negotiation often involves a continuing bargaining process, for agreement is never actually reached and terms are usually insufficiently defined. Thus, while [we] devote much effort to shaping the guidance program in directions it regards as more congenial, the schools are busy subverting the home visiting program."

The movement for real community voice in the public school unavoidably contains potential for conflict, not only in ideological terms but also in more earthy currency. The public schools are a major enterprise, possessing all the elements that surround vast corporate undertakings—a physical plant, millions of jobs, contractors who depend on the schools for commissions, textbook publishers, and various forms of organizations concerned with their own perquisites and positions. In the simplest sense, the public schools are an enterprise with a nearly $30 billion annual budget and more than 2 million teaching and other jobs, both constantly expanding; the money and jobs—both are at issue.

The public schools have, for the most part, emerged from the era when they were a prime trough for the spoils systems, but they are still (in fact, more than ever) a source of benefit—and profit— to countless individuals and companies. Those who hold these interests above the interest of the education of the school system's children will naturally be suspicious of new forces claiming a significant say in the way schools are organized and run. That is not to say that every school principal, school custodian, and building contractor is automatically an enemy of community control. It simply recognizes that they are likely to be wary of changes in the *status quo* and fearful of community and parent spokesmen who declare themselves in favor of full-scale reform of the school system.

At the same time that community and political forces are pressing toward a confrontation on the issue of control of the schools, the professional world of the educator is in ferment. Critics and theoreticians of education, as well as the strategy-minded practitioners, have been in deep debate over the proper approaches to the worsening educational system. The Supreme Court decision and the rising civil rights movement had drawn all manner of "outsiders" to the scrutiny of the nation's vast educational enterprise. Psychologists intensified and sought new paths to research on learning theory. Political scientists began probing the behavior of the public school system as an organ of government and as a form of decision-making organization. Sociologists were peering into the dynamics, goals, and habits of the rulers and clients of the system. Economists, journalists, even novelists were increasingly drawn to the enterprise. Cracks in the professional educators' monopoly, then, had already begun to develop.

At first, the noneducator reformers, students of education from other disciplines, and planners were united in their distrust of the prevailing system and its entrenched hierarchy. But, in time, differences arose among them, too, over theoretical and strategic approaches to the restructuring of education—particularly on the most effective means of reaching and teaching the "disadvantaged." Just as the opening chapter of the drama of community control was about to unfold, two developments all but shattered the remainder of unity among the reformers, critics, and planners. One was the leveling off of federal expenditures for educational improvements and innovations, due to the escalating financial demands of the Vietnam war. The other, cutting ever deeper and marking a landmark in the history of American education, was publication of the Coleman Report, which had been commissioned by Congress in the Civil Rights Act of 1964.

The movement for real community voice in public education, therefore, began gathering force just as underlying assumptions in the main efforts to overcome educational poverty were being fractured. What these assumptions were and the strategies to which they gave rise are the subjects to which we now turn.

2

Alternatives to School Reform

> Whenever we have in mind the discussion of
> a new movement in education, it is especially
> necessary to take the broader, or social, view.
> Otherwise, changes in the school institution
> and tradition will be looked at as the worst
> transitory fads, and at the best merely im-
> provements in certain details—and this is
> the plane upon which it is too customary to
> consider school changes. It is as rational to
> conceive of the locomotive or the telegraph
> as personal devices.—JOHN DEWEY (*The
> School and Society*)

Early school reformers, exemplified by Horace Mann, were, like
James B. Conant in the current era, "stirred to action by the 'so-
cial dynamite' they saw in the slums." These reformers saw the
American public school as a tool for combatting poverty.

Yet, it is questionable whether this egalitarian ideal of the public school was ever accomplished. There is evidence that, far from
offering equal opportunity to children of the poor, public schools
have actually favored the children of the more well-to-do. There
is more myth than substance to the widely accepted notion that
the schools served the immigrant children so admirably in the
late nineteenth and early twentieth centuries. Citing studies in
six major cities since the 1890's, Colin Greer of Teachers College
has pointed out that failure rates of students were so high that in

no school system did the so-called normal grade-level group exceed 60 per cent, while in several instances it fell as low as 35 per cent.

"The public schools have always failed the lower classes—both white and black," says Greer. "In virtually every study undertaken since 1898 . . . more children have failed in schools than have succeeded, both in absolute and in relative numbers." What is different today is that the job market places a premium on education and skills, that the price children pay for school failure has escalated, and that criticism, once confined to reformers, is now being pressed by the parents of the victims of educational failure.

One indication that Horace Mann's public school revolution was far from complete was the zealous reform energy of the progressive-education movement of the early twentieth century. Progressive educators sought to transform not only the public school, but society as well. As one leading exponent, George Counts, argued, it was the school that would dare to rebuild the social order for the betterment of mankind. Unfortunately, progressive education never took hold in the United States, despite favorable results.

All the efforts at improving public education left the basic system unchanged. They strengthened the *status quo,* enabling the system to serve better those it had always served best. The heart of the present crisis in public education is the realization that the system has failed the individual needs of a major segment of the population. This failure did not come to full public awareness until the nation took official cognizance of poverty amidst affluence, and until the nonwhite fourth of society's economic underclass began to assert its civil rights and demand a full share in political and economic opportunity. Long before widespread racial rioting and the issuance of the Riot Commission Report, national *awareness* of a crisis in urban education—as opposed to concern, let alone action—had, in fact, developed. The country was not blind to the failure of the schools to place millions of black children on the ladder of economic and social mobility. It was an isolated or calloused educational leader who would not acknowledge ten years ago—if the subject happened to come up, though it seldom did—what the Riot Commission said in 1967: "Particularly for the children of the racial ghetto, the schools have failed to provide the educational experience which could help to overcome the effects of discrimination and deprivation."

Our present preoccupation with low-income pupils, however, has not diverted some penetrating critics from concluding that the total system is incapable of meeting the challenge of providing excellent education for a diverse student population. Consequently, the mission of fundamental educational reform is not for the poor alone, but for all.

There is little agreement regarding the locus of the problem of school failure. At one extreme is the assumption that the cause of any child's failure to learn lies primarily with him—with his physical, economic, cultural, or environmental deficits. As Charles A. Valentine (in *Culture and Poverty*) has pointed out, the much-publicized theories of "culture of poverty"—found in the writings of such scholars as Oscar Lewis, Nathan Glazer, Daniel Patrick Moynihan, and E. Franklin Frazier—have been exploited by nonscholars to blame the poor for their poverty in general (including educational deficiency) and to discourage attempts to correct the condition.

That most educators and public officials regard shortcomings in children as the major educational problem is reflected in the account of the first year of the billion-dollar Title I of the Elementary and Secondary Education Act (ESEA): "In practice, the goal of Title I is to provide 'compensatory education' for the millions of school children whose *crippling background* offers them little hope for successful schooling." (Italics added.)

At the other pole is the notion that, if pupils are failing, the school system itself is in need of fundamental rehabilitation. Under this assumption, the school's obligation is to diagnose what the learner needs and what concerns him, and how he gains knowledge and responds to external influences, and to adjust its program accordingly. In the early stages of concern about the learning problems of the disadvantaged, the searchlight shone almost entirely on the shortcomings of learners. As attempts to rehabilitate the learner failed to close the gap in achievement between the "disadvantaged" and others, a shift began to develop toward a diagnosis of the entire teaching and learning system as well. A spectrum of "prescriptions" developed—alternative types of intervention designed to reform the process and practice of public education.

Concurrently, data on the "disadvantaged" have mushroomed, yielding valuable insights but also a curious ambivalence even among severe critics of existing school systems. Particularly on the basis of the data of the Coleman Report that indicate that black children do worse in school than white children, some of the critics seem to revert, implicitly at least, to the notion that *nothing* will work with the black child. Indeed, we have recently had a revival of the ugly, pseudoscientific theory that, from time to time, has dotted American racial history—that something is awry in the genetic heritage of the Negro that renders him incapable of learning as well as his white brethren. Without subscribing at all to the myth of genetic damnation, even an observer like Christopher Jencks does say that we must reckon with the fact "that while black children go to many different sorts of schools, good and bad, integrated and segregated, rigidly authoritarian and relatively permissive, their mean achievement level is remarkably similar from school to school."

Such despairing analyses may well be supported by data on the circumstances of the past and the recent present. But they ignore the vast changes underway in the attitude and self-image of the Negro. They also gloss over the fact that what appear to be great variations in existing schools may be limited distinctions rather than fundamental differences. The more refined the data become, it seems, the more they reinforce a prophecy of continued failure. They may also have an intimidating effect on innovators and creative reformers. The more radically future designs for education are drawn, the less proof they receive from past data that they have a chance to succeed. Bold blueprints are, therefore, vulnerable to charges that they are "unsupported," for only a fair trial of the proposed reform (which means a few years at least) will produce data that prove or disprove the concept. The movement for community control of the schools as an approach to educational reform is no exception. Since the movement has coincided with the black power movement, the community control groundswell is usually viewed in political terms alone—as a clash of forces, each vying for dominance, or at least for a weakening, of the other. That the politics of community control is a *means* toward educational reform is usually drowned out, or deliberately ignored, in the clamor over the tactics and battles that attend the establishment of community control.

If the strategies of educational reform were left to academic observers and professional reformers, therefore, the community-control strategy might never be attempted. As it turns out, of course, the option is being seized by those most directly affected. That, in itself, does not guarantee its success where other approaches to intervention have failed, but it is a significant departure from other reform thrusts, which have come not from the victims of miseducation but from the middle-class reformers and the professionals. To understand the basis and singular character of the community-control movement, however, one must first examine the forms of intervention into regular school-system patterns that preceded it in the last decade or so.

Five basic approaches to intervention may be identified: compensatory education, integration, model subsystems, parallel systems, and total-system reform. With the exception of compensatory education, these concepts have not been applied widely throughout any large urban school systems over a sustained period, but in some cases—model subsystems, for example—the few existing examples are sufficient to provide a basis for examining the likelihood of success or failure.

Compensatory Education

Compensatory education—the congeries of attempts to overcome shortcomings in the learner—is the most prevalent form of intervention designed to raise pupils' academic achievement. The first thing that must be said about it, regardless of one's estimate of its effectiveness, is that it was tragically belated. So thick has been the flurry of special educational programs for the Negro (so much thicker the flood of rhetoric and written analysis of the "disadvantaged learner") that there is a tendency to overlook how shockingly late were the awareness, the programs, and even the rhetoric.

Compensatory education was the motif of such early efforts as the Ford Foundation–supported Great Cities School Improvement Programs, Title I of the ESEA, and New York City's early Higher Horizons Program, and the more recent More Effective Schools program. Compensatory measures seek to attack a spectrum of defects in the learner that presumably prevent his participation in the learning process. These defects include, of course, the supposition that the learner's family does not appreciate the value of education, and that, therefore, he is less motivated in school than his middle-class counterparts. Experience and insight have begun to discredit this simplistic guidepost to educational policy, but it dies hard. As late as December, 1967, for example, a Presidential panel urged establishment of a Learning Corps, in which financially successful families would volunteer to accept poor rural or inner-city youths into their homes for one year or more to demonstrate a setting where "education counts" and middle-class goals operate. The advice came from an *ad hoc* Vocational Advisory Council (headed by the Ohio state superintendent of education) that was named to review the Vocational Education Act of 1963, a major piece of federal legislation. President Nixon's 1970 Message on Education acknowledged that "the best available evidence indicates that most of the compensatory education programs have not measurably helped poor children catch up."

In addition to grafting extra education onto the regular school experience, proponents of compensation have attempted to nip deficiencies in the bud through preschool programs like Operation Head Start. The growing interest in compensatory education has been accompanied by a great expansion of research in early childhood development. Not altogether unpredictably, this new wave has brought fresh, more detailed evidence of the importance of the early years on later development. In turn have come proposals for shaping the child's intellectual development, not just in the immediate preschool years of four and five but earlier. In the frenzy to make up for lost time, various approaches to preschool education have arisen, from the rejuvenated Montessori system to Head Start to a system by Bereiter and Engelmann, known as the "pressure-cooker approach," which emphasizes hard-hitting drill in concentrated units of instruction. Overzealous interpretation of "stimulation" sometimes includes coercion of children, ridicule, and exaggerated competition. Some learning specialists are even experimenting with programs that seek to assure the unborn child of a better educational chance by special counseling for his parents-to-be. Such efforts arouse some fears of a "brave new world" in which genetic manipulation will determine lifetime careers; what is more likely is that a state of mind akin to infant damnation will develop, in which if children do not enjoy the proper environmental and intellectual stimuli before they enter school, they are considered all but doomed to academic failure. Few educators are conscious of this trend, and fewer still alarmed by it.

Most research on early childhood deprivation has been psychosocial, calling for increasingly earlier intervention to overcome the alleged deficiencies of black children and, in the case of Bruno Bettelheim, for total removal from the home into kibbutz-like controlled environments.

But studies by some anthropological and linguistic researchers maintain, as Stephen S. and Joan C. Baratz put it, that intervention programs that view black children as verbally, environmentally, and linguistically destitute are a form of "institutional racism." *Differences* in black children (and in others, for that matter) are not *deficiencies,* and the schools should capitalize on the differences instead of bemoaning them as deterrents to learning.

Operation Head Start, one of the most popular of the compensatory programs, is, in several respects, an exception to generalizations about compensatory education. First of all, it operates largely outside the regular public school system. It affects children before they enter the public school system, and it is well established that low-income children gain most from Head Start before they enter school. Controversy over the program focuses on the durability of the experience. Some studies point to a sharp fade-out once Head Start children enter the public schools, unless there are specific follow-through programs modeled on Head Start approaches. (Critics of the regular public school system allege that follow-through in the regular school is a contradiction in terms, since one of the salient features of Head Start is its freedom from restrictions and traditions that are part of the failure of the regular public school system). But much seems to depend on the *kind* of school Head Start children enter; research indicates continued improvement if Head Start children enter middle-class public schools, while Head Starters who enter schools in depressed areas tend to level off, permitting non–Head Starters to catch up to them. But even this finding has to be qualified, according to researchers, because the test scores are taken in one dimension only—that of intelligence measurements. Attendance rates and motivation and interest in learning, for example, continue to be much better among Head Start graduates than among other children in the same class. An aspect of Head Start that is often overlooked by partisans, who cite the program's success as an argument for the compensatory approach, is the parental-participation component.

For the most part, however, compensatory education is a prescription that deals with *symptoms;* it provides strengthened doses of prescriptions that have not proved effective before—more trips, more remedial reading, etc.—without real differences in kind. It is, essentially, an additive or "Band-Aid" approach to the standard educational process, seeking to bring the strays into the fold and to fit them into the existing school mold. The assumption is that the schools need to do something more for "disadvantaged" pupils, but not that the school itself is in need of wholesale re-examination.

Enormous effort, ingenuity, and funds have been invested in compensatory education, but the evidence emerging from even the best efforts indicates that they are having little significant impact on the problem of low achievement among "disadvantaged" children. The proponents of continued compensatory intervention argue either that not enough effort and resources have yet been applied or that greater attacks must be made on factors external to the schools (typically, family stability, housing, and income), or both.

Until recently, the controversy over compensatory education raged on in terms of its effectiveness in place of unattainable racial integration. Thus, the exhaustive report of the U.S. Civil Rights Commission, *Racial Isolation in the Public Schools,* declared: ". . . the compensatory programs reviewed here appear to suffer from the defect inherent in attempting to solve problems stemming in part from racial and social class isolation in schools which themselves are isolated by race and social class." Former U.S. Commissioner of Education Harold Howe II sought to dispel the either-or arguments:

> We are told by some that compensatory education is not working and that we must therefore reject it in favor of massive efforts at integration. We are told by others that integration is an impractical goal and that the only way to improve education in the central city is to make massive expenditures for the schools there without regard to desegregation.

The Office of Education does not accept either proposition. We look at compensatory education and integration not as mutually exclusive enterprises but rather as parallel goals, both to be pursued at the same time.

Howe maintained that Title I's compensatory efforts were making a vital contribution to American education; that, without it, thousands of schools would be in deeper trouble than they are; and that more and more schools were learning how to use the funds it provides to good effect. "We are quite willing to concede," he added, "that there has been no wholesale breakthrough in the problem of ghetto schools, but we think it naïve to expect any such development in two years' time." But, like some other educational leaders, Howe had begun to broaden the definition of compensatory education to include stronger parental participation—in his words, "new involvement of parents and community in the affairs of the schools."

One reason Howe and others have continued to advocate greater investment in compensatory measures is the hope that they would help improve inner-city schools to the extent that, "in time," the schools would attract white suburban children. One of the most ambitious of such efforts is Pittsburgh's. By a massive high school rebuilding program and by honors programs and other improvements, it is struggling to win back the middle class, who, as in other cities, have been abandoning the city for the suburbs. Pittsburgh's compensatory program—based on team teaching and massive expenditures of federal funds—may be coming closer than most cities to producing success in its black schools. But it has shown no evidence of paying off, other than the subjective judgments of the teachers and staff.

In Berkeley, California, too, even under the tutelage of the highly regarded former Superintendent of Schools, Neil Sullivan (now Commissioner of Education for Massachusetts), the compensatory approach fell far short of its promise. Sullivan, earlier, had provided inspiring leadership and opportunity for the black children in Prince Edward County, Virginia, who had, literally,

been left schoolless, when authorities closed the public schools
rather than submit to Federal orders to desegregate them. He
said of the Berkeley effort:

> As have most other school districts in the nation, Berkeley has
> sought to "pull ghetto children up by the bootstraps" through
> compensatory education, Head Start, Follow Through—the full com-
> plement of enrichment, remedy, and experiment, including individ-
> ual tutoring, perceptive counseling, team-teaching, and nongraded
> programs.
>
> Disappointing data came after three years of continuing compensa-
> tory education, four years of strong emphasis on reading (both
> developmental and remedial), three years of Head Start, and three
> years of special small-class instruction in the ghetto schools.

The compensatory approach is viewed with increasing distrust
by parents, both because the techniques used are not achieving
the desired goals and because these parents reject the premise
that the fault lies in their children. But only a few urban educators have abandoned the view that the main trouble lies in the
child and his environment.

Proponents of compensatory education argue that it cannot be
counted a failure, because it has not yet had a fair test. What
would a fair test be? Working from data collected for the Elementary and Secondary Education Act—covering some 8 million
pupils—David Cohen of the Joint Center for Urban Studies
(Harvard-MIT) calculates, conservatively, that a $6.9 billion
annual increase in instructional expenditures alone would be
needed to apply to all disadvantaged schools the formula used
by New York City's MES experiment. Applying this formula
across the country, he notes, would increase expenditures *for the
disadvantaged alone* from 8 to 43 per cent of the present total
annual spending for *all* children. And that would not include
additional outlays totalling $5.8 billion for college training of
the extra teachers needed and for more classroom space. One can
argue passionately that these sums pale in comparison with
expenditures for war, cosmetics, cigarettes, and alcohol, but to

little avail. The federal outlay for compensatory education is not going to multiply fivefold in the near future. Compensatory education must be judged not by a distant potential but mainly on its several years' performance to date.

Putting aside the genuine educational grounds on which the merits and demerits can be argued, compensatory education has also been used politically to fend off pressures for integration. Mrs. Louise Day Hicks, for example, the Boston school board member who gained national prominence as the city's staunchest defender of the neighborhood school principle, salts her warnings of the damage that children can suffer from being bused from their neighborhoods with strong endorsement of compensatory measures for the disadvantaged and of programs for returning dropouts and retarded children.

Nothing has challenged and confounded the advocates of compensatory education more than the Coleman Report. One of its prime conclusions was that "disadvantaged children" gain in learning skills and self-esteem when they associate with children from more fortunate (higher social class) families. At the same time, the report tended to discount the effect of compensatory inputs into predominantly Negro schools. Drawing from very different data than the psycho-sociological underpinnings of the 1954 Supreme Court school desegregation decision, the Coleman Report nevertheless implied the same action: more integration to produce better education for the "disadvantaged." If anything, the Coleman implications went further, to include not only integration of color, but integration of social class, too. Finally, the report strongly suggests a degree of *intra*school integration that very few demographically integrated schools have been willing to enforce—the abandonment of the tracking system. The stark and powerful message of the report confronted educational policymakers just at the time when they had almost universally concluded that school integration in large cities was virtually impossible in the foreseeable future. Integration was still held out as a desirable goal, but, in city after city, the facts showed that inner-city schools had become more, not less, racially segregated since the Court's decision. Thus, stalemate appeared to have developed: as the bloom began to fade from the rose of compensatory education, realistic hopes for attaining racial integration in urban schools grew dimmer than ever.

Integration

A year after the Coleman Report, the U.S. Civil Rights Commission, in its exhaustive review of integration efforts and educational disadvantage, was unequivocal in stating: "Negro children suffer serious harm when their education takes place in public schools which are racially segregated, whatever the source of such segregation may be. Negro children who attend predominantly Negro schools do not achieve as well as other children, Negro and white."

But long before the Coleman Report and the Civil Rights Commission Report, the evidence of the positive effects of integrated education on minority-group youngsters was strong enough that educational reformers saw desegregation and integration as the major vehicles for overcoming educational disadvantage. Moreover, there was good evidence (or, at least, the absence of contrary evidence) that white youngsters would not lose in terms of academic achievement by proximity to Negro youngsters. And when the social benefits of interracial experience were counted in, integration was actually seen to have enormous value for white youngsters as well as for black.

One of the most recent research surveys on the question, undertaken by the Phi Delta Kappa Commission on Education, Human Rights, and Responsibilities, confirms earlier findings. Meyer Weinberg of the Chicago City College, director of the study, declared, "There is simply no other means developed thus far [than integration] for improving the achievement of Negro children that even comes near [being adequate]." The studies show that white students, at the least, hold their own when their schools are integrated, that Negro self-esteem and motivation increase in an integrated school climate, and that white-black student relations were usually marked by "toleration and respect." While Weinberg was disappointed at having found little evidence that the achievement of white pupils did not, as did that of black pupils, rise after desegregation, later studies of integration experiments—in Rochester, New York, Hartford, Connecticut, and Boston, for example—do show improvement among white children in terms not only of tolerance and acceptance but also of curiosity, although the researchers conceded that these matters are less easily measured than academic achievement and less reassuring to white parents worried that integration means their children will suffer academically.

The pace of desegregation has been slow, South and North. By 1964, ten years after the Supreme Court decision, fewer than one-fourth (23.5 per cent) of the school districts with Negro and white children in eight Deep South states called "recalcitrant" by the NAACP had desegregated. Fewer than 10 per cent of the Negro children in those states were attending schools with whites, and, in five of the states, fewer than 1 per cent were. By 1968, the percentage had advanced only to 14 per cent. Southern desegregation has not even kept up with population increases; as a result, more students attend totally segregated schools in the South today than were attending them in 1954.

In the North, despite great moral appeals and the growing store of educational evidence, integration has not moved appreciably faster. In most urban settings, integration has proved elusive, if not impossible. The failure to achieve integration to any significant extent was due, first, to massive white resistance. Now, it is even less likely to occur in this generation because of the growing concentration in the inner city of blacks and other minorities. New York, Washington, Chicago, Cleveland, Detroit, Philadelphia, and St. Louis all have majority nonwhite elementary-public-school populations.

By 1969, whatever national insistence there had been that schools desegregate had nearly vanished, and there was serious question as to whether the national administration would continue or relax governmental pressure for desegregation—even in the face of the Supreme Court's 1969 decision calling for immediate integration of schools.

The pressure for integration from civil rights groups was rarely matched by equal support from educational administrators. School superintendents like Carroll Johnson in White Plains, New York, and Neil Sullivan in Berkeley were the exceptions. In most cases, administrators have blown with the winds of majority sentiment in the white community, to which most school boards, on this issue, are hypersensitive. Several studies have indicated that, even when local boards and/or superintendents have announced integration plans, they have been undermined by middle-management staff.

The failure to achieve widespread school integration is a bitter pill for liberals and some leading educators to swallow. Some still cling to the hope. But, even assuming progress (and the point is arguable), little prospect of integration remains for millions of minority-group children in the large cities, where educational failure affects the largest number of children. One of the Nixon Administration's first domestic controversies raged about the relaxation of desegregation guidelines and deadlines for Southern school districts. The Supreme Court and the Justice Department now appear to be in conflict over the possibility of implementing the desegregation decisions within a reasonable time. The President himself has sealed the fate of integration in many sections by declaring his opposition to busing as a means of eliminating segregation, as have state legislatures and governors in many states.

Despite the pronouncements of federal education officials about the harmful effects of school segregation, federal practice itself has reflected, rather than overcome, local unfavorable political climate to integration in the North. As most clearly embodied in Title I of the 1965 ESEA, high priority, in the form of unprecedented funds, has gone toward improving education in existing segregated schools through compensatory measures.

When the federal government has attempted to flex its fiscal muscles, some school districts have forgone millions of dollars in federal funds rather than integrate their school systems, and not only in the South. Boston, even under the threat of having $4 million in state funds withheld, resisted pressure to reduce *de facto* segregation. Its school board also refused to alleviate overcrowding in ghetto schools by transporting Negro children to underutilized schools in mainly white neighborhoods. At one point, when the U.S. Office of Education threatened to use its financial leverage to compel Northern cities to desegregate more aggressively, political pressure, notably by Mayor Richard Daley of Chicago, beat back the attempt. It remains to be seen whether the $1.5 billion carrot offered in the President's 1970 message on desegregation will be any more effective in advancing integration than the fiscal sticks used by previous administrations.

Even with commitment and leadership at the state level, urban school segregation has not been halted. In 1965, Massachusetts became the first state to enact a law stipulating that no more than 50 per cent of any public school may be nonwhite. Yet, by the end of 1968, racial imbalance had spread to seven more schools, bringing the state total to sixty-seven, fifty-seven of which are in Boston. Since the law was enacted, racial imbalance has spread to five more schools in Boston and to two more in New Bedford, where there had been four before the law.

Pittsburgh, among other large cities, has even abandoned the rhetoric of planned desegregation through such unpopular methods as busing or redistricting, for fear of frightening away the dwindling number of whites. Instead, Pittsburgh's entire integration program is aimed at significant change not in the immediate future but several years away. As noted earlier, it is hinged on a program for reconstructing and educationally improving five Great High Schools. The school system will use the existing high schools as intermediate institutions and abolish some of the old ghetto schools. Education officials hope eventually to rearrange the ethnic composition of the remaining institutions to achieve a somewhat better balance. But, at best, the

Pittsburgh effort will have no effect in desegregating the elementary grades, where it is known that integration has its greatest positive effects. In this respect, Pittsburgh is no different from most other communities, North or South. Flying in the face of the evidence, the direction of whatever integration has been achieved is from the upper grades down, instead of from the bottom up.

One of the more recent plans proposed for achieving integration in large cities (and some smaller ones) is metropolitan integration, across present school-district boundaries. Given the intensity of white opposition to milder approaches to desegregation and, in most instances, the rebuff given by whites to plans for metropolitan cooperation in many less emotionally charged functions (waste-disposal for one), the proposal seems politically unfeasible, if not impossible. It should be noted that total political metropolitanism, as logical and desirable—and even righteous —as it may appear in the context of a good-government theory, in effect means dilution of the nonwhite political power that is building up as urban centers become increasingly nonwhite. Metropolitanism has made strides in attacking such problems as scarce or specialized resources—as, for example, in vocational education, or schooling for the mentally retarded, or joint ventures in curriculum and materials. But considerably less success has attended efforts across political boundaries in the intense human problems of education, particularly integration and the disadvantaged. Here and there around the country (Hartford, Rochester, Boston, for example), several hundred black children are bused into predominantly white suburbs, but, elsewhere, the suggestion has drawn bitter fire from parents, school boards, professionals, and, more recently, some Negroes. Philadelphia's progressive school board president, Richardson Dilworth, for example, has been called a "madman" for suggesting city-suburban exchanges of pupils and services. The occupants of respective rungs on the socio-economic ladder are, apparently, bitterly protective of their relative exclusivism against those one or more rungs down. Separate political jurisdictions, down to small, Balkanized units, whose demise many political scientists urged a decade or so ago, have, if anything, become more deeply entrenched by issues of race and poverty, and by public school issues, in particular. In the mainly well-to-do and reputedly liberal New York suburb of Great Neck, for example, voters rejected three-to-two a school board proposal to bus in forty-five to sixty children from New York City ghetto schools. The issue bitterly polarized factions within the white community. According to Ronald Smothers of *Newsday*, Negro parents already in the district (about 3 per cent of the school district's 9,000 pupils are Negroes) share a feeling of minority alienation within an affluent white community. One black parent, Mrs. Betty Brumfield, while she approved the plan, believed that the teaching staff also needed to be integrated. "How would you feel if you were a black child and almost all the teachers you saw were white?" she asked. More Negro teachers were needed, she said, so that children "will know that Negroes aren't only maids in the homes of their classmates."

Moreover, there is a growing shift of emphasis by minority-group members themselves away from integration at the option of the white majority. Most programs to integrate schools have been oriented toward movement of pupils in one direction only, away from the Negro community. One of the most publicized "integration" successes, for example, is White Plains, where no white exodus has occurred and where Negro children are reported achieving far better than in their former, predominantly black, school. Yet, the integration there was achieved several years ago by transporting the Negro children to schools in middle- and upper-middle-class, white residential areas. The more recent Negro reaction to such plans may be noted in the Norwalk, Connecticut, case, in which both CORE and the NAACP filed court charges against one-way busing of Negro students as a means of increasing school integration in Norwalk. They say the implication is that black neighborhoods are inferior to white neighborhoods as sites for integrated schools.

Another technique, open enrollment, tends to drain off from all-black schools children whose parents have either the means or the strongest motivation to escape from ghettoized education. But it leaves still-segregated schools behind. The educational park concept, too, seeks to make integration less unpalatable for the white community by locating integrated schools outside Negro neighborhoods. The one-way movement is cultural as well as physical. The receiving school is bent on absorbing Negroes into its predominant culture and value system. Rarely does it make an effort to acknowledge—much less make affirmative educational use of—the culture of the minority-group child. Implicitly, such one-way integration says about the minority children, their families, and their community what three centuries of enforced inferior status have imprinted on society: that what is black is, intrinsically, less worthwhile and less desirable than what is white. For the vast majority of white parents, and, perhaps, for most blacks until recently, schools in depressed areas are stigmatized. It is not bigotry alone that persuades parents who can to avoid them and to resist efforts to transfer their children there; they do so also because they believe such schools provide unequal educational opportunities.

Thus, the shift of many blacks away from concentrated efforts for school integration involves matters beyond, and quite different from, a desire for separatism. First, and most simply, after fifteen years of frustration, dashed hopes, and broken promises, many blacks (like many white liberals) have simply tired or despaired of continuing the struggle under present circumstances. Second, many blacks have perceived that the post-1954 struggle for integration was, despite many instances of sincerity, clothed in condescension. For proof, they point to the fact that under current power arrangements, integration is an option of the white community.

Third, they believe that the dependent status of the Negro in American society is perpetuated by the notion that the only way to help the black child is to seat him alongside white children. Beneath this mood is a quest for stronger racial identity and pride, and a desire to gain more control of their own destiny. The Negro drive for integration was based, rather, say many Negro spokesmen, on their belief that parents in predominantly white schools exercised enough power to insist and ensure that the school offered quality education, in which black pupils should share. Unless they linked themselves to such power, Negroes faced further destruction of identity and increasing disconnection from the larger society.

One implication for public education in these Negro attitudes toward more than a decade of incomplete and inadequate integration efforts is greater participation by blacks in predominantly black schools. This is rather different from the "separate but equal" doctrine, since some "black power" exponents reason that, when Negroes achieve quality education under their own aegis, they will then be prepared to connect (integrate) with the white society on a basis of parity instead of deficiency. A good school then would be defined not by the kind of children who attend it, but by the quality of the education offered.

The community-control movement, therefore, does not imply abandonment of the goal of school integration. Rather, it acknowledges the past failure to achieve integration and shuns integration of vastly unequal parties. Instead, it calls for a broadening of the goals of integration to restore a quality that has been sidetracked in the emphasis on the basic-skills–achievement goal of desegregation. That is, school integration must reaffirm the commitment to connect different groups with one another *as human beings*. Under the new goals, diversity and differences must be viewed as assets, rather than unfortunate barriers to homogeneity, and this view must be valued as having as positive an effect on human growth and development as the teaching of academic skills.

About these new goals, Dr. Kenneth Clark has said:

> The suggested shift in emphasis from desegregation to quality of
> education is not a retreat into the blind alley of accepting racial

separation as advocated by the Negro nationalist groups. Nor is it the acceptance of defeat in the battle for desegregation. It is rather a regrouping of forces, a shift in battle plans and an attempt to determine the most vulnerable flanks of the opposition as the basis for major attack. The resisting educational bureaucracies, their professional staffs, and the segment of the white public which has not yet been infected fatally by the American racist disease are most vulnerable to attack on the issue of the inferior quality of education found in Negro schools and the need to institute a plan immediately to raise the educational level of these schools.

This suggests that Negro demands for participation in public education are actually aimed at attaining greater *connection* to society, not separatism. It may not be a coincidence that some of the same groups responsible for impeding plans for integration have turned their energies to opposing plans for community control. But the Riles Report, a recent high-level study (by an Urban Education Task Force appointed by HEW Secretary Robert Finch) that insists on the necessity for integration, defends the eventual compatibility of the movement for community control of schools with integration.

Model Subsystems

In an effort to explore improved learning strategies and techniques, educators create experimental units in which they hope to improve training, retraining, curriculum, and methodology patterns that may be disseminated throughout school systems. A subunit may consist of one or a cluster of schools. Projects under the Elementary and Secondary Education Act are seeking to create regional subsystems, through consortia of institutions.

Under Title IV, for example, twenty regional educational laboratories were established "to link the ivory tower of research and a classful of youngsters." The laboratories have sought to develop, test, and refine a range of techniques from computer-assisted instruction and individually paced curricula to televised "micro" lessons that permit teachers to observe and evaluate themselves. The results are then supposed to be adopted in school systems. Initially, according to some Office of Education officials, it was necessary for some laboratories "to initiate projects for the purpose of building regional good will and as entrees to more extensive innovative work," and the effort was widely criticized for pursuing too many dead-end ideas or rehashing the obvious. More forceful federal guidelines later stimulated the laboratories into what appears to be more venturesome work. However, none of the laboratories' projects have been concerned with the governance of the public schools, and a disproportionate number appear to be directed toward schools serving predominantly middle-class white college-bound pupils. By mid-1969, several of these laboratories had closed down.

Although some colleges and universities have, for many years, maintained experimental undergraduate subsystems (honors colleges, for example), the trend toward this mode of intervention in public schools may have started with a progress report (by a panel headed by Jerrold Zacharias) to the U.S. Commissioner of Education in March, 1964. The report led to the creation of a model subdivision in the Washington, D.C., public schools. At about the same time, the Syracuse public schools (in the Madison Area Project), and later the Boston public schools created subsystems in a deliberate attempt to provide the total system with a development and training conduit for successful innovative practices.

The most recent and most visible instances of model subsystems in a large urban establishment are three experimental school clusters in Manhattan and Brooklyn (including an I.S. 201 complex). These differ from earlier subsystems in that they are governed by community-based boards, although they must still seek ultimate approval on any number of basic decisions from the central board of education.

Many see the subsystem as a means for involving new institutions and persons outside the educational establishment with the urban schools. In New York City, for example, New York University, Teachers College, Queens College, and Yeshiva University have "adopted" single public schools. Antioch College helped start an experimental subsystem school in Washington, the Adams-Morgan School. Such links help bring the teacher-training institutions a step closer to the public schools than the laboratory schools many of them have maintained for years. The university-based laboratory school serves three purposes: as a training ground for prospective teachers, as an alternative to the public schools for children of faculty members, and as a hothouse in which education innovations may be nurtured. Both the conditions and student bodies of the laboratory schools and the surrounding urban schools have differed so markedly, however, that the hothouse function has often proved ineffective in reforming urban school systems.

In addition to colleges and universities, community agencies, research and development centers, Peace Corps and Vista vetterans, private industry, and the professions are seen as possible sources of new talent and ideas to be introduced through model subsystems.

Some corporations that have expanded into both the software (curricula and systems) and hardware (teaching machines, textbooks, and other instructional devices) markets have opened up their own schools, which they use both as testing grounds and as demonstration centers for the programs they are trying to sell to public school systems.

Intervention through model subsystems represents substantial progress toward a realization that "more-of-the-same" approaches have limited effect. It represents a refreshing intellectual concession that the educational process and system may share responsibility with the learner for his failure to achieve. It also borrows a leaf from scientific, technological, and industrial enterprises in its commitment to research and development. The vogue for subsystems is developing rapidly, despite scant experience with them and even scantier evidence of success. There are intrinsic constraints in the organizational framework within which *dependent* subsystems seek to explore the avenues of change.

First, experience suggests that the model lacks the autonomy and freedom to follow its findings through to their ultimate conclusion. More likely than not, explorations into new school patterns call for breaking the rules, and the mother system is frequently unwilling to give her precocious, adventurous children much latitude. As in the human body, the new organ tends to be rejected by the natural host. In the search for other harbors of connection—colleges or foundations, for example—the subsystems may consume so much energy as to weaken their efforts to innovate. Subunits also depend too often for their new energies and resources on imported consultants, who do not become integral members of the existing structure. And, as a practical matter, the educators selected to head subunits are often irreversibly captive to bureaucratic rigidity; their underlying identification is likely to be with the central system that sanctioned the experiment—that is, with the *status quo*—rather than with the new territory the experimental subunit seeks to explore.

The pitfalls of some such attempts are given in exaggerated form in an account of a pilot program in the Boston public schools. Called Operation Counterpoise, its purpose was, in the thoughtless terms of one of its architects, to "compensate for the parental lack of values." For example, training sessions for teachers ignored the ethnic background of the students and the implications of ethnicity. The teachers assigned to the program were, for the most part, the same teachers who had failed "to turn the kids on" in the first place. The in-service training program for Counterpoise teachers did nothing to challenge these teachers' attitudes about their students.

Even without such clumsiness, dependent subsystems can run up against a blank wall. Carl Dolce, former New Orleans superintendent of schools, regarded as one of the country's more enlightened urban educators, describes a model subsystem in the New Orleans public school system as follows:

> We have isolated several of our schools and we have said to them, "You are an autonomous section of this school system. Throw out the established curriculum, throw out the things you don't want, you do the job, and here are the resources."

What is happening to children? Not much! We have thrown out the crutches that educators have used for a long period of time. One of the crutches is large class size. Okay, we say, we will reduce class size. And then we are told, "Well, we don't have enough supplies and equipment." So we pump in supplies and equipment, and now what we are getting is, "Well, the problem is the community." Where does the rationalization stop? And where, and at what point, are people expected to produce?

As for college- or university-operated subsystems, it has not proved easy for a college to operate a project in one school, much less extend it to others. John H. Fischer, president of Teachers College, has analyzed some of the pitfalls as follows:

University groups have been willing merely to use the schools to serve their own research interests or as convenient populations from which to draw samples. School systems, on their side and often with justification, have resented outside research as an intrusion upon the normal, and in their view more important, activities of the classroom. If school-university association in research and development is to be as productive as present needs require, we shall have to move beyond the practice of viewing each project as a separate *ad hoc* exercise. We must establish mutually agreed-upon long-range policies that respect the needs, interests, and resources of all participants. We must lay the groundwork for continuing and flexible cooperation at levels ranging from small studies with a few children to large-scale experiments involving entire schools and school systems.

Most experiments have brought in primarily white professors or teacher-trainees, and some residents make little distinction between them and the white people who have been running their schools for years. A highly publicized Bedford-Stuyvesant project, supported by the Ford Foundation, sought, in a junior high school, both to train teachers sensitive to needs of ghetto students and to enlist university resources for improved teaching. The school's seventh grade was divided into six clusters, each headed by a leader from the participating college. Instead of going their separate ways for different courses, the pupils in each cluster stayed together for all classes.

Four months after the start of the project, one-third of the N.Y.U. personnel had resigned from it. The teacher-leaders, who had been trained in ghetto schools, found their experiences in J.H.S. 57 "shattering." Students were an average of two and a half years behind grade norm. A twenty-three-year-old black teacher, for example, who had himself come from a broken home, recalled that he had thought of school as a home but did not believe present-day schools were providing ghetto children with the same shelter. Cluster teachers disagreed about teaching goals, some considering social skills and subject matter more relevant to the children's lives and more important than academic skills. Other teachers laid heaviest stress on reading skills (some seventh grade students could not identify differences between letters of the alphabet). All of the teachers ran into obstacles erected by the school administration. The breakdown in the school was given notoriety in a film titled "The Way It Is," shown over educational television stations throughout the country. "Somewhere and somehow the schools destroy the kids, especially in the ghetto . . . something happens to the kids in the classroom," the film's narrator said. The film concluded that teachers in such schools must throw away the rule book in dealing with situations to which the school system's rules do not respond or, indeed, exacerbate. It also called for community participation in school affairs. Describing teachers as "taken out of the antiseptic university situation and put in the combat zone," it said they have to be "turned on" and free to use creative methods.

Washington Post education writer Susan Jacoby sympathized with some students' complaints that the chaos inside the school was worse than the chaos in the surrounding slum. On the theory that the school's pupils have too short an attention span, class periods were 20 to 30 minutes shorter than in most schools elsewhere, and loud gongs signaled class changes every 35 minutes. "They leave a painful ringing in the head for several minutes after they subside," she reported, "a pain which becomes more or less constant as the day wears on." Classes were interrupted frequently by announcements by the principal over the loud-speaker system about rule violations. Fights between students and with teachers were frequent during class changes.

Professor Jack Robertson, the project director, says the project narrowed its objectives after the first year: "We were going to surround the school but it surrounded us. Now we've given up on trying to change the school and are trying to carve out an island in the midst of chaos for the kids we're working with." N.Y.U. had, in the school, eight teachers, thirty-eight student teachers and nine additional support personnel (social workers, an educational psychologist, a coordinator for the student teachers, and two community agents who lived in the neighborhood). The incumbent educators regarded the very presence of the university reformers as an indication that someone thought they had been doing a poor job. During the second year of the project, the school principal requested that the university leave the school. "How can you say these people are dedicated when so many of them left?" he asked. "I don't believe they've made any significant improvement in the school at all. Anyway, should an educational experiment last forever?"

In reply, the resident director said the university's biggest problem had been lack of cooperation from the school administration:

> The major problem . . . is that the community has not yet been able to force [the schools] into a state of accountability. Because of the publicity our efforts have received, we have produced a situation in which many more people have become involved with the school. Our big mistake was not involving the community with planning for this project from the beginning.

Experimental subsystems also are under pressure to produce results quickly. The mother system, which itself may be in disarray due to years or decades of decline, nonetheless is impatient to evaluate the subsystem, and vested interests are sometimes only too ready to label it a failure if it does not turn out an impressive record of achievement in a year or two.

Whether a subsystem is dependent or largely autonomous, it is not likely to affect an entire system that is governed by an adept and hierarchy-hardened bureaucracy and conditioned by fixed patterns of behavior. Moreover, the educational substance of subsystems has, up to this point, been fragmented. The experiments tend to concentrate on one piece of a school system—team teaching, new careers for the poor, role playing, teacher training, or reading, for example—but seldom with the form and structure of the total system.

Notwithstanding, model subsystems continue to be established. Among the more recent are designs growing out of Model Cities legislation. For example, a new community is being planned in Washington, D.C., to be called Fort Lincoln New Town. The heart of the New Town is its proposed altogether new educational system, as described in *Designing Education for Tomorrow's Schools* by Mario Fantini and Milton Young. While it will still be a part of the District of Columbia public school system, it has been given a special experimental status that will allow it to depart from the conventional educational practices.

Parallel Systems

One set of approaches to quality urban education amounts not so much to intervention as it does to an escape into various forms of parallel systems. Such approaches assume that, if the poor (or others) cannot reform public education, they should be afforded options to it. The proponents of this approach, known also as the market strategy, argue, too, that schools that needed to compete for students would be more likely to be responsive to their students' needs and parents' wishes. The competition would stimulate innovation and experimentation by the schools. According to the father of the market approach, University of Chicago economist Milton Friedman, "Parents could express their views about schools directly, by withdrawing their children from one school and sending them to another to a much greater extent than is now possible."

Dozens of privately managed schools have been established in urban ghettos, and several others are in the planning stage. Precedents for such schools exist in Southern Freedom schools (notably Neil Sullivan's school for Negro pupils in Prince Edward County, Virginia). Among the better-known Northern counterparts are Harlem's Academies of Transition (Street Academies), whose enrollment consists mainly of hard-core rejects and dropouts from the public school system and whose aims are to send most of these students on to college. (Harlem's Urban League–sponsored academies are sending more than 75 per cent of their students to college.) Other well-known privately supported schools located in urban ghettos include the New School in Boston's Roxbury section, the East Harlem Block School, the West Side Community School in New York, and Highland Park School in Boston. Among other basic differences from most public schools, these encourage a strong and direct parental role. Operation Head Start schools, though government financed, are "private" in the sense that they exist apart from the public school system and are not subject to its rules and regulations, governing personnel, curriculum, and other matters.

Of considerable potential significance to urban education is an act approved by the Massachusetts legislature late in 1967 that enables the state department of education to assist and sponsor experimental school systems planned, developed, and operated by community-based private, nonprofit corporations. Assuming a greater role in education and urban problems, states could establish yardsticks, "educational TVA's," to measure the effectiveness of different forms of education innovation. The first of the Massachusetts schools opened in the fall of 1968 under the auspices of the Committee for Community Educational Development, assisted by state funds. A bill has passed the Pennsylvania legislature providing an estimated $20 million in public funds for privately operated schools (including parochial schools). The bill has successfully undergone its first court test of constitutionality.

One of the most breathtaking arrays of parallel school systems has been sketched by Kenneth Clark. In the light of Dr. Clark's unswerving dedication to the improvement of the public schools, both through integration and through strong community participation, one may suspect his frequent espousal of these far-out systems either as a hypothetical challenge to conventional public education or as a genuine expression of despair at the prospects of public education ever serving minority youngsters with quality education. Whatever the case, he has suggested the possibility of: regional state schools that would be financed by the states and would cut across present urban-suburban boundaries; federal regional schools, financed by the federal government out of present state aid funds or with additional federal funds, cutting through state boundaries, and providing for residential students; college and university-related open schools, to be financed by colleges and universities as part of their laboratories in education yet not restricted to children of faculty and students; industrial demonstration schools—not vocational schools, but schools offering a full academic program—for company employees and selected members of the public; labor union–sponsored schools, though not exclusively for the children of the union's members; and army schools, for adolescent dropouts or educational rejects but not necessarily as an integral part of the military, and subject to quality control and professional accountability maintained and determined by federal and state educational standards and supervision.

Unquestionably, nonpublic schools have flexibility. They do not have to deal with distant and entrenched bureaucracies, with school boards unfamiliar with their particular needs, or, as a rule, with teachers' unions. They are free to hire teachers from a variety of personnel pools and to sidestep rigid credential-granting procedures. They may even abandon such practices as tenure and retain, promote, or discharge teachers purely on the grounds of merit and performance. If the schools are governed by boards with a substantial representation of their pupils' parents, they are likely to be more responsive to the children's needs and thereby encourage better rapport and partnership between the home and the school. In the most general sense, they afford parents the choice of educating their children elsewhere if they are dissatisfied with the performance of the public schools. If enough private schools were available, and if they were so financed or equipped with scholarships as to give the poor the same choice that is open to many middle-class urban parents, the pattern would usher in an entrepreneurial system in which parents could choose, cafeteria-style, a range of styles of education—Montessori, prep school, Summerhill, and others.

Carried to its logical conclusion, the parallel school approach would reduce the scope of public education, if not dispense with it altogether. One of the more extreme proposals along these lines is Christopher Jencks', which calls for allowing "[black] nationalists to create their own private schools, outside the regular public system, and to encourage this by making such schools eligible for substantial tax support." Jencks maintains that the urban school crisis is similar to the conflict a century ago when Catholic immigrants confronted a public system run by and for Protestants. Indeed, he suggests that a black private school system should "ally itself with a parochial system in demanding federal and state support for all private schools." But Jencks seems to contradict the concept of "separate" school by maintaining that "the state should not subsidize any school which is not open to every child who wants to enroll—regardless of race, religion, or ability." (Incidentally, Jencks, under an OEO grant, is presently conducting a study of the voucher concept. Vouchers would provide direct payments of government funds to parents, permitting them to choose schools for their children. One of the obvious problems in the voucher arrangement is that it would benefit the middle class more than the poor.)

The establishment of private schools sufficient to handle significant numbers of poor children would require public support and, in effect, establish a private system of publicly supported schools. Middle-income parents would demand similar privileges.

Whether sophisticated fiscal arrangements could be devised to permit the parallel school approach to become widespread in the foreseeable future is very much an open question. So is the extent to which the scheme could overcome political, if not constitutional, hurdles.

A foretaste of political reaction to a concerted drive for direct state aid to private education is given by Coleman Young, a Negro state legislator from Michigan. Such a drive, if successful, could, he says, "mean the end of public education as we know it." He explains further:

> It is a very real threat, based on serious and honest philosophical contentions, which are not to be easily dismissed. And here again we run head on into the question of racism.
>
> It is not coincidental that some of the southern states in our nation, faced with the Supreme Court decision on integration, were the first to raise this question of direct public subsidy of private educational institutions. [Michigan has] passed a bill which, in essence, provides for private schools all the auxiliary services that are provided for public schools—such as nurses for health service, transportation, remedial reading, etc. This year we are confronted directly with the demand: 'Let the tuition follow the child.' . . . The minimal $21 million subsidy called for in the present bill would quickly become accelerated to about a quarter of a billion dollars, which is what it would cost in our state to subsidize private schools on the same level as public.
>
> This demand comes at a time when there is obvious emergency need to reorganize the fiscal structure for our public schools, which are in danger of complete collapse.

And, since private schools would not be subject to public control, there would, as a matter of public policy, need to be guarantees against the maintenance of publicly funded private education run by special-interest groups for ends inimical to a free and open society. Support of such enterprises at public expense would be intolerable. For alternate school systems, of course, have not always been designed to serve the purposes of reform. In nine Southern states, 200 new private schools, enrolling some 40,000 youngsters (as of January, 1968), have been established as the federal courts have begun to force desegregation of public schools. Private school enrollment is increasing at a rapid pace in Northern cities, too. In many of the large cities, between 20 and 30 per cent of the school population is now in private schools.

Jencks, at least, is candid in acknowledging that his proposal is more political than educational: "These schools would not, I predict, be either more or less successful than existing public schools in teaching the three R's. But that is not the point. The point is to find a political *modus vivendi* which is tolerable to all sides." Furthermore, he joins that group of urban observers who see no fundamental solution to the urban school problem without a general transformation of the ghetto: "After that, the struggle to eliminate the ghetto should probably concentrate on other institutions, especially corporate employers."

Some educators, of course, question the basic premise of proposals to replace the public schools with publicly subsidized and competitive independent schools. Thus, John Fischer says: "I know of no evidence that for any given group of students independent schools can provide a better education than well-staffed and well-managed public schools. Nor, as far as I can tell, do the advocates of the proposal have any such data."

Be that as it may, to push parallel school systems seriously as a major solution to the urban school crisis is possibly misleading in that it may divert attention from the main job of reforming the public school system. Worse, if pressure builds for public support of these schools, it may provide legislators with a rationale for deferring or eliminating necessary increases in public school expenditures. These arguments are, of course, no reason to discourage programs that enable more low-income pupils to attend private schools. Private schools can serve a valuable yardstick function, if they are run under conditions that simulate the resources and inputs of public education—particularly comparable per capita expenditures, and admission policies that should embrace a range of low-income pupils, including the so-called disruptive. But, at least for the short run, that is the limit of their usefulness as a major alternative to improved public education, for there is no ready prospect that they could serve more than a small number of the children of the poor.

Total-System Reform

As we have seen, the compensatory approach has apparently failed, integration is not a realistic short-range prospect, model subsystems do not give much evidence yet of realizing their promise, and parallel systems are, basically, an avoidance of the challenge to reform the schools where most children continue to be educated. The latest and one of the most promising approaches to intervention is reform of total school systems, structurally and otherwise.

There are several varieties of total-system intervention. One approach is to provide new leadership for the system as a whole, while leaving the system's form and structure basically intact. This approach is exemplified by trends in Philadelphia, where a reform-minded central school board, including former Mayor Richardson Dilworth, and a new superintendent of schools with a record of innovation, have, for the last four years been attempting to strengthen the effectiveness of the old system with the infusion of new staff and new styles. Pittsburgh, too, is trying to improve the efficiency of the existing system, within the operational definition of quality education as achievement according to norms. Washington, which, as noted, has started on the reform path through the model-system approach in a few schools, has been urged to reform totally; the Passow Report on the District's schools recommended a total-system reform by decentralizing the system into eight subsystems of approximately equal size, but the report has not been implemented.

Another form is the proposed merger of the school systems of two entire political jurisdictions. Such was proposed, for example, between the city of Louisville and Jefferson County. It would have differed markedly from the piecemeal metropolitan experiments noted earlier. In this case, the new metropolitan school system would have consisted of a number of subdistricts, each with considerable autonomy yet federated into a single system to preserve the best of the worlds of bigness and smallness. The Louisville–Jefferson County proposal did reach the Kentucky legislature, but was defeated in 1968.

In subsystems, models of excellence must swim against the tide of the *status quo* system. The total-system approach has no such constraint; there is no boring from within, for everyone starts at the reform gate at the same time. In a federation of autonomous subsystems, each with an equitable share of the resources, instructional practices would operate in an open, competitive market. The most successful models would be on display as a challenge to the other subsystems to adopt their approaches or surpass them in performance.

The difficulties to be faced in achieving systemwide reform cannot be minimized. Such efforts must take into account the vested interests in maintaining the system and the political forces that naturally would be aroused by any movement toward fundamental change. The history and traditions of large-city school systems have successfully insulated and isolated the school professionals from outside review. Reform of the system would seriously threaten these traditions.

A realistic approach to school reform demands analysis of the present school structure and the nature of power in the system as it now functions. Unless we can pinpoint where and how policies are made, and the sources of potential conflict, we cannot expect to determine the means for effectively changing that process.

3

School Governance and Policy-Making

> If it is believed that the elementary schools
> will be better managed by the Governor and
> Council, the Commissioners of the Literary
> Fund, or any other general authority of the
> Government, than by the parents in each
> ward, it is a belief against all experience.
> —THOMAS JEFFERSON (Letter to Joseph Cabell)

Common to all parts of the nation is a tradition of public education as a governmental activity of great practical and ideological value. Although U.S. public education in the sense of free compulsory schooling is hardly a hundred years old, and although public education through to the completion of high school for a majority of the eligible age group is only a twentieth-century phenomenon, the founding fathers set great store by an educated electorate. Their concept was limited, of course, by the fact that the electorate was initially restricted to property-holders. Thus, the public education ethos in the beginning may have been more elitist than egalitarian. But the egalitarian flavor has predominated unmistakably since the great waves of European immigration from the middle of the nineteenth century to World War I. The school was the indispensable ladder to mobility. It was, also, the acculturating instrument, through which immigrants were transformed into good American citizens.

Despite the increasing public attention paid to school affairs in the post–World War II era, the subject of school governance attracted little attention. Dissatisfaction was usually expressed in attacking the incumbent governors of the system or in replacing one set of decision-makers with others more reflective of the views and wishes of the opponents. Little attention, and less action, was applied to the *means* of governance. Less, still, was applied to an analysis of who really governs.

As Kenneth Clark has noted:

> Public school systems are protected public monopolies with only minimal competition from private and parochial schools. Few critics of the American urban public schools—even severe ones such as myself—dare to question the givens of the present organization of public education in terms of local control of public schools, in terms of existing municipal or political boundaries, or in terms of the rights and prerogatives of boards of education to establish policy and select professional staff . . . the relevance of the criteria and standards for selecting superintendents, principals, and teachers, or the relevance of all of these to the objectives of public education—producing a literate and informed public to carry on the business of democracy—and to the goal of producing human beings with social sensitivity and dignity and creativity and a respect for the humanity of others.

Urban School Districts and Their Demi-politics

The school district is as varied a government unit as the American political system has to offer. It may contain two schools with 680 students or it may contain, as does New York City's, some 900 schools and 1.1 million pupils. A district's annual budget may be as low as $300,000 or as high as New York's $1.2 billion.

Some districts coincide with the political boundaries of cities or counties. Others overlap to take in parts of two or more jurisdictions. Some contain only elementary schools and contract with other districts for secondary schooling of their residents' children. Others contain not only elementary and secondary schools but junior colleges and a variety of technical schools as well, including extensive adult education activities and such services as day-care centers for children of working mothers and preschool centers.

A school district may be independent or it may be a part of other local units of government, most often a city or county. Among independent districts, the degree of independence varies. Some may levy taxes with no more legal restraint than limits set by the state legislature in terms of a percentage of real estate valuation. Others are limited in their budget-making to approval by direct vote of all voters in the district. Regardless of their status under law, however, all school systems reflect an ideology and tradition of education as being independent of the political process.

In city school systems, the ethos of independence is manifest in the special legal status of the school district as a completely independent government, or, in some instances, as a semi-autonomous administrative structure under the state government. Even when a city school system has no taxing power, it is administered under a board of education that is separate from the city government, whether it is elected or appointed. The tradition is reflected, too, in the fact that, of the twenty largest cities (with school enrollments of more than 100,000), fifteen boards of education are fiscally independent.

But fiscal independence is not synonymous with autonomy, less dependence on city government, or indifference to the politics of the city. For example, following a Chicago teachers' union victory in obtaining a $1,000 raise plus ample fringe benefits, a school board member said that teachers had won their battle in the mayor's office by threatening to strike and that for the school board to negotiate with the union was pointless. "Why suffer through all the negotiations?" he said. "In future years we can skip all this nonsense and get to the crisis—and the mayor's office —right away." The member reported that the mayor "got purple, raised his voice, pounded the desk," in order to bring reluctant school board members around to agreement on the settlement; all eleven members of the board are nonsalaried appointees of the mayor. The pressure of increased financial needs and the constant need for voter approval of tax increases require school district leaders to work directly with city officials. The benefit of financial independence is also questionable, since the independent districts generally suffer a loss of state aid.

With the heightening of the urban crisis, the role of big-city mayors in education is coming full circle. Once mayors played a major role in the public school system through the dispensation of patronage and favoritism in employment and the award of school-building contracts. Until the turn of the century, large-city school boards were openly political—with some members appointed by the city council, others put in their posts by ward machines, and some directly elected.

In an account of a notorious case of political interference in school matters, Professor Robert H. Salisbury of Washington University, drawing on material studied by George Counts, has shown that political demagoguery may, sometimes, be the outward sign of deep-seated discontent with educational administration for which there are no other outlets. The case involves the 1927 mayoralty campaign in Chicago, in which the winning candidate promised to fire the superintendent of schools on the irrelevant charge that he was "pro-British." Behind the candidate's flamboyance, however, was the fact that the superintendent had discouraged vigorous teacher organizations, alienated labor in general, and generated class conflict by introducing the junior high school, which some construed as a step toward separate vocational training for working-class children. With considerable support from teachers, the demagogic mayoralty candidate won, and, in time, the superintendent was fired.

Counts himself, one of the deans of American professional education, said in another context:

> Rather than seek refuge in the cautious counsel of removing the school from politics, we should move forward under the assumption that the real business of politics is to provide the channels through which the living energies of society may flow into forms and patterns. The great desideratum . . . is to devise some means of making the school responsive to the more fundamental social realities and of enabling it at the same time to maintain an even keel amid the clash and roar of the contending elements.

The era of professional hegemony was quickened as the political mooring of lay influence weakened with the decay of ward politics. When reform insulated the personnel process and much of the construction gravy from city halls, mayors shunned the public school arena as having little political payoff and considerable potential headache.

Historically, there has been confusion and misapprehension over the meaning of the "politicalization" of education. It has usually been thought of either as exposing education to party influence or, in a more technical sense, as making educational systems regular line departments of city government, with directors appointed by the mayor to serve at his pleasure. Periodic recommendations that have emerged, particularly from academic sources, to abolish boards of education and establish education as a division or department of city government under the mayor have always been short-lived. They faced strong opposition from several quarters, particularly from the professionals in the system.

Actually, the separation of politics from education was never complete. It eroded further as education made compromises in order to receive increasingly larger shares of city budgets and as mayors in several cities were forced to take a central role in settling disputes on such matters as teachers' salaries. The merit system has only internalized school politics and shifted its arena. Today, despite the possibility of reprisals by the voters and accusations of interference from the professionals, the tradition of independence is giving way to greater engagement by large-city mayors—not so much because the issue is politically more attractive but because growing numbers of minority voters are looking to their highest elected local official for redress of grievances against inadequate schools and restrictive procedures that exclude them from the system. Ghetto residents have no reason to honor the purity of mayoral independence from school affairs.

Insulation of the schools from the rest of local government has prevented the integration of education policy with other urban activities. For example, the schools and agencies that are concerned with child and family welfare have much to offer each other, in the process of coordinating services with the pupil's school work to form a deeper understanding of the child and his environment. With the advent of antipoverty programs, inroads have been made toward overcoming the schools' insulation from other government agencies; school systems have been required to have representatives on mandated coordinating agencies, but the ethos of separation from the rest of government—from "politics" —dies hard.

On the key urban school issue of the late 1950's and early 1960's—racial integration—most mayors managed to escape central involvement, despite the efforts of some civic groups to win their leadership in improving racial balance in the schools. On the current issue—community voice in public education—mayors cannot be so nimble. For the community issue is entwined with a new grass-roots awareness that is of immediate and direct concern to city hall; moreover, it has become an important factor in Model Cities planning and implementation, which large-city mayors cannot afford to ignore.

In general, pressures are coming from several directions toward more political engagement in the urban school crisis. As a Michigan state legislator, Coleman Young, said recently,

> I find it somewhat amusing that many educators are hiding behind the self-constructed retreat of professionalism and looking down on politicians. If we are looking for solutions to the problems of education at the hands of some omnipotent mediator, we had best cast elsewhere and look to partisan struggle as the answer.

Anatomy of School Boards

The commonplace target of attempts to reform or rejuvenate the school has been the school board, which is the legally designated decision-making body and the agent of the highest education authority in the state, the regents or the state board of education or public instruction, as the bodies are known.

Assuming, for a moment, that school boards are, in fact, the governors of the schools, what are their characteristics? One attribute common to boards is that they are unpaid lay members of the community. No major school system is presently governed by paid professionals equivalent to the city manager or by paid commissioners.* Some school boards are elected, others appointed. Most large cities—New York, until now, having been the largest exception—elect their boards. However, the elections are at large, a factor, as will be noted later, that is crucial to the crisis of accountability in urban education. In more quiescent times, especially in smaller communities, a tradition of nonpartisanship was followed in school board elections, generally held in election off-years. The schools were said to be above politics, and, often, small, self-appointed groups of civic leaders chose one of their own number to stand for election, the prestige of the group being strong enough so that their choice was, generally, unopposed. Such benign selection is now largely a thing of the past, except in the most homogeneous and affluent suburbs.

Another reflection of the unique status of the school board as an arm of government is, in nonelective systems, appointment by a political authority—by a mayor, say, or, as in Philadelphia until 1966, by a group of judges. Appointment still is the method of school board selection in one-fourth of the large- and medium-sized city school districts. It is an approach that, presumably, insulates the school board from the partisanship associated with election contests but, in practice, it often places the matter squarely into the political realm. To mediate direct political influence, reformers seem to favor another system—the interposition of a screening mechanism into the appointment process. This system, presumably, obliges the mayor or other appointing authority to choose school board members from a pool of candidates screened and certified as capable and willing. The panel itself may be composed of prestigious and influential members of the community—college presidents and heads of civic organiza-

* Under 1969 legislation, however, New York City board members are paid on a *per diem* basis.

tions, for example. The final choice in this two-stage process, then, is political only in the sense that it is made by the mayor. It is presumed to be basically nonpartisan because the mayor is permitted to choose only candidates certified by civic leaders as having the best interests of the community at heart. The shift from direct mayoral appointment to appointment through a screening panel was viewed as a significant reform in urban school processes. Chicago and Philadelphia have adopted the panel process, and New York City similarly changed its system, as a result of an act of the 1961 state legislature that, following a series of school-construction scandals, removed the incumbent board. New legislation in 1969 switched New York to a mainly elective system (for five of seven members). A study by one of the authors indicated that, in practice, the selection panel made little difference in the appointments in any of the cities that used it.

Until recently, the focus of discussion of school-board selection and composition was on procedural matters. The pros and cons of elective vs. appointive methods were extensively debated. Those favoring elected boards argued for the ultimate fairness and wisdom of voting as a democratic process; taking the bad elective choices with the good was as much worth the risk in school government as in the government of the state or nation, they maintained. Proponents of appointed boards, on the other hand, said analogies with elected political office were unwarranted. Membership on a school board pays nothing, for one thing. For another, education is a unique function, in which the contention and partisanship that accompany elections ought to be avoided. Furthermore, high-minded men and women might be discouraged from serving on school boards if they had to go through the trouble, expense, and possible personal abuse of an election. Rarely argued, however, were the questions of how substantial the authority of the school board actually was and how representative a central school board—elected or appointed *at large*—could be, especially in large and ethnically and racially diverse areas.

If a community is an organic whole, with a single public interest in education, there is little reason to serve subcommunity, "selfish" interests by guaranteeing particular groups in the community (labor, ethnic minorities, etc.) seats on the board of education. But, in cities where the nonwhite proportion of the general population has grown and where the nonwhite proportion of the public school population has increased even more sharply, nonwhites are underrepresented on citywide school boards. The proportionate volume of nonwhite voting is still substantially below that of other groups. Moreover, white communities are generally better organized to elect their candidates, particularly in citywide elections. Minorities also tend to be underrepresented in appointive boards. In either case, the result, commonly, is a lack of accountability, of responsiveness to the needs of the non-white community—or, almost as important, a lack of *belief* within the nonwhite community that a body on which it is not represented, or is poorly represented, can be responsive.

For that reason, then, Negroes in some cities have proposed that the boards be elected on a district basis, to more accurately reflect the needs of the people in the community. A school board member elected at large, they argue, by virtue of being responsible to everybody, is really responsible to nobody, and where there is no responsibility, there is no responsiveness.

Regardless of the method of election, the composition of school boards in urban areas is markedly different from the over-all population of most large cities, and the contrast is even starker if the board is compared in its makeup to the parents of the children in the public schools.

Throughout the country, school board members, whether appointed or elected, have more formal education by far than the average for all citizens. For the most part, the members of the boards of education are recruited from the middle and upper classes, having established some prior role in political or educational circles. The last comprehensive national review of research, by the U.S. Office of Education in 1962, found that the larger the community, the higher the educational level of school board members. In districts of 25,000 pupils or more, for example, 72.6 per cent of the school board members had graduated from college, compared to 43.1 per cent of members in school districts with under 3,000 pupils (still above the 7.9 per cent of the total adult population who were college graduates). The average for all school boards was 48.3 per cent. Regional differences come into play, too: boards in the Northeast have the highest level of educational preparation, the South the lowest (though, again, higher than the national average for the total population). Only in the South, and there only by one measure, was any evidence found that elective boards contained significantly fewer less-educated members than appointed bodies: 50.3 per cent of elected Southern boards had at least one member who did not graduate from high school, compared to only 27.7 per cent of appointed boards. At the other end of the scale, at least one college graduate was found on 88.6 per cent of the appointed boards, compared to 71.6 on the elected boards.

Business and professional people dominate school boards the country over, according to the Office of Education survey. They account for more than three-fifths of the members. Housewives account for 7.2 per cent and skilled and unskilled workers for 9.4 per cent. The highest proportion of business and professional membership (75.2 per cent) was found in larger school systems. In general, appointed boards had an even larger proportion of business and professional men and women than the elected ones.

In 1967, one of the authors examined school board composition in six major cities (Detroit, Chicago, Philadelphia, New York, Baltimore, and St. Louis). She found that two-thirds of the members of all the boards were over fifty years of age. Each board takes into account the need to represent ethnic and religious groups, but the typical Negro board member is, usually, a professional not intimately identified with civil rights causes. Detroit had the highest proportion of nonwhite members (two out of seven) and Chicago the lowest (two out of nine).

In all six, women board members are representatives of established women's civic groups. Each board includes representation of the three religious groups, although not necessarily in strict proportion to the population of the city. The religious balance appeared to be a more sensitive issue in New York City than in any of the other cities. The adoption of the panel-selection device in Philadelphia, New York, and Chicago had made little difference in the composition of the board as compared to earlier boards in the same cities or as compared to the boards of other cities.

Nearly three-fourths of all board members were college educated, and about half had advanced or professional degrees. The most common advanced degree of board members was the law degree. In each of the cities, at least one and usually more of the board members were lawyers. Chicago, New York, and Detroit had labor represented on the board, indicating the importance of unions in those cities. In St. Louis, labor was unrepresented on the board.

Detroit, Philadelphia, and St. Louis had religious leaders on the board. The business community was represented on five of the six boards, most heavily in St. Louis. New York City had six board members with a background in professional education, St. Louis and Baltimore had three members with an education background and Philadelphia had one. Teachers were not represented on any of the boards.

In another day, wide social and economic disparities between governing bodies and the electorate were not so suspect. But such benevolence does not prevail in a climate of educational failure and suspicion by low-income, minority communities of the effectiveness, and even the motives, of school authorities, especially when a large school system's power is concentrated at the center.

But Who Is in Charge?

As a result of recent research into school policy-making, a more subtle issue has now come to the fore: Is the school board in the

large cities the strong branch of government its legislating and
policy-making powers would appear to make it? Effective school
board power is offset not only by such forces as accrediting agencies, the colleges and universities, and the National Education
Association and its galaxy of professional education associations
but also by centers of power closer to home. Other powerful
agents in the government of schools are the teachers and administrators. The more complex and sprawling a school system, the
more independent of the board a school bureaucracy may, in fact,
be. The board, which seldom has much of a staff directly and
wholly responsible to itself, must rely on the superintendent and
other school professionals for most of its information and recommendations. Weakness or ineffectuality of a board of education
is, in part, attributed to this lack of staff and to the limited time
available to board members as part-time, unsalaried officials.
Joseph Pois, a Chicago school board member, in his book *The
School Board Crisis,* notes the frustrations of school board members in the face of overwhelming problems and the lack of time
and resources. Often, the school board will be caught up in a
minor administrative problem and neglect long-range policy issues.

But, even in their own domain, policy-making, school boards
often are not the final masters. As a visible and handy target, the
superintendent himself is not likely to subvert or delay implementation of board policies, for, if his opposition is too blatant,
the board has the ready remedy of its power of removal. Under-
cutting by the rest of the professional bureaucracy, however, is
another matter. By inertia alone or non–decision-making, they
can thwart board intentions. In several studies of school integration in New York City, the failure of the bureaucracy to implement board policy has been shown as decisive in the final outcome.

With respect to parents and civic groups concerned with citywide educational policies, the administrators, having both control of information and insulation from public accountability,
can effectively fence off the public from an influential voice in

policies and practices in a variety of functions, from budget-making to curriculum.

Various organizations of principals, district superintendents, and other administrators in the New York system banded together in 1963 in a Council of Supervisory Associations, which, from time to time, has engaged in open rebellion—including lobbying, newspaper advertising, and other techniques of persuasion—against policies of their own chief administrator (the superintendent of schools) and the board of education. Supervisory and administrative dominance of decision-making in other cities, in some degree or other, has been attested to in several studies.

Large-city school systems are composed not only of vertical hierarchies of supervisors—from the superintendent of schools, at the pinnacle, to assistant principals or secondary-school department heads, at the bottom—but also of a horizontal structure of specialists. Specialists preside over dozens of services (such as audiovisual instruction), over curriculum areas (languages, the sciences, physical education, etc.) and, more recently, over involvement in federal aid programs. American schools are more lavishly administered than any in the world. James Koerner has remarked, "No other system can come even close to matching the numbers of full-time, non-teaching school administrators that run our local school systems . . . many of whom are more highly paid than state governors, university presidents, or our most distinguished scholars."

The specialists make policies for the system as a whole, implemented through headquarters-based directors to principals and field staff. In some cities, curriculum coordinators form a bridge between headquarters and the scene of action, but, often, the system flows—or crawls—in a stream of paper, some of it inhibiting, some of it ignored, and some of it irrelevant to many schools in the system.

Of course, any system with hundreds of employees, to say nothing of thousands, is, by definition, a bureaucracy. This term, of course need not be pejorative. But, as applied to school systems, it invariably has negative connotations. It is not the sheer size, alone, that casts the term in opprobium. It is, also, the style of the specialists and the crisscrossing of levels of authority. In most large school systems, promotion to supervisory rank is defined not so much by genuine merit as by the trappings of merit—formalized credentials and prescribed standards. Too often, the credentials and standards, presumably designed to assure quality, have hardened into barriers and restraints, limiting promotion to men and women ready to conform to a rule-ridden system and tenacious enough to pass through fixed hurdles that are legitimized more by age than by purposes that meet the fundamental needs of the system's clients, the children. The more complex the rules of the game, the more it pays the players who aspire to success to have been on the scene from the beginning of their careers. Thus, the system does not need to erect formal fences against outsiders, although it often does. It is *de facto* exclusive and inbred. The structure is further complicated by a web of guildlike organizations of specialists—of department chairmen, of principals at the elementary and secondary levels, of guidance personnel, of secretaries. More often than not, the guilds' roots lie in school politics rather than in professional concerns. They function as lobbies to protect or advance their status as against that of other guilds. In many ways, these associations serve as participants in policy-making through public statements and direct pressure on the board of education and on city and state officials. "The school administration, not the local board and not the teachers, remains the primary focus of control over educational policy and over its implementation," Koerner says.

Thus does the professional educator wield his power. In benign circumstances, the gains of the entrenched professional bureaucracy do not inflict great losses on others—except, of course, to the taxpayer, who must meet the cost without guarantees against nonproductivity. But that is, after all, true in many civil service structures, and in private organizations, too. But, when the circumstances are dynamic—when, for example, the makeup of the student population has changed drastically, or the society is gripped by social upheavals—the system then exacts a far greater toll. For changing clients and changing circumstances call for changes in the system, and a highly structured, inbred, and protective system does not change voluntarily. Usually, when change is thrust upon it, it accommodates only after bitter resistance. In such a contest, the other parties—in the case of schools, children and their parents—are lacking in power, initially unorganized, and easily intimidated by the authority of the professional. That is the political setting of the movement for community control, although, as noted elsewhere, the educational underpinnings are quite as powerful, if not ultimately overriding.

Administrative Decentralization

Over the years, the administrative staffs of urban school systems have increased in complexity and in numbers, the latter increase disproportionate to that of the student population. To alleviate the sheer weight of sprawling headquarters staff, many large-city school systems have established field administrative units, which may range in number from three (Baltimore) to thirty (New York). Mounting concern in recent years with an allegedly unresponsive headquarters staffs has resulted in the delegation of somewhat increased discretion in decision-making to field administrators. In other words, some administrative decentralization has been under way.

However, the mere delegation of responsibility is not a guarantor of responsiveness to community needs and desires. There is no redistribution of power under these arrangements. First, headquarters personnel retain strong controls over citywide policy. These administrators, in general, are the products of strict merit and seniority systems. Even a reform-oriented superintendent of schools often cannot choose his own administrative assistants and personnel staff. He must rely on people who have risen within the system.

Analysts of a reform administration in the Philadelphia public schools, for example, noted that the new superintendent, Mark Shedd, while he brought in a group of young, bright assistants, picked the top bureaucrats as his own men:

> He left the old Establishment intact. And the Establishment was not going to move the system forward. Some say that Shedd did not so much select these people as just close his eyes to their existence. There is a considerable body of thought in Philadelphia that the only way to truly deal with the administration building is to bury it. It contains 1,500 people, many of whom could be stacked in drawers and never missed.

In most urban school districts, the administrative hierarchy comes from the teaching ranks. Promotion to headquarters is based on either further required examination or experience as a school administrator. This procedure closes off the system to outsiders and nonschool administrators. Headquarters staff are generally experienced field personnel who have been promoted into these positions. With very few exceptions, nobody can be a superintendent of schools in the United States—no matter how distinguished he may be intellectually or as an administrator of other public institutions—who has not been through a stipulated training program in a school of education.

Further, there are limitations on the policy-making delegated locally to field administrators. And, even given some delegated authority, district officers still have an eye cocked upward, to headquarters and administrative superiors, and not across, to the community they are assigned to serve. Their eyes tend toward the distant, high direction even when decentralization includes local advisory boards of education. For example, years before murmurs of community control began in New York City, the board of education established a system of appointed local school boards. Although these boards have, at times, provided a useful forum for discussing school-site selection and other subjects, and, some-times, exerted decisive influence on substantive matters, they have lacked decision-making power. They could hold no one *responsible*—not the district administrator, not the central authority—for the performance of the schools in their district.

Martin Mayer, who served on a district school board in New York City for five years, has described the dead end to which many dedicated men and women have come under this structure: ". . . there was almost nothing I could do for the people who called me, and little of substance could come out of our meeting. . . . This giant empire is almost completely insulated from public control." Leading civic organizations, notably the Public Education Association, the Women's City Club, and the United Parents Association, have commented on the lack of community participation available under the advisory boards. And, as recently as 1968, a report of the board of education's own advisory committee on decentralization said that, despite the latest improvements in *administrative* decentralization, a sampling of local advisory boards showed the vast majority of members did not feel their advice was significantly influencing the district superintendent's actions. The conclusion was based on a nine-month survey of five districts varying in socio-economic composition but each having some contact with "disadvantaged" children.

Many local school boards, the report noted, were experiencing difficulty in overcoming professional inability or unwillingness to relate to the parental and subcommunity groups. Although district administrators were quoted as approving the concept of administrative decentralization, they expressed fears even over the increased status of the existing local school boards, which were a far cry from what proponents of full decentralization and meaningful community participation have in mind.

Most professionals (not just those in education) would prefer to be left alone by laymen. The public ideology of school professionals is that parents are apathetic about education, that, if they cared more and took a more lively interest in their schools, their children would do better. Such attitudes apply particularly to ghetto parents, whose poor attendance records at PTA meetings is often the object of tongue-clucking by school personnel and by "interested" middle-class parents.

The parent associations sometimes contribute to incidental improvements and occasionally exert pressure or persuasion on a substantive curricular matter. But their power is quite limited. Fundamentally, they are another reinforcement of the system and its needs, as distinct from the needs of students, which do not always coincide. PTA's are ridiculed for cake sales and preoccupation with trivia and sociability, but their effect is far more significant, in the negative sense. They exist as an elaborate structure at the local, district, state, and national levels, enrolling millions of members and putting forward the illusion of parent representation in public education. The effect of all this is regressive in at least two ways. First, it has often preempted or precluded the formation of other public groups with a direct policy role. Second, it has been supportive of the prevailing educational order.

Teacher organizations and unions have proliferated over the last several years and have emerged as another significant professional influence in school affairs. Although financially weaker than the NEA (a $2 million annual budget in 1967 compared to an estimated NEA budget of $25 million), the American Federation of Teachers is growing in strength; it has more than 650 chapters, and, beginning in the late 1960's, conducted strikes in several large and medium-sized cities. Union leaders have become important participants in school policy-making, and the union contract is one of the more important documents of school policy, particularly in such matters as working conditions, salaries, and fringe benefits. Priorities for the allocation of school funds are greatly influenced by the settlement of wage and salary levels for teachers. In several of the larger cities, unions and other teacher organizations have been directly involved in other related areas of school policy, often with the result that such provisions become an integral part of the contract arrangement. Such matters as team teaching, class size, and compensatory educational programs are becoming issues for negotiation. The American Federation of Teachers, in fact, has adopted a national policy favoring the More Effective Schools program (the compensatory education program initiated by the United Federation of Teachers in New York) and is seeking its adoption in several cities. Teacher organizations and unions have worked with school administrators on problems of recruitment and training as well.

The confrontation between the union and the ghetto community in New York City over the community-control issue indicated the enormous power that the union could exercise on local and state officials when it felt compelled to do so. There is no question but that teachers' unions have emerged as major participants in the politics of education in urban areas.

In addition to the formal organizations of professionals in urban communities, some important informal participants group together to influence school policy-making. Special education interest groups are usually reform-oriented citizens who watch over the school system on a citywide basis. Some have a small professional staff to carry on organizational or public relations activities, and they occasionally engage their own researchers for particular studies, some of which have proved valuable. More often, though, these groups support the system and serve to help in securing more funds for school purposes. They are seldom critical of the total system but may attack a particular program or encourage adoption of a new approach or project. Boards of education, superintendents and school administrators are usually in close contact with these groups and use their good offices to reinforce their own positions. On occasion, there is an interchange of personnel as well. In New York, for example, the former chief executives of two main education interest groups are now employed by the board of education.

Since racial integration became a lively issue in public education, civil rights and *ad hoc* local groups in urban areas have, also, become directly involved in education issues. In fact, many of the school systems have established human relations divisions to cope with the increasing pressures in this area. While civil rights groups have concerned themselves largely with the integration issue, they are, also, more directly involved than other citizen groups with other matters related to minority groups and compensatory educational needs. Their influence has, however, been of limited effect.

The analysis of power in school policy-making is particularly relevant to the movement for school reform—primarily because the concentration of power in the central bureaucracy in urban school systems is so basic to the lack of responsiveness of the system to changing circumstances and needs, but also because it greatly influences the ability to achieve change. Those in power have a vested interest in maintaining the system, while those who are powerless are striving to effect adjustments to allow their voices to be heard.

Community frustration with the public education system has manifested itself in the movement toward the community school, and this movement, of course, fits in with a general effort to achieve a redistribution of power to allow the public a greater voice in the development of educational policy.

4

The Community and the Schools

> We both consider the people as our children
> and love them with parental affection but
> you love them as infants whom you are afraid
> to trust without nurses and I as adults whom
> I freely leave to self-government.—THOMAS
> JEFFERSON

So long as the schools appeared to perform adequately, the growing distance of the policy-makers from the clients was too abstract an issue to arouse intense challenge. Parents, by and large,
considered the system (if they had occasion to consider it at all)
responsive and adequate, or better. In other words, the system
was responsive to felt need, if not expressed desire.

To be sure, the professional educators, not too long emerged
from an inferior status, remained mindful of potential parental
activism. School administration has always demanded political
acumen, if only as a matter of self-defense. "Community relations" has long been a staple of the curriculum for future school
principals and superintendents, and such institutions as the PTA,
open school week, and isolated school-visiting days are community relations devices. That they are devices aimed at giving the
illusion, and preventing the substance, of actual parental voice in
school decisions is an open secret, celebrated in what used to be
humorous commentaries about the impotence of PTA's.

The distance between school and community became a prime
educational issue only after the schools began noticeably to fail

in delivering a satisfactory product to large numbers of pupils, especially low-income urban racial minorities. However, initial recognition of massive pupil failure as a school responsibility instead of—or at least along with—defects in the learner and his home environment, did not crystallize all at once in community demands for control of the schools. An interim response was the development of "community schools."

The community school concept reflected growing concerns not only about educational disadvantage, but also about delinquency, poverty, and general urban decay. Such a school serves the community as a center for a variety of educational, cultural, recreational, and local social-development activity, for youngsters and adults. Ideally, such a school also uses the community as a laboratory for learning and organizes the curriculum around the processes and problems of living. And according to Edward G. Olsen, a leading analyst of the community school, it is designed to "practice and promote democracy in all human relationships," by encouraging "citizens, parents, teachers, pupils, and administrators [to] work together in the formulation of policy." The community school also has an economic motivation—to make more efficient use of the school plant. It is supposed to remain open day and night and to provide a center to which adults can come for advice and training, in areas ranging from literacy to skills development. In this interim stage, the community school continued to be governed mainly by educators but augmented by specialists in employment, homemaking, and other fields. The role of the community remained that of a client. Harold Gores, former superintendent of schools in Newton, Massachusetts, and now president of Educational Facilities Laboratories, observed that

. . . the young need to be served, but the schoolhouse committed only to the young is too specialized for the city's good. Indeed, if all parts of our cities are to become good places for people to live, committing the schools solely to the young is too slow a process. Adults need the schoolhouse as much as children do. And adults determine what happens now, not a generation hence. To put the matter in bluntest terms, the schoolhouse in the slums should be the people's college, their town hall, their cultural center, their country club, their school.

The foremost post–World War II model of the community school concept is the New Haven public school system, but there were prewar antecedents. One, the Flint, Michigan, program, arose from a noneducational and external impetus. It was initiated by Charles S. Mott, a wealthy automobile executive, to combat juvenile delinquency through recreation. Rather than construct separate facilities, Mott persuaded the Flint public schools to keep their buildings open afternoons and evenings in return for private support of youth programs. The program quickly expanded to adult education as well, and now includes enrichment classes for students, vocational advancement, hobbies and crafts, high school credit courses, and adult reading programs. The Flint program is said to have inspired the creation of community schools in more than 100 other localities. It has established a community council, composed of adult organizations within the schools and of clergy and businessmen within the attendance zones of each school. However, the community council role is advisory and confined to requests for after-school classes and sports.

The New Haven version of the community school added the dimension of distribution of social services. It was envisioned, wrote Mitchell Sviridoff, president of the board of education when it was initiated there, as "a neighborhood center where [counseling and services in such fields as health and employment] could be coordinated to meet the needs of the people in a specific area; and where, hopefully, the people themselves could initiate programs to help themselves." The schools house dozens of programs ranging from courses in black history for parents and teachers to tutoring and senior-citizen activities. Each school has a neighborhood service coordinator from the local antipoverty agency as well as staff from municipal health and recreation departments and private service agencies. "The point is that in the modern city people have needs which are closely connected," says Sviridoff. "People need good education and good health in order to achieve good employment . . . good employment in order to afford good housing. Good housing and good recreation are necessary for good health. And good physical and mental health are important if one is to get a good education."

Ironically, one of the most articulate exponents of the earlier style of community school was a New York City educator, Leonard Covello, principal of Benjamin Franklin High School, located in what was, at the time, a heavily Italian neighborhood and is, now, predominantly Negro and Puerto Rican. Covello, who was also one of a courageous few who organized a teachers' union in 1916, wrote:

> Formulation of school activities, planning of curricula, school administration, classroom techniques, and so forth, result in positive achievements only if and when all educational procedures are developed under constant awareness of the extra school educational forces active in the background of the students.

As Preston R. Wilcox, one of the latter-day theoreticians of community-*controlled* schools, notes, Covello used the concept to enable local residents to use the schools for dual functions:

1. To acquire the coping and elevating skills—educational, social and others—to enable them to move into the corporate world
2. To help deepen their understanding of the Italian culture as a tool for contributing effectively within their own private world

According to Covello:

> . . . the school must have a thorough understanding, not only of its aims, but of the needs and potentialities of its students. We have discarded the idea of the subject-centered school and developed, as the next step forward, the child-centered school because we realized the futility of emphasizing subject matter instead of child development. But there is one more step forward. In the concept of the community-centered school, we have, it seems to me, the ultimate objective of all education because it deals with the child in connection with his social background and in relation to all forces, disruptive as well as constructive, that contribute to his education.

Covello's efforts were mainly designed to enable Italo-Americans to undergo the process of Americanization without experiencing ruthless assimilation. Unconsciously anticipating a later generation and another culture, Dr. Covello introduced Italian into the curriculum.

A further stage of the community school embraces all the elements of the New Haven and Flint models, but includes a more active role for the community—for example, the use of parents as teacher aides, the use of skilled residents as resources in instruction, and, perhaps, the strengthening of parent associations or other groups in advisory or consultative capacities. In the modern urban environment, the school functions as an acculturation tool, an educational instrument, and a community center attempting to make viable connections between different homes and different cultures in a climate that respects and cherishes creative differences. It also nurtures similarities. The usual school pattern is to attempt to emphasize similarities and to obliterate differences —the melting-pot approach.

Another contemporary vision of the community school is the "education park," which enjoyed a great vogue—in plans and conferences, if not in bricks and mortar—in the mid-1960's. The education-park concept was advanced primarily as a less painful method of racial integration than the transportation of Negro and white pupils into one another's neighborhoods. It was also promoted on grounds of educational efficiency and as a center for community services. Thus, Harold Howe II, while commissioner of education, said:

> Such a school would be part of a school system that could afford to surround the building with recreation space, sponsor a community orchestra, organize sports. It would exist in the midst of the business and cultural life of the city; while training people to participate in the one, it would enrich the lives of its students with the other. It would be open day and night to serve both children and adults.

Finally, the most advanced concept of the community school includes all the foregoing elements but features a fundamental change in the role of the community. Now, the community par-

ticipates not only as a client, not only in an advisory role, but
also as a decision-maker. It joins with professionals in planning
and operating the school. The clients no longer accept, on faith,
the idea that the school serves the community; they take an active hand in determining the nature of the school's services and
in ensuring that it is continually responsive to their needs as they
see and feel them.

Models of the Community-Controlled School

The evolution of a classic community school is illustrated by
the Morgan school in Washington, D.C. The case has its roots in
the frustrations and fears of black and middle-class white parents.
Discontent with the public schools of the nation's capital had
long been brewing. The causes had been known in a piecemeal
way for many years, but it was not until September, 1967, that
they were exhaustively laid out in public view, in the 593-page
report of a two-year study of the Washington public schools directed by Dr. A. Harry Passow of Teachers College, Columbia
University. The study was no different, in most respects, from
reports of ghetto education in other cities. It documented the
failure of public education in Washington with both data and
intimate accounts of classroom and school experience. Most of its
recommendations replayed familiar themes—for example, a call
for massive remedial programs for pupils with learning problems
and for preschool programs for all four-year-olds from disadvantaged areas. But, in one respect, the Passow Report did break new
ground: Buried in its recommendations was a proposal that the
Washington school system be decentralized into eight subsystems
of approximately 20,000 pupils each. Each subsystem was to be
governed by an elected community board of education, each to
choose its superintendent of schools from a list of candidates submitted by the central superintendent of schools. The local boards
were to be given "considerable autonomy," for "if the boards are
restricted to serving in an advisory capacity, tokenism and scarcely
any real decentralization will result." The report continued:

"The District schools tend not to be in touch with the communities they should serve. . . . The varieties of services and leadership should be responses to joint planning by school and community."

In the meantime, a modest but symbolically significant step had been taken toward closing the gulf between Washington's citizens and its policy-makers for the school system. Congress had passed a law calling for an elected ten-member central board of education to replace a nine-member board appointed by district court judges. The first elections were to take place in November, 1968.

The Passow Report's findings legitimized the need for innovation and decentralization in Washington, and its recommendations were supported by all major forces in the district, but, in point of fact, the seed of the Morgan Community School Program had been growing for more than a year before. The Thomas P. Morgan Elementary School is located in the ethnically- and socio-economically–mixed Adams-Morgan section of Washington, but 730 of the school's 750 students are black. (Before the 1954 Supreme Court decision, the school was *legally* segregated.) The neighborhood, two-thirds of which had been an exclusive white residential area until World War II, had a postwar tradition of community efforts even before the school issue became paramount. Interestingly, parental organization had been stimulated, to a great extent, by the principals of Morgan and another elementary school in the area. The organization they formed obtained a grant under the Housing Act of 1954 for a two-year demonstration project, under the supervision of American University, to halt physical blight by combining volunteer citizen action with stepped-up services from city government.

The successor organizations included an activist middle-class group, the Adams-Morgan Community Council, which struggled to unite the diverse neighborhood sufficiently to go beyond physical problems and develop programs that might penetrate to the root causes of spreading social decay. The process, covering a six-year period, was slow and painful, but it succeeded in establishing block organizations, a walk-in science center, a storefront art center, an "alley" library, a community preschool, a summer program employing 200 people, and a neighborhood house. The Morgan Community School, the council's most noteworthy achievement, was a response to a range of educational shortcomings—from overcrowding (four separate classes had to meet in the auditorium) and lack of a school library or lunchrooms, to the feeling of Negro parents that they were not shown respect at the school and were unable to visit and talk to teachers without making appointments. Parents also wanted to work with educators and explore the possibilities of team teaching, ungraded classes, individualized instruction, and other approaches.

Pressure by the community council won an experimental status for the Morgan School in May, 1967, with the stipulation that operation of the school would be contracted out to Antioch College, within a framework of strong community involvement. (Officials of the Antioch-Putney Graduate Center in Washington lived in the Adams-Morgan community.) Shortly after school opened in September, 1967, an election was held for a Morgan Community School Board. The Antioch group had suggested that the coming fall was too soon for the project to start, but the community council overruled a proposal for a one-year postponement. Dissatisfied with the Antioch project-director, the community council fired him. They had dubious authority for this action, but Antioch never replaced him. The community also opposed Antioch's desire to turn the Morgan experiment into a training ground for its students and staff. The Antioch ties diminished while community cohesiveness grew.

Then, on September 18, 1968, while the New York City school system was paralyzed by a teachers' strike amid growing conflicts over decentralization, the Board of Education of the District of Columbia met in public session and voted its support and approval of the Morgan experiment. Busloads of community people packed the meeting. Superintendent of Schools William R. Manning delivered a formal and eloquent appeal for decentralization, setting the stage for board endorsement. He said the administration would encourage individual neighborhoods to develop plans for their own schools "rather than superimpose them from the central office as in New York." The president and other key leaders of the Washington Teachers Union were present to reinforce their previously stated commitment to decentralization and community control. "Teachers' rights may well be more closely protected in a community-controlled school than [in one controlled] by the downtown administration," a union policy statement said. The District's other teachers' organization, the National Education Association affiliate, had also backed decentralization.

Having gained board of education approval, the local Morgan board assumed additional responsibility and a second election was held. Community support grew and was enhanced by the new principal selected by Morgan's community board, Kenneth Haskins. Haskins had no traditional credentials as an educator—he held a master's degree in social work and had served as a school-community liaison worker in an integrated Northern suburb—but his geniality and ability to establish a rapport won the respect of the teaching staff and parents. Most of his carefully selected teaching staff were affiliated with the Washington Teachers Union. William Simons, head of the union, foresees that, eventually, there will be twelve to thirty subsystems in Washington, and he is ready to negotiate special subcontracts with them, while tenure, salary, and conditions of work will remain protected by regulations binding on all schools.

As the governing body, the Morgan Community School Board sees itself as controlling, as far as possible, staffing, curriculum, financing, outside resources, and use of the physical plant. "It cannot be merely an advisory or consultative body to an administrator who is basically responsible to a larger system over which the community has no control," the board says of itself. In personnel, for example, "the Community School Board must choose its own staff and determine the number and type of personnel. . . . Qualifications . . . will be determined by the Community School Board and other bodies." Moreover, "The school should take its character from the nature of the people living in the community and from the children that use the school, rather than defining itself as an institution accepting only those people who already fit into a set definition." In turn, "the school should affect the community . . . The school should be, in a sense, a small community within itself, providing all the kinds of interaction that the larger community provides."

The Morgan School academic program features team teaching and the organization of all children in vertical grouping, with seven overlapping age groups rather than grades. The development of subject specialities among teachers is encouraged. The curriculum has strong affective overtones, discouraging competition and punishment, but the school claims that its students are progressing better than previously in terms of conventional performance criteria, too. Children in the upper-age groups conduct self-evaluations and evaluations of the school and its programs. Staff development emphasizes home visits and other means of drawing teachers closer to the children and their families.

After one year, the community board's appraisal of its professional staff is measured but positive. It details their willingness to experiment, their extra efforts, and long hours: "[The staff] were usually able to put the needs of the children above their own," says the board's first annual report. "[They] felt a certain responsibility to the school and to the entire community . . . The way the staff accepted this responsibility is most encouraging." The high degree of teacher cooperation that now marks the project was not present at the start. Half of the teachers resigned early in the project, and, by 1969, the school had virtually an entirely new staff.

The school has drawn from a variety of resources—ranging from the Urban Service Corps, which provides volunteers, to a

Friends group and other private organizations, which provide summer camping and field programs. The Morgan School was one of the few in Washington where pupils' reading scores on standardized tests rose markedly during the year (1968). Truancy has declined sharply, and vandalism to the school building has dropped to a new low.

But opposition (both black and white) has prevented expansion of the Morgan Community School concept. The governing board had hoped to bring in three neighboring elementary schools and the local feeder junior high school but it encountered strong parental objections. These seem to be grounded in conservatism, including adult skepticism of the freedom permitted pupils in the school, which is interpreted as a lack of discipline. The principal of a neighboring school said, "Our parents don't want their children involved in that kind of freedom."

Chicago offers another example of a relatively mild community-control experiment that lost national attention amid the din of New York City's dispute. Understandably, Chicago officials are cautious about equating their project with New York City's. It is less ambitious, both in the number of schools involved to date and in the degree of community participation. But the thrust is unmistakable—to let parents in on the educational decision-making process. In November, 1968, just as the New York City schools were struggling back to "normal" operations in the wake of their ten-week strike ordeal, Chicago's less visible and less controversial experiment was unveiled. The site of the experiment is Chicago's South Side, where, over a period of 20 years, a predominantly Negro neighborhood, Woodlawn, has developed next to the University of Chicago campus. The neighborhood was the scene of one of the earliest confrontations between an urban university seeking to expand and its low-income, Negro neighbors. Intense university-community differences in Woodlawn were on the way to resolution before community conflict throughout the country reached the deep bitterness of the late 1960's. Residents had called in Saul Alinsky, a controversial sociologist and community organizer, to guide their self-help efforts. The Woodlawn Organization, mainly the fruit of his work, was described, in 1964, by Charles Silberman in *Crisis in Black and White:* "The most impressive experiment affecting Negroes . . . a living demonstration that even those living in the worst sort of slum can be mobilized to help themselves, and that when they are, neither the Negro community nor the city as a whole can ever be quite the same again."

Two federations of some 100 organizations had achieved earlier successes in school matters—having persuaded the board to eliminate double shifts in the schools and to reduce overcrowding and having negotiated with the university for a nursery school program. Woodlawn's experimental school district, developed with the help of university personnel, is much more cautious than New York's in its exploration of what can be done to bring the schools closer to the community in decision-making. Willard Congreve, the first director of the experiment, not only denied that he had a "model" for local school control; rather, he said, "I do not even want to say that we have the beginning of a model. We have something, however, which is working, which is developing, but it is in the very early stages."

The governing board of the Woodlawn District operates three schools—the Wadsworth Elementary School, the Wadsworth Upper Grades Center, and Hyde Park High School, with a total of about 3,300 students. It has a federal grant of $1,353,000 for the first year, renewable for two more years upon application. The board has twenty-one members—seven appointed by the Chicago Board of Education, seven by the University of Chicago, and seven by the Woodlawn Organization. Two teachers from each of its schools sit in on board meetings as advisers, and two elected student observers attend and speak at all board meetings. Each seven-member segment caucuses and casts one vote, and no action can be taken without unanimous consent. Failure to achieve unanimity simply means that the board goes on deliberating the issue.

The legal authority for the experiment comes from a memorandum of agreement signed between the local board and the Chicago Board of Education in August, 1967, under which the local board has full authority over all federal funds and considers all matters relating to the three schools—such as finances, curriculum, teacher appointments, school programs and community relations. In theory, it only makes recommendations to the board of education, which then must take the official action on any program. So far, the board of education has acted positively, and without dissent, on every suggestion from the Woodlawn Experimental Board.

The experimental board began by screening all teachers appointed to the schools under its jurisdiction. This practice has raised some questions within the Chicago Teachers Union, but the union has not yet made any formal objections. One attempt by the board to fire teachers was vetoed by the university representative. The local board also claims the authority to move some teachers out of the schools by administrative transfers without prejudice to the teachers. While all sides recognize the possibility of conflict, so far no one has been moved against his will.

Community control is appearing in a number of other schools as well, private and public. The most recent governmental impetus comes from Model Cities legislation, whose educational component requires some degree of community participation in planning. Under the legislation, formal plans in Philadelphia, Dayton, and Gary create community-control school districts. Unofficial arrangements whereby parent committees in individual schools are involved in the selection of programs and personnel exist in various other cities. Several Follow-Through and Head Start schools have created parent boards and emphasize direct parent roles in adoption of policy and in the selection of personnel.

In addition, community control is a feature of most of the new private schools that have arisen in the last few years to provide more creative alternatives to the public schools, especially, though not entirely, in urban ghettos. Many are characterized by less structured and less authoritarian teaching styles. Most operate on a shoestring and several have already failed because of lack of funds. But more keep arising, and an estimated 300 now exist; they held their first national meeting—the Conference on Alternatives in Education—in April, 1970, together with representation from experimental colleges and "free universities." Also, a National Association of Community Schools was formed in June, 1969, by representatives from twenty-three community schools.

Defining Community Participation—and Control

At this stage, the community school concept—which has its roots in American history and has been largely unquestioned until now—merges with the concept of community control. The resulting synthesis is highly controversial, for it seeks basic structural reform of the system as a means toward quality education, and its hallmark is meaningful community participation. Beginning in New York City, the development bids fair to overshadow in intensity the somewhat analogous struggle that raged around client participation in antipoverty programs; it may be foreshadowing similar movements in other governmental services—law enforcement and welfare programs, for example.

A knotty semantics has evolved around the definitions of community control, parental participation, and school decentralization. But the concepts are not so much obscure as they are controversial, and some of the confusion that has attended discussion of them may be deliberate on the part of opponents of meaningful participation. It is worth discussing each of them briefly.

We have already dealt with the nonparticipatory community school. As far as parental participation in the vast majority of traditional schools is concerned, that has declined steadily, due to professionalization of the educator, as noted, and to two other forces. One, common in the days of large-scale European immigration and persisting in the urban ghetto, has been the low level of the parents' own education relative to the teachers'. Regardless of their desire for education for their children, most ghetto parents are not prone to challenge the assigned authority represented by a better-educated teacher. The other factor, of course, is the growing size and impersonality of the public school systems in large cities. Even well-educated, middle-class parents who seek to engage in *meaningful* school decisions are deterred by the inertia of the system or by the aura of professional exclusivity. Even the atmosphere in school buildings discourages parental presence, and most parents visit the school mainly in response to trouble. Also, the schools have carefully drawn boundaries as to how far parents (singly or in parent-teacher associations) may go, even in asking questions of professionals. A sophisticated PTA member may nag at a school board that does not offer French in elementary school, but she will rarely ask for research results (or for research to be initiated) on the effectiveness of the school's language instruction. Still less is she apt to ask for such information as the school system's criteria for teacher selection or for evidence of its aggressiveness and imagination in recruiting teachers. Even when probing questions are asked, information is often safeguarded as being in the professional's domain. Only now are some school systems beginning to accumulate and release performance data on a school-by-school basis.

Most educators define the participation concept in one-sided terms. Elaborate structures and devices have been fashioned—parent-teacher associations, visiting days, American Education Week, parent education programs, dissemination of information—ostensibly to "inform" the parent. The administrator who seeks a "happy" school (or "tight ship," as the case may be) will see that his parents are paid some attention or even a degree of deference. He will be patient in explaining, say, homework policy. At best, most professionals feel their role is to interpret the school to the community; at worst, they are indifferent to the community. The chief motivation in their community relations is usually to make *their* system work more smoothly. From the parents' point of view, their concept has a basic flaw: When a school system is dysfunctional, the community is acting against its own interests and those of its children in maintaining the system and failing to criticize it. In short, the existing concept of parent and community participation in education is basically misdirected toward supporting the schools' *status quo*.

Real parental participation covers a wide range of involvement, but the irreducible minimum is a part in the selection of those who govern the schools. Meaningful participation stands between arm's-length, professionally circumscribed participation, on the one hand, and total control, on the other. It calls for a parental and community role in such substantive matters as budgeting, personnel, and curriculum. The vehicle of participation may be structures at the individual-school level or elected bodies on a neighborhood basis. In either case, one of the chief criteria is proximity of educational decision-makers to the affected schools. The chief political criterion is accountability of the professional and the school system to the community.

The concept of parental participation is fraught with fears, however, on the part of incumbent educators and others. Thus, Christopher Jencks says: "The distinction between 'participation' and 'interference' is largely a matter of where you think parents' rights end and staff prerogatives begin." But interference is not what the advocates of community control of the schools have in mind. David Spencer, of the I.S. 201 demonstration project in New York, declares: "What we are talking about is not parents coming in and becoming teachers and principals. We still feel the professionals must be there, but let them be the professionals of *our* choice, the professionals that have ideas along the lines of what we in our communities think is best for our children."

The idea of parental participation has been described in more detail by the Public Education Association, a reform-minded, middle-class New York City organization noted for its dispassionate and authoritative analysis of public school problems. The PEA envisions

a system under which community districts' Boards of Education, composed of lay people, are elected by the local community. The

Board of Education then acts as a representative of the community and, working with the help and advice of a professional staff, establishes policy, maintains the schools, plans the budget, and appoints professional personnel. It holds regular public meetings at which citizens may speak, and it usually maintains close contact with parents' associations or other parent groups and the general public. It must make its aims understood, it must reflect its community's needs, or the community will vote the board out of office.

Of course, the rudiments of community control have long operated in suburban school districts where voters elect school boards and pass on referenda for major construction or school budgets. However, parent involvement in such districts is often minimal, in part because long-term recontracting with school superintendents tends to reinforce a monopoly of professional control. In some districts, however, community control does work in the ideal terms suggested by the Public Education Association, as a composite of "three forces: the community, the lay board it selects to represent it, and the professional staff [each with] its responsibilities and limits of power."

The out-and-out opponents of community control charge that the demand for participation is the product of militants' agitation aimed not at achieving better education but rather at gaining for themselves control of the community. Moreover, says the head of New York's CSA, Walter Degnan, "The average citizen has neither the time nor the inclination to engage in 'participatory democracy' on a permanent basis. . . . Community control is not being demanded by the average parent, whose attendance at school meetings averages about 1 per cent."

To which David Spencer replies:

They say the parents won't get involved. Why? Because they have been depending on you [educators]. Parents have been taking it for granted that you knew what you were doing, and now we find that you *don't* know what you are doing. So we are not telling you to get out and you can't do it—but we *are* saying that we want to be in there to see that you do the job of educating our children.

To be sure, part of the fear of and opposition to community control stems from the disbelief among the white community (and among some middle-class blacks as well) that low-income blacks are capable of determining school policy. This attitude depends, to some extent, on a racial stereotype—"those people don't care about education"—which, though persistent, has been refuted by several studies showing that minority-group parents make quite high demands for academic achievement. One observer has gone so far as to say that the parents' aspirations are "in the nature of wishful fantasies, in the sense that the parents do not know how to implement them," although he adds, "the aspirations have consequences in that they somehow get conveyed to the child as expectations he is supposed to fulfill."

But many people who would reject the racial stereotype harbor more subtle—and fundamentally paternalistic—feelings that low-income blacks cannot manage their own affairs and lack the intellectual and verbal experience and sophistication necessary to deal with educational issues and educational systems and staffs. An answer to this view was formed by a group of black parents and educators who formed an unexpected caucus at the 1968 annual conference of the National Committee for Support of the Public Schools:

> We may make some mistakes. However, these mistakes can hardly be more serious than the ones being made at present. They certainly will not be as long-standing. Because we, holding the welfare of the children as our only criterion, will effect change as soon as we or they deem it to be necessary. When people have an opportunity to be really involved in more than *cake sales* and *teacher luncheons,* when they know that they can be part of making decisions that have meaning, we will not have to worry about parental apathy or student disinterest. When members of the school board know that they are accountable to all the people whose children they serve, and to the students themselves, they will gear their activities toward responding to the needs and desires of these groups.

The act of assuming control over his schools, then, is valuable to the minority-group member in two respects. It offers him an opportunity to improve the school along lines he deems best for his children and it is a sign of his own power to affect his destiny without the white man's intervention. As the black caucus statement continued:

> We cannot any longer *afford* to worry about *even those* whites who have been our allies, because that alliance has not proven strong enough to endure bigotry that has defeated us. There is a role, however, that our white friends can still play. They can work *within their own communities* to support our efforts, and for the needs that will develop from our efforts—additional budgetary support, understanding of our goals, etc. We feel our responsibility now is to *our* community alone. Our white friends must tackle their community.

What parental involvement may also mean is suggested by former U.S. Education Commissioner Howe:

> It means jobs for parents as teacher aides. It means schools which are open evenings, weekends, and summers, and available to adults as well as children. It means frank and frequent talk among teachers, principals, and parents. It means local employers lending a hand with work-study opportunities, job counseling, big brother and big sister relationships and teaching help. It means student governments that govern from a base of responsibility and participation. It means literally and figuratively that the fence must come down. The informal participation in the life of the school is an important power relationship of citizens to their schools in suburbia. We need an analogous effort in the cities.

Both the schools and the parent and community participants themselves benefit from their active involvement in the education process. Their very act of meaningful participation—a sense of greater control over a decisive institution that influences the fate of their children—contributes to parents' sense of potency and self-worth. ("If I have a voice, if what I say counts for something, I am somebody.") Armed with the experience of acting effectively and with a heightened sense of self-worth, they become, for their children, better models and "teachers" of that part of the "curriculum" that is theirs exclusively—rearing in the home.

The fact that the parent and community agents themselves undergo growth and development in the difficult task of participating in the education process is inherent in the concept. Moreover, since the inflow of parents into participatory roles will be continuous, the danger of institutional rigidity should be averted (the schools will serve as "open" rather than "closed" institutions). The participants' own development should help to assure that the reformed system will be readily inclined to adjustment and change—standing in sharp contrast to professionally dominated, bureaucratized school systems, which are rigid in their functions and habits, and highly resistant to change.

Participatory democracy in education should also instill in parents and the community a new respect for the complexity of the professional problems in urban education. Responsibility comes with the power of effective voice, and, in its train, should follow judgment, stability, and dedication to constructive purposes. The classic pattern of the revolutionary is that, when he takes power, he shifts from destroying institutions to building order and new institutions (of his own kind, to be sure). It is not likely that parents who have gained admission as true partners in the educational process will oversimplify and lay the blame for failures solely on the professional. As things stand now, low-income communities outside the system understandably lay the blame squarely on the assigned professionals: "You are paid to teach, to deliver a certain product. When overwhelming numbers of our children fail to learn, you are not delivering. You are not meeting your professional obligation." The syllogism is simplistic: It ignores the fact that professional talent can be thwarted by a system, and it does not take into account extraschool factors in teaching and learning. But it is an altogether natural response from parents to whom the system provides no access and offers but two alternatives: total resignation and apathy or anger, protest, and, sooner or later, some form of retaliation. As Samuel Shepard, Jr., the St. Louis educator, said: "Nor should we forget the difficult, almost insurmountable problem of parental fear of, and disgust toward, the school and school people. This fear, often manifesting itself as indifference, apathy, or even outright hostility on the part of disadvantaged parents, makes the school appear to be an unwanted alien island."

As to the qualifications of low-income, poorly educated parents to engage in educational decisions, the question should involve not what parents know now about the technicalities of education, but what they can come to know. That they want to know is suggested by the few instances in which they have become more or less equal partners in the process. Indeed, the processes of training of, and participation by, parents and community residents fulfills one of the tenets of American democracy: the existence of an *informed* electorate. Participation affords direct knowledge and facilitates understanding and insights far more effectively than attempts to learn and understand from a distance. Experience is the great teacher. One of the surest guarantees that parents and the community will govern responsibly is the fact that they will be able to know the education process from the inside, through personal involvement. They are less likely to be susceptible to propaganda, personal charisma, and other diversionary political devices that are common in elections in which the voter's knowledge of the issues is distant and rarely touched by personal exposure.

Preston R. Wilcox has described the difference between the parental role in a community-controlled school system and that of the parent aide in a traditional system:

> They become "teachers" outside the school and "foster parents" within the school. An important part of their function is to help individual students in their efforts to bridge the gap between school and home. Naturally, they would expend a majority of their efforts on those students or in those situations where their roles are not already being fulfilled by an interested parent or teacher.
>
> Unlike teacher's aides and assistants who, for all intents and purposes, are extra arms and legs for the teachers, the foster teachers carry out community-parent functions, being advocates on behalf of the community, not the school.

Decentralization has become confused with parental involvement and community control because of its relationship to the community-control dispute in New York City. But decentralization in and of itself is only an administrative device, a reaction to the inefficiency and unreality of a massive bureaucracy. It does not necessarily result in a more responsive system or one in which the community has a determining voice. "A decentralized structure can create the environment in which meaningful change can occur," as the New York Board of Education advisory committee reported, but it does not provide the sanctions and instruments whereby the school system can be held to account for failure to change.

The frustration and failure that led to the community-control dispute in New York City actually built up during a period when the city's schools were more administratively decentralized than ever in their modern history. In a survey by the aforementioned board of education committee, the majority of parents' association presidents in twenty-two schools indicated their belief that little effect had been felt in their schools (predominantly white and middle class) as a result of the board's administrative decentralization policy. Among these presidents, the report noted, "there appears to be considerable confusion as to what decentralization really is all about." PA presidents in one district said that, although the district superintendent still did as he wished, he tended to give the impression that he was consulting the local board.

The varied definitions of decentralization are much like concepts of federalism; the difference is in the range, from limited to autonomous powers for the local districts. At one end of the scale, the outer limits of school decentralization are set by "administrative" decentralization—the delegation of powers to district superintendents. At the other end, complete control forms another parameter—the independent school district, without city supervision and relating only to the state education department. Even the latter calls for some outside control, but the supervision is shifted from the city to the state.

Everyone appears to endorse some measure of community involvement in local school districts. But the shades of difference are crucial. Some favor participation but not power in making school policy for local communities. Community groups espouse a concept of "community control" that implies local discretion in a wide range of policy areas, especially in capital and expense budget, curriculum, personnel, appointments, transfers, and reviews. They seek locally elected boards and limited central supervision and authority.

Urban community control can only be created through some form of decentralization; however, decentralization does not necessarily entail community control. Any decentralization plan that delegates decision-making power to a locally selected board falls within a general frame of reference in which the community is given a role in the policy process; the balance between the degree of local control and the maintenance of central powers will determine the extent to which community control can be exercised.

For those who support a redistribution of power in the school system, the evaluation of any decentralization plan relates to the extent of community control. If the local public power (translated into the power of the local board) is completely circumscribed by a central authority, then community control is virtually nonexistent. Effective decentralization cannot occur without some delegation of power to locally selected boards. Whether local school districts are stronger, even as part of a citywide system, will be determined, in large part, by the nature of their delegated power.

New York City's first major attempt to move toward a more meaningful community school concept for the entire city led to the plan for decentralization prepared by the Bundy Panel in 1968. Much can be learned from an examination of that experience, and the document itself might well serve as a standard for city school reform throughout the country.

5

The Bundy Report

It is because modern education is so seldom
inspired by a great hope that it so seldom
achieves a great result. The wish to preserve
the past rather than the hope of creating the
future dominates the minds of those who
control the teaching of the young.—BERTRAND
RUSSELL

"It used to be," recalls a suburban school superintendent, "that
when a New York City schoolman stood up at a session of a national educational meeting, the audience hushed in churchlike
silence. Teachers or principals from other parts of the country
hung on his every word. They listened in almost reverential awe,
for here was a man from the very pinnacle, from the educational
version of the City of God, and from the pedagogical avant-
garde. He was not only a romantic figure, not only a 'star' celeb-
rity, but also an object of deep respect. Whether the particular
New York educator was in his own right worth all this, it was
given him because of the system he represented. The sheer size
of the New York schools had something to do with it but not
everything, I think, and not even most. What set off New York
like a precious jewel was its reputation for professional quality,
in program and staff. Its programs were fabled for their daring
and effectiveness, and the staff had a legendary collection of
supermen and women. It was said to be so difficult to qualify as a

teacher in New York that Ph.D.'s were a dime a dozen, even in
the elementary schools."

Whether the reputation was deserved is beside the present
point. What matters is that it was believed, so that New York was
the nation's educational pacemaker in a way that not even Evans-
ton (Illinois) Township and Newton (Massachusetts) became after
World War II. The "golden age" of public education in New
York reigned in the 1920's and 1930's. By the 1950's and 1960's,
the image may have changed to that of the Blackboard Jungle,
but what happens in New York still sends tremors throughout
the web of education across the nation. Educators everywhere
still have an eye cocked on New York. For one thing, the 900-
school system is responsible for the education of nearly one out
of every forty public school pupils in the entire United States.

Thus, passions were ignited far beyond the borders of New
York when, on November 9, 1967, a report entitled *Reconnection
for Learning* was published. Better known as the Bundy Report,
it dealt with the problems of the New York City school system
and proposed that the *path* toward solution (*not* the solution
itself) could best be opened up by decentralizing the system and
admitting parents and the community into a partnership with
professionals in educational decision-making.

Understanding the Bundy Report and the storm that followed
is crucial, therefore, for at least two important reasons: first, because the concept and practice of citywide decentralization and
strong community engagement in urban education developed first
in New York; and second, because the New York schools are still,
to an important degree, the cynosure of American public education.

The report was drawn up by a committee created in response
to a request of the New York State Legislature. This committee,
headed by McGeorge Bundy—president of the Ford Foundation,
former Presidential Assistant and a former dean of faculty at Harvard—took as its basic premise the legislature's pointed assertion
that "increased community awareness and participation in the

educational process is essential." This seemingly bland idea, well-grounded in the traditional American concept of local responsibility for free public education, became, in turn, the controversial theme of the Bundy Report.

In surveying New York City's vast school system, the committee found problems to be so severe and the breakdown of school-community ties so advanced that it called for fundamental structural changes in the administration of the schools. "If this proposal is radical," asserted *The New York Times* in response to the report, "it is justified by the fact that the situation is desperate. If the cure is drastic, it is necessary because a long succession of moderate reform efforts has failed to halt the deterioration of New York's gigantic school system."

The heart of the Bundy Report was a plan for massive decentralization that was expected to have far-reaching educational and social implications. Before attempting to describe the plan, however, or to interpret its implications, we must look briefly at the circumstances that gave rise to it.

A Deteriorating System

By the time of the report, the New York City school system had long since begun to sag under the weight of its own sprawling bureaucracy, with a corresponding drop in its ability to respond effectively even to normal demands, to say nothing of crises. Quite apart from the issues of parental control, racial conflict, and massive educational failure, the overcentralized, rigid system itself had become a commonplace target of analysis and criticism. Indeed, administrative decentralization of the New York school system had been urged for at least a quarter of a century. The first tangible step was taken in 1961, when a new citywide board of education was installed following the disclosure of scandals in the awarding of school-construction contracts. Existing but basically moribund local districts—each headed by its own board—were reorganized and reduced in number. The power to appoint district school board members was shifted from the anachronistic borough presidents' offices to the central board of education. In turn, the central board was required to seek the advice of local screening panels chosen by the presidents of the parents' associations in the various districts.

All this looked fine on paper, but the plan had basic defects. First, the selection method involving the advice of parents' associations was less effective in low-income areas than in middle-class sections. (The "parents' association," as then and now constituted, is essentially a middle-class device and is not consonant with the style of low-income, poorly educated minority parents.) Second, these local school boards possessed only advisory powers, and their efforts to respond to community demands were often frustrated by the long chain of command leading to the central board headquarters.

Moreover, the central board itself was less than enthusiastic about the plan. As one of the present authors, Marilyn Gittell, wrote in her analysis of decision-making in the New York schools (*Participants and Participation*), "The Board of Education has been reluctant to delegate powers to local boards for fear that they would encroach on its own authority." Not until 1967 were these local boards even provided with office space, and they remained largely without professional or supporting services.

The failure of this partial decentralization to make the schools more responsive to parental and community needs did not pass unnoticed. Grievances focused not only on children who were failing in school, but also on thousands who left school before being graduated. The largest group were the dropouts—an estimated one-third of the high school population (for the 1967 graduating class, some 20,000). In ghetto schools, dropout rates were averaging 70 per cent. Besides dropouts, an estimated 12,000 students (in the 1966–67 academic year) were "pushouts"—suspended students—many of whom were left to their own devices after their suspension from school. These included students classified as mentally retarded or emotionally disturbed; but other students were suspended for disciplinary reasons—ranging from failure to do homework to fighting with other children. According to a 1967 report by fourteen civic and civil rights groups, many students were suspended without receiving a fair hearing. Several years earlier, Mobilization for Youth had attempted to assure hearings and the right to legal representation for students threatened with suspension. Failing on the administrative level, MFY brought a case in the federal courts on behalf of a junior high school student. The district judge ruled on behalf of the plaintiff, finding that a pupil's suspension hearing in a district superintendent's office was a critical matter that could violate his First Amendment guarantees, and that, therefore, attorneys should be present. The judge enjoined the board of education from conducting suspension hearings without the student's lawyer being present, but the decision was appealed and, on December 7, 1967, it was reversed by the U.S. Court of Appeals. However, the principle was embodied in a new board of education bylaw early in 1970.

Many other indexes pointed to the need for fundamental change. Dissatisfaction with the schools and with discredited professional education officials was matched by growing distrust of the lay leadership provided by the board of education. Bitterness toward the board was fanned, over the past decade, by its successive rollbacks on promises of integration. For the board's part, its distance from ghetto communities grew. In the summer of 1967, for example, while the Bundy panel deliberated, the board declined to attend a hearing by the citywide antipoverty council on whether the board or ghetto communities themselves should have charge of some $69 million in federal funds intended for the improvement of schools in disadvantaged neighborhoods. Every one of dozens of Negro and Puerto Rican leaders who testified at the hearing—including parents and black school teachers —argued that they would rather see the city return the money to Washington than have it handed over to the board, which, they said, would use it against the interests of minority children. Reflecting decentralization sentiment already in the wind, some of the speakers wanted the federal money spent on an alternative school system, run by local communities within the city.

By this time, too, the vaunted experimental projects and pilot innovations that the New York system seemed to adopt as quickly as the latest fall fashions, had lost their luster and credibility. They were, as David Rogers has written, "uncoordinated, overlapping, and often inadequately evaluated [and] virtually none that have been tried have worked." The discontents were magnified during the two-week teachers' strike at the beginning of the term in the fall of 1967, which convinced some parents that teachers and administrators held their group interests above those of the children.

Furthermore, parents, and especially ghetto parents, began to resist official explanations that placed the burden of failure on the child or his family. Rather, there was an increasing tendency to place responsibility on the schools. Parents accused the schools of being either unwilling or unable to respond to the special needs of ghetto children. They asserted that many teachers and administrators were hostile or negative toward children who did not conform to essentially middle-class styles and values. Expressions of dissatisfaction ranged from talk about a "lack of accountability" on the part of the school system to charges that New York City educators were "colonizers sent down among them by a central office."

The collision between tense community forces and the central board of education was not long in coming. The clash took the form of strikes, boycotts, and demonstrations. There were meetings and petitions, charges and countercharges, even an invasion of the board of education headquarters by a self-styled "People's Board of Education," headed by Milton Galamison, a well-known Negro minister and civil rights activist. In 1966, the "People's Board" brought suit in the courts to prevent adoption of the regular school budget, complaining that the city's regular school board had "yielded its policy-making authority to the school system's professional staff." Less than two years later, the Reverend Galamison was appointed by Mayor Lindsay to the expanded central board of education.

A Plan for Real Reform

It was in this context that the New York State Legislature, in the spring of 1967, passed an education money bill to which a significant string was attached. The bill granted the New York City schools a bonus of $54 million in state aid if the monolithic school system could be split administratively into five school districts—one in each of the city's boroughs (which are weak political units that coincide with the five counties within the city borders). This five-borough approach had actually originated in the education section of the report of a group appointed by the previous (Wagner) administration, the Temporary Commission on City Finances. Mayor Lindsay adopted the decentralization idea and suggested it to the legislature as a formula to gain more state aid for the city.

At that time, decentralization was regarded purely as a paper reorganization. But there is reason to believe that the mayor had substantive reorganization in mind as well. Earlier, he had sought to make city government in general more responsive to community needs—for example, by proposing a civilian police-review board and by attempting to open a series of vest-pocket "city halls" in various parts of the city.

Later, more than a year after the Bundy Report had been published, he had the following to say about the play of forces in the city's schools:

> There just isn't any one group powerful enough to control New York. Because of the size of this city many of our institutions have become so huge that in their groping for even more power they tend to collide with each other. . . . The City's schools, for example, over the years . . . have been subjected to two powerful groups—the Superintendent of Schools and the Board of Education, to whom the city turned over one billion dollars every year without a check or double check, and the United Federation of Teachers. These two

groups became so totally engaged in their own contest that they bypassed everyone else. Look over their past contracts and you will see a pattern whereby the two groups often dovetailed. They were inextricable. It became very difficult when parents and children began to demand a place at table because the mountainous bureaucracy began to groan.

To the surprise of almost everyone, the legislature, aware, of course, of the controversy that had been raging in the city, adopted the mayor's proposal and carried it one step further. It attached the condition that the mayor present a plan for greater community participation in the governance of the city's schools. In effect, the legislature asked the city to develop a new plan for real—not paper—decentralization. The influence of State Commissioner of Education James E. Allen is said to have weighed heavily in the legislative opening toward decentralization, but, whatever the cause, the fact that the legislature bypassed the board of education and laid the challenge for a reform blueprint at the mayor's door presaged a storm even before the study began.

Amid cries charging political interference with the schools, Mayor Lindsay moved to meet the legislature's request by appointing a blue-ribbon advisory panel to produce such a plan. The panel members included: the president of the board of education (then Lloyd K. Garrison, subsequently Alfred Giardino); Mitchell Sviridoff, then head of the city's Human Resources Administration, a new superagency that sought to coordinate health, education, and welfare efforts throughout the city; Francis Keppel, president of General Learning Corporation and former U.S. Commissioner of Education; Dr. Bennetta Washington, a Negro former high school principal, head of the Women's Job Corps and wife of Mayor Walter Washington of Washington, D.C.; and Antonia Pantoja, a social work professor and prominent leader in the Puerto Rican community. To chair the panel, the mayor called upon McGeorge Bundy, as a previous mayor (Wagner) had appointed the previous president of the foundation (Henry T. Heald) to head an earlier major school inquiry (1961). A foundation-staff member (and one of the present authors), Mario Fantini, was appointed staff director of the study.

The membership of the panel was determined by the mayor and four members of his inner circle—Deputy Mayor Robert W. Sweet, Chairman of the City Planning Commission, Donald H. Elliot, Mitchell Sviridoff, and Lewis Feldstein, an assistant to the mayor whose tasks included liaison with the board of education. The group considered but quickly dismissed any idea of doing the study within the city administration: staff time was not available and, more decisively, the study needed the aspect of detachment—the cachet of a group at some remove from the city government. The mayor himself proposed Bundy as someone of unexceptionable status whose recommendations would command a hearing in all communities.

The mayor's staff felt that the panel must include one black and one Puerto Rican. Antonia Pantoja was an almost automatic choice for the Puerto Rican community. Various men and women were considered as possible representatives of the black community. Kenneth Clark's name came up and was passed over, because of various differences between him and the Puerto Rican community. Bennetta Washington was decided upon because she could add the experience and perspective of a teacher and school principal and because of her special familiarity with the problems of school dropouts. Keppel was picked because of earlier experience as commissioner of education, his new role in the "education industry," and the fact that, five years earlier, he had served on a committee to select a new superintendent of the city's schools. Sviridoff was to be the mayor's representative on the panel. After some hesitation, it was decided that, since the legislature's mandate strongly implied changes in the board of education's powers, a representative from the board of education had to be involved; there was also the practical consideration that, in its work, the panel would need information and staff assistance from the Office of the Board of Education. Accordingly, the president of the board was asked to represent it on the panel.

In the months that followed its appointment, the panel and its staff solicited proposals for decentralization and met with hundreds of individuals and lay and professional groups. It examined the educational problems and studied the demographic, fiscal, legal, and political implications of various organizational configurations. It analyzed the functions of the school system—personnel, budgeting, curriculum, etc.—in terms of the forces having an impact on each function and of the effectiveness of each in meeting educational goals. It reviewed the effects of city government and the state department of education and state law on school policies and practices. As its proposals began to take shape, it discussed them with various interested parties—particularly civil rights groups, the United Federation of Teachers, and the Council of Supervisory Associations.

In the end, when the advisory panel issued its report, Mr. Giardino, who emphasized that he was serving not as an individual but as a representative of the board of education, expressed basic disagreement with its findings. Arguing that the board was already committed to parent and community participation and to decentralization, he declared that

> serious problems must arise in recasting, in one quick stroke, the largest educational system in the world. We must be reasonably sure that a plan will be successful and [we] do not feel sufficient assurance in the plan submitted. Rather than a rigidly timed and mandated set of procedures, we prefer a more deliberative process of movement and evaluation. Moreover, we believe there are constructive legislative alternatives that can achieve many of the same goals without as many dangers.

Mr. Giardino filed the panel's sole dissent.

The basic recommendations of the Bundy Panel can be summarized as follows:

1. The New York City public schools should be reorganized into a community school system, consisting of a federation of largely autonomous school districts and a central education agency.

2. From thirty to no more than sixty community school districts should be created, ranging in size from about 12,000 to 40,000 pupils—each district large enough to offer a full range of educational services yet small enough to maintain proximity to community needs and to promote diversity and administrative flexibility.

3. The community school districts should have authority for all regular elementary and secondary education within their boundaries and responsibility for adhering to state education standards.

4. A central education agency, together with a superintendent of schools and his staff, should have operating responsibility for special educational functions and citywide educational policies. It should also provide certain centralized services to the community school districts and other services, upon the districts' request.

5. The state commissioner of education and the city's central educational agency should retain their responsibilities for the maintenance of educational standards in all public schools in the city.

6. The community school districts should be governed by boards of education selected, in part, by parents and, in part, by the mayor from lists of candidates maintained by the central education agency. Membership on these boards should be open to both parents and nonparent residents of a district.

7. The central educational agency should consist of one of the following: (a) a commission of three full-time members appointed by the mayor or (b) a board of education with a majority of members nominated by the community school districts. In the latter, the mayor should select the members from a list submitted by an assembly of chairmen of community school boards; the others should be chosen by the mayor from nominations made by a screening panel.

8. Community school districts should receive an annual allocation of operating funds, determined by an objective and equitable formula, which they should be permitted to use with the

widest possible discretion within set educational standards and union-contract obligations.

9. Community school districts should have broad personnel powers, including the right to hire a community superintendent on a contract basis.

10. All existing tenure rights of teachers and supervisory personnel should be preserved as the reorganized system goes into effect. Thereafter, tenure of new personnel employed in a particular district should be awarded by the district.

11. The process of qualification for appointment and promotion in the system should be revised to give community school districts freedom to hire teachers and other professional staff from the widest possible sources, so long as hiring is competitive and applicants meet state qualifications.

12. Community school boards should establish procedures and channels to facilitate the closest possible consultation, at the individual school level, with parents, community residents, teachers, and supervisory personnel.

13. The central education agency should have authority and responsibility for advancing racial integration by all practicable means. The state commissioner of education should have authority himself, or through delegation to the central education agency, to overrule measures that support segregation or other practices inimical to an open society.

14. The community school system should go into effect for the school year beginning September, 1969, assuming passage of the necessary legislation in the 1968 legislature.

15. The main responsibility for supervising the transition from the existing system to the community school system should rest with the state commissioner of education. The principal planning and operational functions should be assigned to a temporary commission on transition, which should work closely with the current board of education, the superintendent of schools, and his staff.

16. The transition period should include extensive programs of discussion and orientation on operations and responsibilities

under the community school system and on educational goals. Community school board members should be afforded opportunities for training and be provided with technical assistance on budgeting, curriculum, and other school functions.

These recommendations dealt with four main problems: the nature of community voice in educational policy, the composition and selection of community boards of education, relations between community boards and higher authorities, and reform of the personnel system. It may be helpful to examine the issues confronting the panel in each of these areas and to understand the reasoning that led to the panel's final recommendations.

Community Authority: Early in its deliberations, the panel concluded that, if it was to go beyond a mere paper reorganization, it had to propose that substantive power in the areas of finance, personnel, and curriculum be given to local governing units.

Since the community school districts were to be quasi-autonomous and would not have taxing powers, they would have to draw their funds from the overall city education budget. But autonomy without control of the purse would be an illusion. Thus, to guarantee that community school districts would have flexibility in the way they spent their funds, the panel proposed that they receive lump-sum allocations from the board of education. This would eliminate line-item restrictions, so that the community boards could determine their own priorities. Only through lump-sum allocation would community school boards have effective power to make their own decisions on pupil-teacher ratios, the functions of personnel, the number and kinds of books and other instructional materials, the conduct of experimental programs, and a host of other needs and educational strategies.

To ensure that districts with special needs would receive their fair share, the panel proposed that these lump sums be allocated by a formula that would go beyond per-capita allotment and take into account such factors as income levels, unemployment rates, and the presence, in particular districts, of either non–English-speaking children or gifted children. To ensure against misuse of funds, the panel outlined a number of auditing and reporting procedures and other safeguards.

Local-Board Composition: The choices open to the panel in the difficult decisions regarding composition of community boards included communitywide representation, parent-only representation, and arrangements that would include professionals. The panel decided on a parent-based system, which, it felt, would be most responsive to the needs and interests of children attending the public schools. Unwritten in the report, but clearly implied, was the converse of this proposition—that is, that "nonparents," including parents of private and parochial school pupils, would have no voice in the direct operation of the community public schools. (Throughout the country, where local boards are elected, voting by nonparents has often proved a problem on such issues as taxation for school expenditures.)

Indirectly, through their political participation in mayoralty elections, nonparents could have some influence, but it would be quite weak compared to the day-by-day active participation available to parents. That nonparents would not be entitled to vote in community elections was not considered constitutionally objectionable because the community districts had no taxing powers.

Seeking to encourage maximum parent participation in the selection process, the panel recommended that a prescribed proportion of eligible parents—"at a level sufficiently substantial to constitute an effective participatory process"—be established, below which elections would not be valid. In such cases, it proposed that a new election or alternative methods of obtaining parental representation should be employed. (The legislation passed in 1969 carried no such provisions, and, as it turns out, only 15 per cent of the eligible voters participated in the initial elections, in March, 1970.)

The panel proposed a two-stage process for selection of the parent members: Representatives of individual schools would be chosen by an assembly of parents; these representatives, in turn, would select the board members on a basis proportionate to the pupil population of each school.

In fixing on a parent-only majority, the panel sought to avoid the danger that these local boards might be dominated by political clubs, by majorities of residents who were not parents, or by sectarian groups that might not hold the interest of public education uppermost. (The 1969 decentralization law did not limit voting to parents, and in the first elections, fears that such organized interests as sectarian groups, the UFT, and political parties would prevail were borne out in many districts.)

The panel leavened its recommendations favoring parents, however, with a provision that five of the eleven community board members be appointed by the mayor. This provision reflected a concern for minorities within districts marked by a strong racial or ethnic character—particularly Puerto Ricans in largely Negro neighborhoods. Thus, the report declared,

> It is a real possibility, especially in the early years of the reorganized school system, that a parentally chosen district panel might wholly exclude representatives of minority groups in that district. While we do not hold with proportional representation on Community School Boards, we do believe that total exclusion of minority representation would violate the spirit of community participation in the educational process.

Recognizing that its proposal trod on new ground in urban school structure, the panel provided for review of the selection method by the state commissioner of education after a three-year period; at that time, an alternative type of board selection or composition could be adopted by a local district through a referendum vote.

The panel decided on the mayor as the agent for choosing the centrally selected members because of his citywide purview and his prior responsibility for the city's schools, notably in the allocation of the school budget from the total municipal budget. Another consideration was to help insure a broadly based representation. Recognizing that this decision would unleash charges of political domination (such charges did develop), the panel nonetheless argued that there were now strong reasons for breaking down the supposed wall between a city's highest political office and its public school system. Nationwide recognition of the urban crisis and its educational component was growing, and traditional strictures maintaining a separation between political and educational authority were weakening.

Both by admitting parents to a more active role in the educational process and by building a closer link to elected government, the panel sought responsibility and accountability—a school system so organized as to be more responsive to the needs of the citizens. The panel also hoped that, through closer ties with city government, the schools would be able to coordinate their programs with other city agencies, such as its sixty existing planning districts and its recreation, health, and antipoverty efforts.

Size and Number of Districts: The establishment of boundaries for the proposed new districts was a politically sensitive matter for which the panel would have had no appetite, even if time and resources had permitted. But the panel urged flexibility in these matters, taking into account the complexity of the city and the likelihood that changes would, in the future, be desired. It suggested the creation of an additional ten to twenty districts beyond the existing thirty (none of which would have to be of uniform size), and a process allowing for the changing of boundaries three years after the establishment of the initial districts.

The creation of additional districts would have helped to insure more representation of minority groups. Under the legislation finally passed in 1969 and amended in 1970, the existing number of thirty districts was retained. This partially accounted for, in the initial elections under the law, the lack of minority representation on the boards of several districts with large minority populations.

Relations to Higher Authorities: While tipping the balance toward far greater responsiveness to diverse community needs, the panel took pains not to destroy the citywide integrity of the school system. The reorganized school system, it said,

> should insure all pupils and all localities the benefits of the numerous and variegated facilities and services that major urban school systems can offer—ranging from special high schools to costly research, technical services, and logistic support. It should couple the advantages of urban bigness with the intimacy, flexibility and accessibility associated with innovative suburban school systems.

Without diluting the essential independence and decision-making of the community boards, therefore, the panel proposed that the community boards have a number of ties with the central education agency (the board of education). These ties would include the latter's authority over pupil transfers (to ensure optimum utilization of school buildings throughout the city), over negotiations of the union contract, and—of crucial importance—over integration policy.

Anticipating charges that a federated school system might lead to sectarian pockets—black power districts, on the one hand, or ultraconservative or segregationist districts on the other—the panel proposed that the central agency be empowered to overrule any actions by a community school board "that are judged to be inimical to a free and open society." But the panel said this power ought to follow guidelines established by the state commissioner of education. It further cautioned that the central power to curb parochialism or sectarianism should not be interpreted to exclude a reasonable curricular emphasis upon the cultural background of groups that were a large element in a given school—an obvious reference to frequent demands in the ghettos for attention to

Negro history and Hispanic and Afro-American studies in the schools.

In view of the city's diversity, the panel provided for the possibility that some districts might wish to continue to draw on many of central headquarters' traditional functions. Under the plan, therefore, a district would have the options of handling its own purchasing, curriculum development, and recruiting, or of relying on the central board of education for these services. Only such clearly citywide functions as pupil transfers, capital budgeting, integration policy, testing, auditing, and information were reserved exclusively to the board of education. The community school districts would be given freedom to contract with other agencies—universities, private research and development organizations, and other governmental agencies.

In disputes between community school boards and the central board of education, referee responsibility would lie with the state commissioner of education. Implicit in the panel's view was a trust in community responsibility, so the burden of proving irresponsibility or improper activity would lie with the central board.

Personnel: The main direct personnel power granted to the community boards would be the right to hire, on contract, a community superintendent of schools. While preserving tenure and centralized collective bargaining, the panel also proposed to place hiring and the granting of tenure at the community level. Its single most important—and controversial—personnel recommendation called for elimination of the central citywide examination system and its venerable board of examiners, established in 1898.

This recommendation was intended to ensure a wider pool for recruitment of personnel and a more flexible promotion system. In New York State, only two school systems, New York City's and Buffalo's, required examinations for teacher certification beyond the state standards. Not only would centralized examinations be inconsistent with the requirements of effective decentralization, the panel claimed, but the system had grown obsolete in a market where the demand for qualified teachers outran the supply. The examination system had also produced an inbred leadership structure that discouraged flexibility and change. The panel called, instead, for "a broadening of the concept of merit and qualification for educational leadership, opening the system to more talents and ability, both from within and without the system." It cited studies that indicated that formal course work, age, length of service in a school system, and prior school-administrative experience—factors given heavy weight under the present system of promotional examinations—bear no positive relationship to the ability of a principal to improve the quality of staff performance. Coincidentally perhaps, a few months later, the board of education announced that, for the first time, one of the national teacher examinations (in junior high mathematics) would be used instead of a city test. It also reduced, by two years, the time required before a teacher could have access to the supervisory career ladder.

The personnel reforms raised the question of adequate staffing. In a system in which each community school district had to compete with the others for staff, would teachers flee the ghettos for middle-class districts? The existing system, whatever its defects, at least guaranteed, by means of an assignment system, an adequate number of teachers in the most "difficult" schools. A UFT statement declared: "[The Bundy proposal] ignores the new power and integrity of the professional teacher who will not continue to teach in any school or district where professional decisions are made by laymen." Nevertheless, for several reasons, the panel was confident that predominantly ghetto districts could attract and hold adequate numbers of qualified teachers. It held that:

1. Removal of rigid entrance requirements would facilitate the entry of additional talented teachers from the city, the metropolitan area, and the nation generally.

2. Despite its problems, the New York City school system's salaries are, competitively, quite favorable, and low-income districts could offer the same salaries as more economically favored districts.

3. The air of reform and innovation under the reorganized system would attract large numbers of men and women ready to accept difficult professional challenges.

Although predominantly Negro and Puerto Rican districts might, at first, seek to staff their schools with more black and Puerto Rican teachers and administrators, the panel—again committed to the proposition that most parents want quality education rather than the exercise of power for power's sake—anticipated that professional quality would sooner or later override ethnic considerations in the selection and promotion of teachers. According to the panel, the best guarantee that the selection of staff would eventually be based on merit rather than race would lie in the improved school and community climate that would grow out of strengthened cooperation between parents and school personnel. Teachers would serve in a given district because they chose to be there and were chosen by the community, rather than having been assigned there without an expression of preference on either their part or the community's.

Opposition to the Plan

The panel took great pains to ensure that the report's language was conciliatory. (It described the failings of the New York schools "politely and precisely," according to the *Saturday Review*.) Despite its tone, however, the hard bite of its proposals made fierce opposition, particularly by those with a vested interest in the *status quo*, inevitable.

Revelations, exposés, and reform plans were part of the way of life of the board of education and the New York schools' administrative bureaucracy. As early as 1933, the panel's report noted, studies had been made that called for increased diffusion of administrative and pedagogical responsibilities to superintendents, principals, and teachers. Just before World War II, François S. Cillie—in a Teachers College report, *Centralization or Decentralization? A Study in Educational Adaptation*—called for decentralization, arguing that instruction could be individualized better, change adopted more readily, and programs administered more effectively under a decentralized system. In 1942, Alvin Hicks, in *A Plan to Accelerate the Process of Adaptation in a New York City School Community*, said that the potential for community participation was being ignored because of the unwieldiness and size of the big-city systems, such as New York's. Dozens of other studies and reports—major and minor, official and private (to say nothing of best-sellers like *The Blackboard Jungle, Up the Down Staircase*, and *36 Children*)—that embarrassed but failed to change the New York school system dealt not only with the centralized organization of the system but also with management, pupil achievement, personnel policies, and, of course, racial integration. So constant had been the attack that school officials "tend to be inordinately suspicious of any outsiders [and the system] has taken on an almost 'paranoid' tone in recent years," as David Rogers noted.

And, yet, the system had not changed much, not only because of the failure of diverse factions in the city to coalesce vigorously or persistently enough to carry through on reform blueprints, but also because of the acquired skill and almost unlimited capacity of the system for resisting protest and change. By "confusing and dividing the opposition, 'seeming' to appear responsive to legitimate protest by issuing sophisticated and progressive policy statements that are poorly implemented, if at all, and then pointing to all its paper 'accomplishments' over the years as evidence both of good faith and effective performance," to use Rogers' metaphor, the system has, like a punching bag, always managed to return to its old equilibrium, regardless of the force or direction of the punches aimed at it.

But the system's antennae sensed in the Bundy Report a challenge of extraordinary, perhaps unprecedented, force. First, as noted, conditions in the schools, particularly in ghetto schools, had deteriorated so gravely that they could no longer be hidden from wide public notice. Also, in contrast to earlier plans for decentralization, the panel's proposals were unique in their urgency and aggressiveness. Not only had the panel been legitimized in its origin under a legislative act, but also its report buttressed its recommendations with specific proposed legislation, ready for enactment. The report suggested in other ways a strong belief on the part of the authors that it was an exercise in reality, not, like most reformist documents, one of noble intent but essential futility. For example, the panel included a timetable that foresaw full implementation by September, 1969. The report's very contents, therefore, bespoke a conviction of speedy enactment. Indeed, the implied optimism may have been stronger than the panel's actual belief in imminent approval, but it, nonetheless, galvanized the opponents into a degree of opposition that a plan of vaguer origin and content might not have done.

The mayor's support was clear:

> This response is more than an experiment in political democracy, although it clearly does make institutions more responsive to the citizenry. It also gives promise of ending the image of the schools as separate from a child or a parent's neighborhood. There is hope for our schools—all of them, in all parts of the city—only if they can rebuild their links to the neighborhoods of New York. And that cannot be done by promises or good intentions.

Approval of the recommendations was expected at the state level, too, since the state department of education, even while the Bundy Panel was still at work, had appointed its own group to consult on and evaluate its proposals.

The intrinsic audacity of the plan overcame the careful qualifications with which the panel sought to surround it. McGeorge Bundy had written, "These proposals will not bring instant educational improvement to New York," and "Decentralization is not attractive to us merely as an end in itself; if we believed that a tightly centralized school system could work well in New York today, we would favor it." But the conciliatory pragmatism of the report's plea for a constructive orchestration of powers—the "reconnection"—could not overcome the fact that its proposals would diminish the powers of those previously in command and strengthen those of the weak.

Finally, although it did not purport to contain much new or original data, the report played a strong spotlight on the failure of other measures—including the great struggle for integration in the city—to arrest the spiral of educational decline. Given a mandate, the panel cut through the enormous complexities that had previously restricted no less brave men and women to piecemeal proposals for reform. It emerged with a proposal as political and social as it was educational. The proposal called for a totally restructured system *within which* particular educational changes could take root, thereby reversing previous reform approaches, which sought to rebuild the system block by block through particular education innovations. Thus, one observer, Jason Epstein, wrote in *The New York Review of Books:*

> Not only had it been a matter for them [the panel members] of forestalling a revolution in the ghetto but of simultaneously proposing solutions to pedagogical problems which have so far perplexed nearly everyone who has tried to think about them. To have had to face these dilemmas within the sharply foreshortened perspective of America's racial agony compounds the puzzle, so that one is amazed to consider that Mr. Bundy and his colleagues agreed to undertake their work at all. That they had also to state their conclusions in the form of legislative proposals elevates their task to a truly metaphysical level of difficulty, made still worse by the gloomy presence of an educational bureaucracy which all the forces of history, concentrated as they are on the ghettos of New York, have been powerless to budge.

Reaction to the panel's report was instantaneous. The existing board of education, represented on the panel by its president, Mr. Giardino, made its opposition felt through his official dissent. Others, too, read in the report an attack on their positions, and elements in the school system that had often contended with each other quickly began to make common cause against the plan. The leadership of the UFT, for example, joined with the board of education and the CSA to oppose the Bundy proposals.* The drive against the proposal was initially spearheaded by the CSA, some of whose constituent bodies assessed their members to raise war chests against the plan. These school supervisors, sometimes described as the mandarins of the system, had risen to their position through what had originated as a merit system but had hardened into a protective guild, called by one critic, "a pyramid . . . so firmly impacted at its base and so remote at its summit that it promises to survive (unless it is destroyed by its angry clientele) longer than the pyramids of Egypt."

One basis of the fierce opposition among the lower supervisory ranks—men and women who had served their time and were on the way up—was the fear that they might lose their place in line for such jobs as principal or assistant superintendent. Another form of insecurity lay not so much in the prospect of loss of jobs (since the Bundy Plan proposed to protect tenured administrators' *ranks*) but in the possibility of disruption or discomfiture, since there was no guarantee of personnel remaining in their present *assignments*. The board of examiners itself called the plan "terrifying in its implication" for white teachers.† There were a small number of significant cracks in the massive opposition of the city's school administrators. One of the highest rank-

* An organization of eighty Negro school supervisors, however, endorsed the plan.

† In the attack of professional educators on the Bundy Report, there are remarkable echoes of the assault of thirty-one grammar school masters of Boston in 1844 on the seventh annual Report of Horace Mann as secretary of the Massachusetts Board of Education. The issues were different, but the battle was drawn along the lines of threatened reform and innovation over established practice. Mann's report was labeled a "pernicious tract." He was accused of being insufficiently acquainted with the Boston schools, and it was said that he had "so far poisoned [the public mind] that great distrust is felt in all teachers of the old school." The injury the school masters perceived, as Michael Katz has observed, stemmed in part from their feelings that they were "career . . . teachers; they were proud of their work and felt that they were the representatives of an honorable educational tradition within the city."

ing school-headquarters officials wrote to the panel within twenty-four hours of publication of the report: "The recommendations are educationally sound and responsive to the political and social realities of the cities. Indeed, I think that this document will serve as a blueprint for change across the country. . . . some of my colleagues were both unkind and unfair; but you must remember that this report hits our ego, our image, and our future."

Another leading official, Deputy Superintendent of Schools Dr. Fred Hill, writing jointly with Dr. Richard L. Featherstone, chairman of the Department of Administration and Higher Education of Michigan State University, while calling the report weak in a number of respects, said it "is strongest in its inherent belief in the democratic procedure whereby citizens have a voice in the control of the destiny of their children through community educational systems." They concurred in the report's rejection of the concept that uniformity, in itself, provides equality: "It is perfectly evident that a city the size of New York with its varied population and myriad of educational needs, simply should not provide a uniform educational program throughout the city." Its weak points, they said, were its exclusion of teachers and other educators from the community boards, and its failure both to consider the mobility of families within the city and to seek from other governmental agencies and from private enterprise suggestions for models of schooling that would not be tied to geographical boundaries. (In fact, the Bundy Report did propose that district boundaries "should be so drawn as to encourage and facilitate greater coordination with other important governmental efforts serving human needs in the city," and spoke further of geographically unbounded models as options under a federated, decentralized system.)

Opponents of the panel's plan blanketed the city with speakers, brochures, and advertisements. They established a "hot line" telephone number, which anyone in doubt could call to find out "facts" about the controversy. The plan would have been a jolt, no matter whose hands had fashioned it. It rankled some opponents all the more because it appeared to be the work of "out-siders." This irritation was not confined to the educational bureaucracy, whose opposition to the proposals was predictable. It was shared, ironically, by some outside the system who had themselves worked long and hard to persuade, nudge, or force the giant system into revitalization. These included sociologists, political scientists, parent groups, educational specialists, and others who had, during their more than ten years of efforts to de-segregate the city's public schools, achieved a kind of *esprit de corps*. The general defeat of these efforts had made the limited integration victories in certain areas where ghettos adjoined middle- and lower-middle-class neighborhoods all the more pre-cious. Thus, many of the embattled integrationists were not so much opposed to the Bundy Panel *per se* as saddened, or angered, by its frank acknowledgement that decentralization would do nothing immediately to advance integration and its candid, methodical recital of the general failure of desegregation efforts —a defeat many could not bring themselves to admit.

All these groups, with some justice, regarded New York City's educational problems as their turf, and there was ample justifica-tion for their feeling that the Bundy Plan was the work of men and women essentially new to the educational wars of the city. If John Lindsay was not a "true New Yorker," in the sense of a battle-tested Democratic officeholder, the panel chairman, Mc-George Bundy, was even less so—he had arrived in the city only a year before. Yet, as president of the Ford Foundation and former dean of the Harvard faculty, he possessed great prestige. Also, he had, in a short time, stepped up the foundation's engagement in civil rights and social problems. But, to some liberals, his concern for and actions to meet the nation's social crisis were offset by his association with the Johnson Administration (which he had left but not renounced), more precisely, by his close association with the early official Vietnam policy.

Those who sought to stigmatize the panel as a group of out-siders would not have their minds changed by the fact that the panel had access to advice and consultation from many of the leaders active in New York's educational struggles. Some of the latter (including Marilyn Gittell) were formal consultants to the staff. Others freely expressed themselves to panel members and/or staff: for instance, Kenneth Clark, Florence Flast of the United Parents Association, and such militant blacks and whites as Ellen Lurie, former head of EQUAL, a mainly white pro-integration group; David Spencer, a key figure in the I.S. 201 experimental school complex; and Roy Innis, head of Harlem CORE and later director of national CORE. So did all levels of the educational structure, from the superintendent of schools and members of the board of examiners to UFT President Albert Shanker, as well as members of the existing appointed local school boards. But none of this stilled the voices that cried foul because the panel itself consisted primarily of non–New Yorkers.

The *ad hominem* argument was employed as a tactical weapon of active opponents and as a parenthetical observation by purportedly objective critics of the community-participation movement generally. As a means of arguing against the substance of the plan, it was obviously irrelevant. But it is relevant in pondering the outcome of the panel's deliberations. Would a panel composed primarily of "true" New Yorkers have reached the same conclusions? In fact, could such a panel have been assembled without creating a conflicting tangle of the many and varied interest groups in the city?

Answers cannot, of course, be given with certainty. As bold as they were, the panel's particular proposals were not bizarre or esoteric. The general notion of decentralization of the New York City schools had been a subject of dialogues and reports for more than twenty-five years. Proposals to combine strong parental participation with meaningful administrative decentralization were already in the wind in various parts of New York, and, as noted, had been presented in an earlier form in the report of former Mayor Wagner's Temporary Commission on City Finances. The choice of a "non–New Yorker" panel entailed a political disadvantage, but it may well have been the lesser of other burdens. For example, if the mayor had selected an equally small number of "true New Yorkers," he might have had to omit important segments of the population and interest groups—for example, the teachers' union, militant elements of the Negro community, and the United Parents Association. Had he attempted to represent *all* major groups and interests, he would have emerged with a panel of a dozen or more members that might have been unwieldy and, more seriously, contentious. Whether taken consciously or unwittingly, the choice of a mainly "non–New Yorker" panel augured well for strong, unequivocal recommendations and may even, on balance, prove to have been wise politically.

In the immediate aftermath of the report's publication, many arguments were raised against it. The chief lines of attack were as follows:

1. *The scheme would Balkanize the city.* The creation of two dozen or more quasi-autonomous districts would penalize children who moved from one neighborhood to another, because curriculums would not be comparable. The system would result in duplication and inefficiency, consuming funds that might better be used for direct improvement of education (for example, smaller classes and more remedial services). Moreover, the panel had been naïve—if not deceptive—in drawing an analogy between the proposed districts and suburban or small-city school districts.

Against these arguments, proponents of the panel's plan noted that each district would be required to adhere to state educational standards and that a pupil moving from a district in Manhattan to a district in the Bronx would incur no more of a penalty than a pupil moving from Buffalo to White Plains. Moreover, the cost of duplication was exaggerated. (The city budget director subsequently estimated it would cost $13 million, or about 2 per cent of the total city education budget.) Besides, backers of the plan argued, the present centralized structure had already far exceeded the size at which it might benefit from economies of scale. Instead, it had turned into a wasteful, educationally un-sound bureaucracy.

As to the charge that it improperly compared the community school district to suburban or small-town districts, advocates of the plan noted that the report made no effort to glorify small districts; it simply pointed out that the proposed new districts, which might range from 12,000 to 40,000 in enrollment, would be sufficiently *large* to be able to offer the same range of services and curriculums as such cities as Berkeley, Norwalk, or Evans-ville.

2. *By creating segregated districts, the plan would deal a blow to integration efforts.* During its study, the panel frequently heard this fear expressed, mainly by whites. The panel report, while supporting the desirability of racial integration in the schools, took the position that, in New York City, integration had become a secondary issue. Ten years of efforts to reduce racial imbalance under the prevailing system of New York City school organization had failed because of white resistance, professional inaction, and population shifts. The panel's recommendation preserved the right of the central board of education to mandate inte-gration policies and urged that the state offer individual dis-tricts incentives to promote integration. But it said that the long-run value of its proposals for integration must be found in their effect on the quality of public education: "Communities which achieve high levels of pupil performance—in schools that have a favorable climate for learning—will be the strongest possible magnet to draw all kinds of parents back to the city. And nothing less will do the job."

3. *The proposals would produce chaos and turn the schools over to "vigilantes" and "racists."* The UFT's Albert Shanker said he feared the plan might open the way for "local vigilantes to constantly harass teachers." Walter Degnan, then the head of the CSA, said, "Schools have been the focus of recent attack because they are the most vulnerable politically and because they involve, next to welfare, the largest sums of public monies."

Columnist Joseph Alsop charged that the decentralization movement was an effort "by the extreme wing of the Black Power movement . . . to take over control of the predominantly Negro schools in a whole series of big cities." Others voiced similar views in more guarded language.

Such fears cannot be discounted simply as tactical arguments. Over 90 per cent of the teachers were white, most of them Jewish, while the student body was half nonwhite (29 per cent Negro and 21 per cent Puerto Rican). In reply, however, advocates of the plan pointed out that the panel had written a number of strong safeguards into its plan—particularly the requirement that the community school districts, no more nor less than independent school districts, would be subject to the state education law and the considerable administrative powers of the commissioner of education. Other checks were provided in the reporting and auditing requirements. The community school boards would not, as the plan's opponents implied, be rump bodies but duly elected and selected official bodies. Those who would be "taking over" would not be outsiders or political extremists but the parents of the school children—those with the greatest stake in the educational effectiveness of the system. Moreover, the panel proposed a timetable and transition mechanism during which detailed plans for an orderly changeover would be made. The subsequent upheaval over personnel transfers in the Ocean Hill–Brownsville district, whose fate, many said, would become the entire city's should the panel's proposals be enacted, actually occurred, largely, because detailed guidelines and regulations did not exist and because the prospects for an orderly, planned transition had been killed in the legislature.

4. *Ghetto parents (if not laymen generally) are incompetent to deal with educational issues.* Lawyer and civil libertarian Morris Ernst, for example, declared that "Few of us are capable in time and background of being intellectually involved . . . We could easily wreck the lives of thousands of our children by giving power to parents who would be called upon to act without . . .

highly sophisticated . . . knowledge [about] the great and ever-lasting problem—the relation of the mind of a teacher to the mind of a pupil."

Proponents of decentralization replied by pointing to the tradition of lay control of public education. They argued that, while members of school boards have the role of reflecting community concerns and needs and of approving educational policy, they are neither required to be versed in the professional aspects of education nor are they supposed to oversee the day-to-day operations of the schools. Even Deputy Superintendent of Schools Hill, who expressed reservations about the report, acknowledged: "Basic are the twin assumptions that local people should have the right to make mistakes, and that, in the long run, they will ultimately evolve educational programs which best serve the needs of their children."

The reaction to statements about ghetto incompetence was expressed by a black caucus from five cities, at a Harvard education conference early the following year: "We consider it an insult to be asked to prove whether we can do a better job in order to be granted the necessary resources and support. We should not be forced into answering the question, 'Can you do it better?' to those who have failed miserably in the past despite their control over substantial resources."

Moreover, one of the least discussed and most innovative aspects of the Bundy panel's plan was its recommendation that prospective board members be given preparatory training. Few local school boards anywhere in the country even now provide such training to prepare incoming members for their responsibilities. The panel furthermore recommended systematic, intensive programs of education for the community at large on the powers and responsibilities of parents and boards in the proposed new structure.

5. *The personnel changes would deprive ghetto schools of adequate staffs and would destroy the merit system.* As noted earlier, the panel advanced several reasons for its belief that

schools would be adequately staffed and, indeed, that staff-community relations would improve. With regard to merit, defenders of the plan noted that teachers still would be required to meet state certification standards and that the present examination systems had produced an administrative structure in which initiative and innovation were not rewarded. Other protections against the spoils system included the requirement that openings be made public and that appointments and promotions be competitive—that is, that candidates be examined (by interview or test or both) and a record be maintained of the criteria by which they were employed or rejected.

The plan specifically recommended that tenure be preserved and that administrative personnel should retain salary and rank. It also recommended that, at the time the plan went into effect, no tenured person should be transferred out of a district without his consent. Despite these safeguards, opponents raised the specter of mass transfers out of newly decentralized districts into what they described as "the Livingston Street Hilton," or "[Board of Education] headquarters hotel."

Actually, the report was only the latest in a stream of studies indicating that the examination system is an outmoded device that rewards characteristics other than educational or administrative merit. As a New York University study, *Teacher Mobility*, noted in 1963, the present system pays off

> those with "stick-to-it-iveness," [those who] plug along, voraciously swallowing every exam that comes along, and become administrators; those who "know the system" and "speak the language" become administrators; the remainder, good and bad, with little success in either passing exams or knowing the system, are denied advancement and fall by the wayside. The school system feeds on its own kind, and many potentially good administrators are lost as a result.

That community control spells ethnic favoritism in hiring is not borne out by the limited experience to date in New York City. Even in the most embattled of New York's three experimental districts, Ocean Hill–Brownsville, the majority of new teachers hired have been white. And in a 1968 survey of the three districts, a vast majority of parents (82 per cent) said it made no difference one way or the other, whether their children were taught mostly by black or by white teachers. Even in Ocean Hill–Brownsville, only one-fifth of the parents said they preferred black teachers.

6. *Decentralization would weaken the teachers' union.* Despite the plan's proposal that labor negotiations remain centralized, union leaders argued that the "breakup" of the system would make it more difficult to bargain forcefully. In New York, the UFT increasingly has gone beyond salary issues into demands for a voice in the determination of working conditions and educational policy. Some union officials believed that this trend would be blunted by the transfer of substantive decision-making powers to dozens of community boards. At the time the Bundy Report appeared, the union's self-confidence was at an all-time high as a result of its success, a few months earlier, in a two-week strike that the union labeled a "mass resignation" in order to steer clear of a state law against work stoppages by public employees; the union won its strongest contract ever—a 26-month, $135.4 million agreement. This strike, however, had exacerbated teacher-community tensions in some areas. Many parents accused teachers of abandoning children for selfish interests. Teachers, in turn, accused parents of serving as "scabs." Blacks kept some ghetto schools open, using mostly parents and a bloc of black teachers who crossed picket lines.

Despite earlier union support for the decentralization concept, Albert Shanker now declared, "Without a strong central authority [and safeguards] decentralization will be a movement toward apartheid, bringing forth extremists (black and white) and the creation of a huge community pork-barrel in which some can improve their economic lot at the expense of their own children." The union opposition to the Bundy Plan, according to a prescient analysis by Joseph Featherstone in *The New Republic,* "has the makings of a tragedy, for parents and teachers may not have identical interests, but they do have interests in common against the school administration." Indeed the UFT had been active in setting up New York's three experiments in community participation. In the Washington, D.C., experiment with neighborhood control, the head of the local teachers' union has declared, "The parents are demanding, and are going to have, a greater say in the operation of the schools whether the teachers are with them or against them. We want to be with the parents and we have no intention of aligning ourselves with reactionary forces that fear community involvement."

7. *Decentralization is a shrewd effort to foist responsibility for the failure of the schools onto the shoulders of the poor.* Some critics saw in the plan a design by the establishment to let ghetto communities stew in their own juice. According to this thesis, the power structure, unable—or, worse, unwilling—to achieve quality education in the ghetto, would, by surrendering control to the communities, also shift the burden of failure to the victims themselves. Furthermore, the surrender would relieve the establishment of the need to allocate more resources to public education. As the notion was put in the union's statement on decentralization, "to turn over a starved school system to local control is merely a political tactic to shift blame for inevitable failure on a powerless local leadership from responsible city and state officials." The theory found credence even in high academic places. As the dean of the Harvard Graduate School of Education put it, "Lower the heat from the community by making the community directly responsible for the mess, the cynic concludes. So does the realist."

There are as few facts to refute this theory as there are to support it. The panel and its supporters asserted that low-income parents, given the substance of participation instead of the illusion provided by the middle-class PTA model, would be motivated to seek high-quality education. Furthermore, the panel asked, what are the alternatives?

Then U.S. Commissioner of Education Howe, who endorsed

the principle of decentralization in testimony before a state legislative committee, rejected the "shift of responsibility" argument:

> I would take issue with those who argue that decentralization of schools is a trap to shift responsibility for the conduct of education onto the shoulders of people who lack power, know-how, and money. It is, instead, an effort to give them a chance to learn the responsible use of power, and to build an access for them to the power exercised for the whole city by the City Board of Education.
>
> You cannot have it both ways: those who demand improvement must be willing to participate in its achievement. There is a role for criticism, but that role must exist within the framework of responsibility and accountability. The alternative is anarchy. Decentralization of control of education in our large cities does not mean handing over money and personnel selection to groups of self-appointed saviors of education who seek their own aggrandizement more directly than they seek new opportunities for young people. Instead, it means making democracy work in an orderly fashion among those who have never had the chance for participation in the affairs of the schools which serve their children.

What ghetto parents now have under a centralized system, others said, is inadequate education. The assumption that they are protected only under a system that purports to do something *for* them denies their potency. A so-called hard-headed view holds that giving poor people a role in their own institutions amounts to romanticizing the poor. The Bundy Panel contended, on the contrary, that, given the freedom and funds, people—poor or rich —will find whatever technical resources they require. The difference is that they will not be at the mercy of a failing, albeit professionally dominated, system. Under community control, it is held, the technicians and professionals would have to perform or be replaced. Of course, a school district might also fail under the proposed reorganization. The point, according to the advocates of decentralization, is that the plan opens a *variety* of routes through which success may be pursued. As things stand now, children march down the single centralized educational road, and, if they fall by the wayside, there is no alternative.

8. *The plan is a distraction from the need for greater comprehensive attacks on all social ills.* This argument, an enlargement of the one just noted, was articulated, among others, by Bayard Rustin, a civil rights leader whose ties to the black community collided with his long association with the labor movement. He had this to say about the New York City schools and the Bundy panel's plan:

> Every year there has been a new gimmick. First it was busses; the next year it was the [State Commissioner of Education] Allen Plan. Now these are forgotten. The following year it was talk about education parks. Last year it was the More Effective Schools program. This year it's decentralization. Next year it will be still another gimmick. The fundamental reason educators have become involved in this gimmickry is that they do not seem to understand that unless there is a master plan to cover housing, jobs, and health, every plan for the schools will fall on its face.

This argument was also pressed by the CSA:

> The approach of the Bundy Report is a superficial one in that it focuses on the schools alone without regard, except for incidental references, to other institutions or forces. It assumes that current social unrest can be appeased by an administrative restructuring of the schools system. The needs . . . for better housing, improved recreational facilities, higher education, job training, and placement, medical care and social services . . . are largely ignored.

The reply of advocates, of course, was that schools were a major instrument for upward mobility and that efforts to reform them could not be suspended until major social and economic needs were met. The Bundy Panel was not blind to these other factors. As the panel wrote in transmitting the report to the mayor, "We think it self-evident that education is only one instrument of progress"; also, as it noted, the panel had been asked to examine school decentralization, "not . . . to settle hard priorities between jobs, housing, and schools."

9. *The plan deals only with administration; it does not solve financial problems or contain any educational innovations.* Har-

vard's education dean said the proposed reorganization would improve the existing system but said flatly, "the system will still not run much better." The system was hopelessly underfinanced, he said, and "without new resources the only thing new will be the objects of criticism, the Community School Boards rather than 110 Livingston Street."

But the panel had acknowledged that "decentralization is no substitute for other deeply needed changes . . . in particular . . . the massive infusion of funds which the school system now needs," and supporters of the plan, while not denying the need for such funds, emphasized that the way the funds were spent was crucial. They noted that pupil failure had continued even while compensatory education funds, teacher salaries, and other school resources had increased. Their judgment was confirmed in subsequent appraisals of Title I (for example, the NAACP's report, "Is It Helping Poor Children?") and in the comments in President Nixon's 1970 education message about the disappointing results of compensatory-education efforts.

Other intellectual critics deprecated the Bundy Plan for its alleged lack of "new educational ideas." Staff members of the Center for Urban Education published a particularly strong "critical analysis" (from which, incidentally, the director of the organization disassociated himself). The failure of the center's staff to see pedagogical innovation in the plan was symptomatic of professional critical myopia. In fact, the Bundy Report did suggest a number of possible innovations. The report, among other things, touched on bilingual instruction, university-contract skill centers in reading and other subjects, curriculum research centers in individual schools, nongraded school organization, and tutorial arrangements. Other possibilities discussed were new career patterns for paraprofessionals and a process in which teacher aides would advance to professional status through the ranks of teaching assistant and associate teacher. The panel did not include any of these in its recommendations, for to have done so would have been to prescribe detailed styles of education for communities, a common error of educational reformers that is precisely inimical to the principle of community self-determination.

What the Bundy Panel did recommend, however—the structural reorganization of school governance—is itself a fundamental educational innovation. Some academic critics fail to see that participation by parents—as equal partners and not through the sufferance of professionals—is educationally potent. As *The Saturday Review* noted, "Inevitably the 'education' that results [from having parents participate] will reach far beyond the classroom—into the homes and local institutions of the community."

The same educators who rail against children's environmental handicaps are doing battle against the entry of those great environmental agents—the parents and the community—into the school process. The school is a system. It needs energy, and parents and the community are great energy sources. Not only has formal education failed to tap them but it has so resisted them that this energy is now increasingly working against the professionals. Society does not know the full potential of this energy for improving the educational system, because it has never been tried, not even in middle-class schools. There is some evidence to be found, however, from Head Start and even from New York City summer school programs in which the regular rule book is thrown away. In such cases, parents perceive the school as "their" institution, and, whether they continue to stay at home or actually work in the school building, they become true partners with the professional, with all that implies for student motivation and incentive. At the very least, it is unlikely that students and their families in a participatory climate will continue to regard the school as an alien institution, indifferent to their needs. Reconnecting the school with the home is an educational innovation of the first magnitude.

"The aim of the Bundy Report is to reconnect the persons responsible for the children and renew the human purpose of education," said *The Saturday Review*. "In a city as vast and anonymous as New York, such communications—rather than high math and reading scores—may be the chief benefit of decentralizing the schools."

While critics of the Bundy Plan rapidly mobilized opposition, support for the plan grew slowly. (It was not until six months after the plan's publication that a citywide committee of respected leaders was formed to organize support for it.) Nevertheless, it was clear that there was a great deal of sentiment for some changes along the lines favored by the Bundy Panel. The United Parents Association, representing some 400,000 members, approved the proposals, with the reservation that the central board should be responsible for curriculum and safeguards against favoritism, bias, or influence-peddling by the local boards. Support also came from such prestigious groups as the Public Education Association and the Citizens Budget Commission, from several members of existing local school boards, and from most civil rights organizations.

Although school superintendents in many major cities gave the Bundy Report a cool reception, both U.S. Commissioner of Education Howe and one of his predecessors, Dr. Samuel Brownell, now a Yale University professor and formerly Detroit Superintendent of Schools, endorsed the proposals. The approach, said Brownell, "holds promise of meeting some of the fundamental challenges and problems that have remained immune to piecemeal, special approaches heretofore attempted."

Support sometimes came from surprising sources. Predictions that the plan would be embraced by the Parents and Taxpayers (PAT), a conservative New York group that opposes the use of busing or redistricting to achieve integration, proved unfounded. Mrs. Rosemary Gunning, leader of PAT forces, termed it an "untried hybrid system" and proposed, instead, a five-borough plan with boards elected by all residents. But California's conservative educational fundamentalist, Dr. Max Rafferty, aligned himself with progressives like Howe. "Every new idea attracts both nutty friends and screwball enemies," wrote Rafferty, "but the [Bundy] proposal is basically a sound one. For too long we educators have been moving in a profoundly unhealthy direction, talking up the advantages of size and numbers and consolidation while at the same time paying lip service to the ideal of education for the individual."

While many critics of the plan opposed it because, in their opinion, it "went too far," there were those who felt it did not go nearly far enough. Some civil rights groups, for example, argued for totally independent community school districts within the city, rather than for the panel's federated plan. They charged that the plan would create a middle-class leadership in the ghettos "whose basic task is to keep the community from getting real control." It was, they said, "a pacification program." This hardly accorded with Alsop's claim that the plan is a surrender to wild-eyed black extremists. The contradiction was seldom noted, however, in the furious clash of opinion aroused by the report.

The suggestion that the plan did not go far enough was also implied in reservations expressed by Joseph Featherstone, who, while writing in general support of the Bundy Panel's design, believed that even districts of the size it suggested do not consti-tute communities in the true sense of the word. He was skeptical about how participatory the board-election process would be and suggested that it may be farfetched to assume that voting in board elections will help parents shed their feeling of powerlessness. In reply, Bundy Plan backers argued that participation goes well beyond the ballot. As the report itself noted, "Voting is not the sole measure of a participatory system. A decentralized school structure should encourage and create other means of parent participation."

Publication of the Bundy Plan was a major chapter in a long political and social dispute that, as of this writing, nearly two years later, is still under way. In that dispute, the plan itself took on as much symbolism as substance. If one or another of its details was sidetracked in the ebb and flow of alternative plans and legislative and administrative struggle, its concept—meaningful participation of parents and community for urban education reform—remained at stage center. The plan, under its name, had become too controversial to serve as the blueprint the mayor presented to the 1968 legislature, but its main components formed the backbone of legislation proposed in both 1968 and 1969.

The panel's plan advocated legitimizing the role of parents and the community in the educational decision-making process. In effect, it would have provided a measure of community control. By no means would it have shifted total power to the community, which some community-control advocates now consider prerequisite to the concept. The decentralization law that was finally adopted by the New York Legislature in 1969 fell considerably short even of the Bundy Plan.

The Bundy Plan *per se* had taken its place in history, but both the proponents and opponents of the new pattern of the New York City schools knew, though they would not publicly acknowledge it, that the plan had mapped out the ground on which the legislative struggle would be waged. A different but parallel struggle followed in the wake of the Bundy Plan. It is to this that the next chapter turns.

6

New York—Crucible for Community Control

> There is no squabbling so violent as that between people who accepted an idea yesterday and those who will accept the same idea tomorrow.—CHRISTOPHER MORLEY (*Religico Journalistici*)

Until real community control of the public schools is established in some large American city, the concept will be associated in most minds with the three "demonstration districts" of New York City. These clusters—comprising eighteen schools, out of nearly a thousand in the city—were the focus of tempestuous events that escalated urban educational issues into a maelstrom of political and social strife and thrust the phrase "community control" into the national vocabulary. In the two and a half years from their feeble beginnings to their scheduled abolition in 1970 by legislative fiat, the demonstration districts have been a microcosm of the thick net of urban politics, of the nation's open racial polarization, and of the difficulty of achieving educational reform in the face of tradition, established interests, and fear.

A review of both the origin of the demonstration districts and the play of forces that led to their demise goes far in illuminating urban educational issues as well as the politics and perils of reform attempts. To begin with, the demonstration districts, whose origin may be traced to a set of extralegal demands, were actually established as legally constituted entities. The demands arose primarily from community groups in East Harlem whose frustrations had mounted during the period following the inconclusive outcome of the I.S. 201 school boycott in the fall of 1966. Elsewhere in the city, there were signs of increasing discontent with school conditions. Parent boycotts occurred at more than a dozen other schools. A predominantly black federation of parents in the borough of Queens demanded that teachers be rated on the basis of the standardized test scores their students achieved. A boycott, centering on the issue of community control, occurred at another Harlem school, P.S. 125. But I.S. 201 continued to be the focal point of a quickening politics of participation—with parents and community groups seeking an unprecedented voice in the schools, school professionals growing increasingly resistant, and other forces (Mayor Lindsay, for example, and, to some extent, Superintendent of Schools Donovan) seeking to mediate by advancing decentralization somewhat beyond the point of mere administrative diffusion of authority. Central to these negotiations was a series of meetings between East Harlem community groups and the superintendent of schools. The board of education itself took no direct part in the negotiations, but officials from the mayor's office and the city's Human Resources Administration were actively seeking to resolve the dispute, as were UFT representatives. Newly arrived on the scene were members of the education staff of the Ford Foundation, who had become acquainted with the dispute in the course of discussing with Teachers College possible education improvement programs in Harlem. Donovan encouraged the foundation's interest. Community groups were initially suspicious of the foundation, because they viewed it as representative of white "establishment" interests, but after foundation president Bundy declined to serve on a task force that they viewed as a delaying tactic, they were more willing to discuss matters with its staff. In fact, distrust of the school system by community groups was so extreme and communication between the two so difficult to maintain that, increasingly, the foundation's representatives (who were sympathetic to the community views yet sensitive to the difficulty of change in large educational systems) became a link between the two.

Donovan's basic position remained that the law prevented delegation of powers to any community group. The Harlem representatives continued to predict further deterioration unless parents were given a voice in the policies for their schools. The compromise was a proposal for the establishment of small demonstration school districts in which some prohibitions against delegation of powers could be waived because of the districts' special experimental status.

The policy under which the demonstration districts were to be organized was announced by the board of education in April, 1967. In its statement, the board expressed a desire "to experiment with varying forms of decentralization and community involvement in several experimental districts of varying size," and asked the superintendent of schools to submit specific proposals for experimental districts designed to "improve the instructional programs for the children in the schools concerned by bringing the parents and community into a more meaningful participation with the schools."

Four communities were actually designated by the board, although only three of these managed to achieve recognition as demonstration districts. The fourth was an area on Manhattan's upper West Side, where white children still constituted more than one-third of the school population. The board never accepted the various proposals submitted by this racially and economically integrated community, one which offered a unique opportunity to test not only parent participation but the elusive goal of "quality integrated education" as well. As a result, the demonstration districts (and, by implication, the very concept of community control) were identified in the public mind as an exclusively black movement.

I.S. 201 quickly took advantage of the board's new policy to form a project involving the intermediate school and the four elementary schools that feed into it. Groups in the two other communities did likewise: the Ocean Hill–Brownsville section of Brooklyn, with a junior high, an intermediate school, and six elementary schools; and a section of New York's Lower East Side called Two Bridges (because it lies between the Brooklyn and Manhattan bridges bordering Chinatown), with a junior high and four elementary schools. Both had been centers of parental unrest: In the former, a rump school board had been established after minority parents charged that the officially appointed district board (covering a much greater number of schools) was not representative, and, in the latter, neighborhood groups had named their own district superintendent.

Community groups in these areas were then being encouraged by the UFT as well as by Yeshiva University faculty and Ford staff members. Interestingly, some union leaders had viewed decentralization as an opportunity to enhance the influence and status of teachers. The theory was that, if local school boards were no longer subordinate to central direction, they would rely increasingly on the staffs of individual schools; parents would thus become the allies of the teachers in disputes with central authorities.

It is important to underscore the board of education's public action in authorizing the demonstration districts. This authorization was a crucial turning point in the history of community control of public education, but it has been obscured by a persistent mythology that later enveloped the demonstration districts as to their origin and status.

The myth holds that the districts were creatures of the new black power movement, abetted by outside forces. But, as noted, the pilot districts actually emerged through the legitimate channel of negotiation with the school system—during a mounting crisis of educational failure in New York City, heightened by the frustrations and broken promises of a decade-long struggle for integration. Born of community pressures and focused particularly by strife at I.S. 201, the movement developed before the legislative call for an official citywide decentralization blueprint, and the board of education's announcement of its policy on demonstration districts preceded by six months the appearance of the Bundy Report (indeed, it was made public three weeks before the first meeting of the Bundy Panel).

The myth that has developed over the demonstration districts' status is that they were illegitimate. Their opponents persistently characterized the districts as rump uprisings or vigilante groups. But, as we have seen, their establishment was negotiated with the superintendent of schools and the union, and approved by the board of education. Superintendent Donovan, in partially meeting community demands, may well have been trying merely to buy another respite from crisis. The board of education, too, anxious to quiet dissatisfaction in several neighborhoods, may well have approved the experimental districts without having the slightest inkling of their significance. Certainly, both suppositions are suggested by one aspect of the school system's past behavior, its habit of taking almost any way out of a crisis, with little regard for future consequences (even though they might be even more serious than the present crisis).

The fact of their official authorization, however, did not, in itself, provide a sufficient foundation on which the demonstration districts could build into strong units or even survive. The districts were beset by challenges to their authority and uncertainty about their duration, and felt threatened by the behavior, if not the intent, of superior authorities—the board of education and the administrative hierarchy of the school system. Also, the districts were troubled not only by two principal adversaries, the UFT and the CSA, but by internal factions and by a few who sought to use the districts for political advantage.

A Shaky Beginning

All three demonstration districts were in impoverished areas or neighborhoods, where income, quality of housing, and level of education were well below the city average. Few residents (13 per cent) held white-collar jobs. Social problems were severe; the 120,000-population Ocean Hill–Brownsville neighborhood had the highest narcotics-addiction rate in the country. The residents were predominantly Negro, except for the Two Bridges area, where Chinese and Puerto Ricans constituted a majority (80 per cent, together) and whites and blacks a minority. Three-fourths of the Negro parents in these areas had come from the South.

Although many of the schools in the demonstration districts had acquired the elements of compensatory education—including low instructor-pupil ratios, Head Start programs, new library facilities, and comparatively high per-pupil operating expenditures —pupil achievement levels were below average.

The differing views of the communities themselves and of outsiders as to what the demonstration projects were all about proved, ultimately, to be one of the shoals on which the projects were wrecked. The variation was evident from the beginning. Leaders of the pilot districts saw them as concrete first steps—a real commitment by the board of education—toward community control. Their first move after receiving the board's "approval in principle" was to plunge into a period of devising plans for gaining board approval of full-scale operation.

The board's pace was languid and half-hearted. No senior official in the school administration was assigned responsibility for the demonstration districts. Requests and decisions, often even on minor matters, had to go to the superintendent of schools himself, with all the delay this entailed. It took two months for school headquarters to assign a full-time liaison officer to the demonstration districts—and he turned out to be unfamiliar with the district areas and unauthorized to make substantive decisions without approval from headquarters. Thus, during that first summer, the leaders of the districts depended, virtually every step of the way, on the Ford representative to act as liaison with the board.

The board did establish its own advisory committee on decentralization, headed by Dr. John Niemeyer, president of the Bank Street College of Education. In its report, this committee, itself, pointed to the cloudy area of authority under which the demonstration districts operated: "The Board did not make clear from the outset which powers could be delegated within the legal limits placed upon it, nor did the Board assume the degree of leadership necessary to cause the projects to succeed."

After the board approved the three demonstration districts "in principle," Ford awarded them planning grants totaling $135,000: for I.S. 201, $51,000; for Ocean Hill–Brownsville, $44,000; and for the Two Bridges project, $40,000. With these funds, the three community groups conducted elections and hired consultants to advise them on curriculum planning, community organization, and legal matters. The last item was crucial, because the board of education, lacking legislative sanction, had long maintained that it had no authority to delegate substantive decision-making powers to any lay bodies. This position had been reinforced by the board's declaration, at the very time it announced its policy sanctioning the projects, that "basic functional relationships would remain the same." The community-planning groups sought to stretch the board's existing powers as far as they could by legal means; in their view, the law should be probed and tested to permit the school system to go as far as possible toward meaningful community voice in educational decision-making.

Thus, activist parents and community groups still saw the board of education as an adversary, as it had long been. A second force—the teachers' union—was also beginning to loom as a likely adversary instead of a possible ally. (This development had first been evidenced in the conflict over the appointment of a black principal of I.S. 201 in the fall of 1966, when the UFT joined the supervisors in opposing such an appointment.) The UFT policy of cooperation with the demonstration districts had been linked with an understanding that the districts would support the union's demand that the board of education expand the controversial More Effective School (MES) program. Designed to saturate ghetto schools with compensatory services, MES was then operating in twenty-two ghetto schools throughout the city; involving smaller classes and extra staff, it entailed an additional cost of about $500 per child. But evaluations of the program by the board itself (and later by the Center for Urban Education) indicated that MES fell short of its goals, and, even before the plans for the demonstration districts were submitted, Superintendent Donovan had announced that there would be no extension of MES within the three districts. Although the Ocean Hill–Brownsville plan did seek an experimental school status that would also have meant additional personnel and services, the union accused the community-planning group of violating its agreement.

The rift between the teachers and the planning group had widened in the fall of 1967, when the union struck the entire school system in a demand for higher wages and a greater voice in school policy. Many parents in the demonstration districts believed that their schools should have been exempted from the strike and that the union's failure to do so was evidence of an intention to weaken the projects just as they were beginning. Parents attempted to keep the schools open, and, in the I.S. 201 district, some of them threatened to "screen" returning union teachers when the strike ended—a threat that later evaporated, but, nevertheless, left a bitter taste.

As was noted in the Niemeyer Committee report, from the point of this early strike on, the union leadership determined that the teachers were to regard their relation with the elected governing boards of the three districts "like any other labor-management relationship." It had been planned that teachers would participate in the governing boards, but suspicions increased, and the union finally advised teachers not to sit on the boards. However, in each of the districts, some teachers ignored the union directive and chose to participate.

It was during this same period, during the fall of 1967, that the union began to realize, as it met with the Bundy Panel in the course of its deliberations, that a strong citywide decentralization plan would probably be recommended to the mayor and, through him, to the legislature. Union leaders were given assurances that collective bargaining would be maintained under the proposed blueprint and that teachers' tenure would be preserved. Notwithstanding, some union leaders evidently felt that their interests would be jeopardized in any plan that involved a transfer of power—even if not of total powers—away from the central source (from which they had become adept at wresting concessions) and to community groups throughout the city. The union's privately expressed resistance to any such plan soon emerged in full public view after the Bundy Report was published in November. The demonstration districts now became a focal point of the campaign against the plan. Community-union tensions had been growing in the demonstration districts, where the union's suspicions were fully matched by those of the parents and other active parties. Acts of noncooperation, teacher absences, and teacher opposition to governing board actions were seen as attempted sabotage of the projects.

To the advocates of community control and those anxious to see the demonstration districts succeed, the union, in October, 1967, threw down an open, unmistakable challenge by joining the organized supervisors of the school system in a court action against the districts. The case was pivotal, because it concerned the issue of whether the governing boards of the demonstration districts could hire as administrators men and women not on the board of education's eligibility list. Unless the governing boards could do this, the "demonstration" status of their districts would have been undermined to the point of absurdity. Even the board of education concurred, and successfully persuaded the state commissioner of education to find a loophole. Whereupon, the CSA brought suit. When the UFT joined the suit on the side of the administrators, it was a significant turning point. If not natural enemies, teachers and supervisors, notwithstanding their common professional status as educators, traditionally had essentially the same relation as workers and foremen. If anything, teachers often were natural allies of parents in the latter's grappling with bureaucratic rules and practices established and implemented by the administrative structure. Now, the teachers and the administrators put aside old differences to wage a united battle against what both felt was a paramount threat to their gains and powers.

The administrators themselves, as noted, had immediately mobilized a campaign against the Bundy Report's proposals. They had also taken measures calculated to hasten the failure of the demonstration projects. In Ocean Hill–Brownsville, for example, most of the assistant principals and principals (all CSA members) chose to transfer out of the district; in the Two Bridges project, principals played on differences among parent groups in the community and ran their schools as though nothing had happened to change the status of the district. I.S. 201 began its first year under the demonstration-district status without its acting principal, and its two assistant principals soon left. The school almost totally collapsed while replacements were delayed because, for two months, the district lacked a permanent administrator. And, in the other schools in the district, many regular administrators who remained hardly gave even lip service to the authority of the local governing board.

An Unfortunate Confusion

At this point, it is necessary to examine the relation between the demonstration districts and the proposed community school districts under the Bundy Plan as revised by Mayor Lindsay. For it was the success of the union in equating the two—despite their key differences—that accounted for a good deal of the strength of the union's campaign against effective decentralization.

The board of education's official stance was that the demonstration districts were experiments, expedient responses to crisis and community pressure. It is doubtful that the supposed experimental status of the districts ever penetrated very deeply into the public consciousness, and the more the fires of controversy were stoked around the districts, the more the public regarded them as illegitimate products of black power. Yet, the districts were, as we have noted, established under a board policy, and the governing boards were chosen in community elections that were supervised by impartial agencies and adjudged by the Niemeyer Committee to have been honest. That they were established under official auspices and that the administrators and teachers on *all* sides of the issue were duly appointed board of education employees were facts generally lost in the verbal melee. The confusion was abetted by those who sought to poison public opinion outside the ghettos against the community-control concept. A certain amount of confusion was inevitable over the Ford Foundation role. The president of the Foundation, Bundy, had been appointed by the mayor to head his advisory panel on decentralization; yet, in serving as chairman, Bundy was acting as a private citizen. At the same time, the foundation had been active in early negotiations for the demonstration districts and had granted them start-up funds. Indeed, one strong reason for Lindsay's choice of Bundy was the foundation's interest and experience in urban education.

Even those aware of the demonstration districts' actual legal status usually examined the districts not in their own right, or in comparison to the state of the schools before the districts were created, but as pilot models of community control. Despite their sympathies with the principle of greater parent participation, some influential commentators were so detached from the struggle of communities to escape educational failure and domination by unresponsive public agencies that they maintained an unrealistic faith in the possibility of fundamental changes being effected in a scientifically controlled experiment. Another group, the university and foundation personnel who helped the districts come into being, hoped that, with proper development and encouragement, the districts might serve as transitions to decentralization and as tentative, but encouraging, models of effective community participation.

But the districts developed neither under carefully controlled laboratory conditions nor in a vacuum. Action-oriented ghetto residents saw the demonstration projects as implicit promises of community control, not as impermanent experiments. And, perhaps most significantly of all, the demonstration projects influenced, and were influenced by, the struggle to defeat in the legislature the mayor's citywide decentralization plan.

One principal difference between the demonstration districts and the community districts proposed in the Bundy Plan was that the former were subject to termination by the board of education. Another lay in the fact that they were islands (and predominantly nonwhite islands) in the vast city school system. In contrast, the plan placed before the legislature would have established permanent districts embodying the principle of effective parental involvement throughout the city.

The demonstration districts were always viewed by those within them and by their friends outside as beleaguered outposts. This feeling of siege, combined with traditional ghetto suspicion of the forces and institutions of the larger society, goes far in explaining the defensive behavior by some of the leaders of the districts. This is not to say that provocation was illusory, for deliberate harassment, normal bureaucratic lethargy in the central administration, and unfavorable publicity dogged the projects from the beginning.

Serious disagreement developed over guidelines on the structure, procedures, and authority of the demonstration districts. Points of contention were the governing boards' power to enter into contracts and subcontracts, their right to apply directly for federal grants without funneling them through the central board, and their exercise of full control over their budgets so that, for example, they could apply money allocated for textbooks and supplies against maintenance needs. Some central board representatives argued against obtaining additional funds from government and other outside agencies on the grounds that this would unduly influence the "experimental nature of the project." Presumably, all was to remain the same, except that parents would elect local boards. One can imagine the effect of this argument on parents desperately seeking every possible source of aid to lift their children out of an impoverished educational status.

A study by the New York Civil Liberties Union dismissed these and other constraints by the central authority as subterfuges: "Once the Board of Education understood that what Ocean Hill–Brownsville really wanted was an experiment in genuine community control, it backed off even before it had begun."

So much emphasis was put on the occasional emotion-laden controversial incident in demonstration-district schools that an impression was created that, before the projects, all had been tranquillity in the city's schools. That the projects had difficulties—of their own making as well as those resulting from external forces—is undeniable. Each of the districts suffered periodically from factionalism among parents, from policy and personality disagreements between governing board and district administrator (notwithstanding the fact that he was a man of the board's own choice), and from intrusion by racist elements. The point is that, by and large, the public failed to place these difficulties in proper perspective—a perspective including the following factors: (1) the demonstration districts were seeking to break new educational and community-development grounds, difficult tasks under the best of circumstances; (2) they were harassed by a variety of forces; (3) they were located in some of the most alienated neighborhoods in the city, if not the country; (4) they were trying to reverse, in a very short time, the damage of years, if not decades; and (5) they were subjected to extraordinary public scrutiny.

All things considered, it is remarkable that the districts survived at all. So much else of an innovative nature in the New York City public schools had, in the past, failed utterly, far outside the glare of public attention. The demonstration districts eventually were to die not of their own shortcomings but under a legislative edict. They did not collapse administratively or educationally; they did not lose community support; they did not fall captive to racist control.

Evaluating the Districts in Context

What are some of the most significant achievements of the demonstration districts? First of all, they produced boards that included direct representation of the poor, an uncommon phenomenon in urban school districts. In contrast, the twenty-four local boards elected under the 1969 legislation have a predominantly middle-class membership that is similar to the makeup of the previously appointed boards. In fact, many of the minority-group communities in New York now have white-dominated local school boards.

Moreover, the demonstration districts surmounted the lock-step, inbred pattern of selecting educational leadership from civil service lists that reflected longevity more than leadership qualities. The governing boards chose their own unit administrators, and, whether the choice proved a happy one, as in the case of Ocean Hill–Brownsville, or an unhappy one, as in Two Bridges, the governing board and the community knew that they bore responsibility for the choice as well as the power of removal. For his part, the administrator had undiluted obligations to the community that selected him and to its children—not, as in the case of administrators chosen by central headquarters, to a distant center of authority. The same held true of the chosen leadership at the next level, the principalships. Many schools in the districts were abandoned by their regular principals after the experiment began, but the governing boards were wise enough, in most cases, to choose leaders who were able to restore the schools to orderly operation and to move on toward increasing their effectiveness. In the instructional staff, too, the demonstration projects proved they could attract sufficient numbers of qualified teachers of the caliber they wanted, despite the predictions of opponents that the projects would be short-staffed. The districts also broke new ground in the use of paraprofessionals. Teacher aides were not uncommon in the New York City schools before the demonstration districts, but they had been confined to clerical and other noneducational tasks. The demonstration districts successfully employed them in classrooms, where they assisted directly in the teaching process.

Evaluation of the demonstration districts must encompass more than conventional educational criteria—test scores of individual students, for example, or quality of staff as measured by credentials and years of service. For the ultimate aim of these demonstration projects is to improve pupil performance. But the specific goals, as stated by those who initiated them (and, implicitly, by the superintendent and the board of education, who sanctioned them), were more immediate: that is, to demonstrate the role of the community in governing its own schools, particularly in the selection of administrators and teachers; to undertake new educational programs; and to create a positive new environment for learning, in which the attitudes of teachers and students are complementary, both directed toward the improvement of student achievement. In experimental terms, the demonstration districts did not have the same characteristics of, say, a vaccine inoculation program, in which the expected outcome could be clearly stated in advance. Instead, as two leading academic critics (Robert S. Weiss and Martin Rein) noted recently in discussing evaluation of social-action programs, "they are concerned first with the impact of the program *on a situation,* and only secondarily with the impact . . . on individuals." Evaluation asks the extent to which predetermined goals are reached. But, in broad-aim programs, as distinguished from scientifically controlled experiments, "how will such goals as increased opportunity, a more responsive institutional system, and a richer cultural atmosphere show themselves?" The negative judgments that have been passed on the demonstration districts are not expressed in these terms— not, in other words, through what these two observers describe as "a more qualitative, process-oriented approach." No such evaluation of the demonstration districts was made—indeed, no evaluation of any sort was made—by the board of education or the state legislature before the districts were given their legislative death sentence.

Each district had to overcome the administrative disarray that it had inherited in its schools or that soon developed because of inadequate support from the board of education or desertions by regular personnel. Ocean Hill–Brownsville, for example, began the first year under demonstration-district status with principal-ship vacancies in seven of its eight schools, and, in a short time, seventeen of twenty-one assistant principals transferred out on the advice of the CSA. Replacements for the assistant principals were appointed by headquarters, so that achievement of some administrative order in the schools was a slow and sometimes painful process.

As far as racial tension is concerned, so much has been said and written of the Ocean Hill–Brownsville district that the public tends to forget that, almost a year earlier, the I.S. 201 district successfully overcame a racially based crisis. A consultant in the planning group—a suspended assistant principal under indictment for conspiracy in an alleged plot to assassinate moderate civil rights leaders—became an avowed candidate for the position of district administrator. Although governing board members who opposed him risked being accused of Uncle Tomism, they prevailed by a narrow margin, and the controversial militant was edged out of his consultancy as well. But this difficult act of responsibility did not, a few months later, insulate the governing board from another barrage of accusations of black racism, after press accounts sensationalized a Malcolm X memorial service at the school. The school was then temporarily placed under central headquarters control—a humiliation for the district less than six months after it had taken its first step toward a measure of community control.

Such difficulties played perfectly into the hands of the UFT and CSA lobbies that descended in force upon the 1968 state legislature, the first to consider a formal plan for decentralization with community participation in educational policy. The brunt of the battle was borne by the union, which not only had superior numbers and funds, but, unlike the organized supervisors, also had direct ties to the New York City (and, to some extent, the national) labor movement. Organized labor is a potent force in New York, not only among its own rank-and-file but also among nonmember liberals who retain warm memories of the New Deal and of the underdog days of the labor movement. When the conflict broke out in the open, one of the union's most potent appeals was for solidarity of union-minded New Yorkers.

Although the plan sent to the legislature by Mayor Lindsay was not as strong as the Bundy Panel's, it was, nevertheless, a target for full-scale lobbying by the opposition. No estimate of the cost of the campaign to defeat the plan in 1968 was reported, but *The New York Times* did report that the UFT spent more than $600,000 to defeat a similar plan in 1969. Against legislators inclined to vote for the bill, the union came armed with more than slogans and promises of a day of reckoning at the ballot box. They had, in addition, purported evidence that the demonstration districts were—as they predicted the entire city would be, if the bill should pass—in a state of chaos. "Vigilantes" were taking over the schools, and black nationalism was threatening to supplant the regular curriculum.

In contrast to the union's forceful legislative effort, supporters of the bill mustered only a feeble and ineffectual one. An *ad hoc* citizens' committee hardly advanced beyond the brochure phase, and its prestigious head, RCA president David Sarnoff, took no personal part in its activities. The city's grass-roots poverty organizations supported the bill but did not follow through with efforts significant enough to influence the outcome of the legislative struggle. The mainly white liberal agencies that, for years, had campaigned against inadequacies of the educational system diluted their effectiveness by advocating bills that departed significantly from the panel and Lindsay proposals. The members of the Bundy Panel themselves, who might have become leading spokesmen for Mayor Lindsay's bill, chose, in effect, to end their role with submission of their report. Leaders in the legislature supported the mayor's bill, as did Governor Rockefeller, but the governor did not use his maximum political capital to swing votes to it.

The union took full advantage of this near vacuum. Many members of New York City's delegation to the legislature, traditionally sympathetic to Negro problems, were persuaded to regard decentralization as nothing more nor less than an attempt to turn over the schools to black militants. "You won't find a white person left on the island of Manhattan if this goes on much longer," one was quoted as saying. "The whites are in mortal terror." Reversing the usual pattern, the relatively conservative upstate Republican bloc supplied the bulk of the votes for the temporary, watered-down decentralization plan passed in the 1968 legislature. Only a handful of reform Democrats in the New York City delegation supported a strong decentralization bill.

The legislature passed a bill (the Marchi bill) that, in effect, delayed a definitive decision for a full year. But the bill was by no means innocuous. The union had succeeded only partially; by some accounts, in fact, it had, by its uncompromising demands, overplayed its hand. The union insisted that the legislature permit no transfer of powers from the central board of education to decentralized districts; particularly, it asked for an unqualified prohibition against delegation of personnel powers. Although unwilling to accept Mayor Lindsay's proposals for mandated decentralization, the legislature so resented the force of the union demands that it passed a bill that threw back to local officials a ball with considerable bounce. The bill it passed did not *mandate* decentralization and community control, but it *permitted* both, if the mayor and the board of education chose to march ahead to them. It provided two openings for possible reform. One eliminated the major legislative restraint against delegation of powers by the board of education to community school districts.

The other enabled the mayor to change the complexion of the board by appointing additional members.

By filling vacancies as well as the newly created positions, Mayor Lindsay attained a board of education whose majority favored strong decentralization. But even this board did not act aggressively to clarify and solidify the demonstration districts' authority, to create public confidence in them, or otherwise to shore up their legitimacy. Was the UFT's escalation of its boycott of Ocean Hill–Brownsville (begun in the spring of 1968) to a city-wide strike (in the fall) meant to discourage and prevent the new board from delegating powers to the local districts under the Marchi bill? Whether planned this way or not, the 1968 strike at the least consumed the board's attention for two months.

Continuing inaction, even by a board reputed to be sympathetic to community needs and desires, was interpreted by the ghetto communities as further bitter evidence that they could hope for little in the way of voluntary grants of the authority needed to determine their own educational destiny. Prospects for new legislation that would *mandate* the transfer of authority seemed even more remote than the year before, and the prevailing mood of the demonstration-district governing boards was to consolidate what they had acquired under their tentative status as experimental units and to exert pressure for more. The legislative defeat, the inaction of the established central authority, and signs that the support from Mayor Lindsay himself was weakening also strengthened the hand of extreme militants. At the same time, the stage was set for the following year's legislative campaign by the union and the supervisors to deal a decisive blow to effective decentralization.

The teachers' strike in the fall of 1968 made that defeat a foregone conclusion.

Focus on Ocean Hill–Brownsville

Although the fundamental issue in the strike was the organized teachers' and supervisors' resistance to greater community

participation in educational policy, the surface issue that precipi-
tated it was the authority of the Ocean Hill–Brownsville governing
board over personnel. The UFT charged that, in seeking to transfer unwanted teachers out of the district, Ocean Hill–Brownsville
was violating due process. The governing board maintained that
involuntary teacher transfers were common throughout the school
system and that denying the demonstration districts the same
practice was imposing a double standard.

The personnel situation had been deteriorating in Ocean Hill–
Brownsville almost from the beginning of the demonstration district, with the union's decision to end its active cooperation with
the project. Friction increased when, under the exception granted
by the state commissioner of education, the governing board
appointed principals of its own choice. The governing board accused some teachers of "sabotaging" the project by excessive absences and lateness, virtual cessation of teaching, and other acts.
Suspicion also centered on several assistant principals assigned by
the board of education after the regular assistant principals had
withdrawn from the district; some of the district's locally selected
principals claimed that the inexperienced replacements were
neither obeying orders nor supporting the project.

When, toward the end of the school year, in the spring of 1968,
the local board was led to believe that Superintendent Donovan
would not approve a request for transfer of nineteen teachers and
supervisors, the local board ordered their transfer to central headquarters for reassignment elsewhere in the system.

The union, over a period of ten years, had succeeded in establishing rules against involuntary transfers, while the board of
education had sought more flexibility in assigning experienced
teachers to more "difficult" schools, usually in ghetto neighborhoods. Notwithstanding union rules, both the union and central
headquarters had long maintained an unwritten truce whereby
principals and other administrators could transfer teachers, but
always informally and without bringing charges. This gentle-
man's agreement had accounted for, by some reliable estimates,

the involuntary transfer of about 200 teachers a year. One of the survival skills of a school administrator in the New York school system was his ability to palm off unwanted staff to other districts without arousing the ire of the union or rocking the boat at central headquarters.

Moreover, in Ocean Hill–Brownsville, the board of education had, earlier, winked at its own rules by permitting a number of teachers to leave the district voluntarily, with little trouble. At the same time, the board made it difficult for experienced teachers who wished to transfer in, and whom the governing board wanted, to do so with similar ease. But now, the Ocean Hill governing board decided to take the initiative in transferring out teachers it no longer wanted, and the central administration would not permit the transfers. The governing board refused to keep the teachers. The union termed the transfers "dismissals." It then called for a boycott of the schools, and most union members in the district walked off the job. Superintendent Donovan thereupon closed three schools, and the governing board closed the remaining five. The issue remained unresolved as the schools closed for the summer recess.

In the fall, the union went on strike, not only in the eight Ocean Hill–Brownsville demonstration schools but throughout the city's more than 900 schools, on the grounds that its members had been denied due process.

Ocean Hill–Brownsville's rationale had been the same employed by the UFT in obtaining approval of teachers transferring voluntarily out of the district—that special conditions in such a demonstration district warranted waiver of transfer rules. It is almost universally conceded now, even by friends of the district, that the Ocean Hill–Brownsville governing board had made a strategic error when, under the pressure of the union's hammering at the due process issue, it agreed to bring formal charges before a hearing examiner, who ultimately ruled in favor of the union. Charges of unsatisfactory teacher performance or behavior are extraordinarily difficult to prove in any school system, except on virtually criminal or mental grounds. Ironically, therefore, the governing board had handed the union a battle cry by following a formal rule (the bringing of charges) for dismissal rather than transfer.

The governing boards of all three demonstration districts had learned, even in their short lifetimes, that the central board was not quite so flexible in dealing with their administrators as with old-line principals and other school officials. Little wonder that ghetto residents—those directly affected by the demonstration districts—and others as well saw the Ocean Hill–Brownsville issue as yet another instance of the use of the white society's rules and regulations against their interests. The prudence and wisdom of one or another of the steps the Ocean Hill governing board was to take in meeting this challenge will long be debated. We believe these are less important than the great political misjudgment that many made, in and outside the ghetto—the failure to realize at the outset that the demonstration districts were on trial and that their opponents were prepared to seize on any misstep in an effort to discredit and ultimately eliminate them.

Thus, for example, when the union struck, the principals and other school administrators throughout the city also walked off the job, reciprocating for the union's collaboration, some months earlier, in the supervisors' suit against the demonstration districts. This action was seen as a clear signal that the educational establishment was determined to destroy not only the demonstration districts but also the community-control concept as a whole.

The strike, which lasted thirty-six school days, took place in three stages, interrupted by two-day and two-week reopenings of the schools, during which mediation efforts took place. In the course of these phases, there were several notable events: the unwanted teachers were taken back into Ocean Hill–Brownsville but denied regular classroom assignments; striking and nonstriking teachers polarized further; at one point, militants and others prevented union teachers from entering a junior high school in the Ocean Hill district, hundreds of police were sent in to patrol the area, and some fought with residents; and the union accused the board and the mayor of failing to enforce agreements whereby the teachers would be received back into the schools without harassment. The board of education placed observers in the district schools to guard against alleged harassment of the union teachers. Ocean Hill unit administrator McCoy and his principals were suspended for three days when the Reverend Herbert Oliver, chairman of the governing board, said that returning union teachers (after the second strike) would not be given their regular assignments. The governing board—though left out of most of the negotiations—was suspended, reinstated, suspended again, and, finally, reinstated two months after the final settlement of the strike.

The governing board's distrust of the board of education and the mayor was aggravated by the suspension, as part of the strike settlement, of three principals. The suspensions were based on an adverse court ruling on the state commissioner's authority to allow the governing board to bypass Civil Service lists in appointing demonstration school principals. However, the board of education could have permitted the principals to remain in office while the court's ruling was under appeal. The governing board and its supporters felt that the suspensions constituted capitulation to the UFT and the CSA. Many community residents also saw it as a penalty against the children, in that it interrupted the continuity of supervision in the schools while the issue of the legitimacy of appointments to principalships was unresolved.

Although Ocean Hill's schools did manage to remain open during the entire strike period, community resentment ran high, what with union demands that the experiment come to an end, the humiliation of having the disputed union teachers returned under police guard, and, at one point, the stationing of a thousand policemen in and around the schools. The settlement that ended the strike included the establishment of a trusteeship, operating directly out of the Office of the State Commissioner of Education, to oversee the district operation. This trusteeship ended four months later.

In the Wake of the Strike

The strike heightened tension and conflict throughout the city. It fractured old coalitions—between organized labor and the civil rights movement, for example. It caused internal ruptures in formerly cohesive groups; the liberal establishment, for one, found itself torn between, on the one hand, its affinity for the oppressed and, on the other, its traditional loyalty to the hard-won prerogatives of labor unions. Some liberals swallowed hard and maintained their loyalties to labor. Others denounced the UFT and the rest of the labor movement in the city (which, at one point, hinted at a general strike in sympathy with the teachers) as unresponsive and protective in the face of legitimate community aspirations. Still others began by supporting the UFT and later turned to support of the community's stand. For many, the third strike was the turning point, because it seemed by then that the union's price for peace had gone well beyond the issue of teachers' rights and become nothing less than the destruction of the demonstration districts, the defeat of decentralization legislation, and the humiliation of the black community.

But the fractures followed other lines, too. Since the majority of New York's teachers and supervisors are Jewish, several Jewish organizations tended to side with the UFT. Their opposition intensified with the surfacing of anti-Semitic remarks and, occasionally, pamphlets. The UFT itself duplicated and distributed one anti-Semitic broadside as purported evidence that the Ocean Hill governing board was condoning, if not abetting, anti-Semitism as a tactic. The administrator and governing board of Ocean Hill–Brownsville firmly denied that they were parties to or tolerant of anti-Semitism, and some civil libertarians criticized the UFT for reproducing the literature.

Not the least of the divisions arose between striking and nonstriking teachers throughout the city. Some younger teachers, in particular, did not regard the union picket line as inviolate. A month before the strike was settled, nearly half the schools outside the demonstration districts were open, many of them manned by parents, with an attendance of slightly over 6 per cent of the pupils and somewhat over 10 per cent of the teaching staff. Some veteran union teachers also remained on the job and accused the union of using the strike as a weapon to break community control. One union vice-president, John J. O'Neill, broke with his colleagues, declaring:

> Is there anyone so naïve as to think that a social movement with the power of the Black and Puerto Rican community (a majority in our school system) can be held back or even turned aside by "teaching them a lesson"? Is there a shred of evidence in all sociological theory to support this proposition? If anything, and, it is already clearly evident, our [the union's] rash action in Brownsville has turned a brush fire into a conflagration sweeping across the city.

For their part, some union teachers could not forgive the actions of their colleagues who had not participated. In one of the city's most prestigious academic high schools, the union chapter voted to post on its bulletin board the names of twenty-three nonstriking teachers "for the future reference of the Faculty." It remained there for seven months.

In the months following the end of the strike, sporadic disruptions occurred, including a demonstration by several hundred high school students protesting the settlement.* But none had anything like the impact of the strike. The UFT and CSA now walked into a state legislature softened up by the reverberations of the strike. The ghetto communities had not only lost the battle of the strike; they had also failed to gain a large enough proportion of the white community to the cause of community control.

Some New Yorkers, while not necessarily sympathetic to the Ocean Hill–Brownsville board, had, nevertheless, denounced the

---

* A number of high school students now view the strike, and particularly the behavior of some teachers and principals during the strike, as a decisive element in their growing disillusionment with the schools.

union for widening a dispute in eight schools to penalize children in the entire system. Parents in some nonghetto neighborhoods broke locks on school doors to reopen schools and crossed UFT picket lines. But a large segment of the white community was more truly represented by residents in conservative white sections who organized mass picketing *against* school openings so long as the strike continued. Those residents were not so much pro-union as they were anti-Negro and Puerto Rican. New York City was thus caught up in the unmistakable early phases of a national backlash against militancy in the civil rights struggle.

It was the New York City school dispute, in fact, that provided one of the tenets of the national backlash ideology—that the affluent elite was engaged in a plot to defuse ghetto unrest by concessions and payoffs at the expense of the white middle and lower classes. Union partisans were bitter in their condemnation of agencies allegedly dominated by socio-economic elites that, in any way, assisted the demonstration districts—the Urban Coalition, private foundations, and civic agencies like the Public Education Association. Even the New York Civil Liberties Union was denounced when it published a report unfavorable to the union position; it then faced a revolt within its ranks by members who supported the UFT strike. The Ford Foundation was a prime target. Following the initial planning grants it had made to the districts, Ford continued technical and financial assistance to the districts through a grant to the Institute for Community Studies of Queens College. Critics of the foundation's role demanded nothing less than a renunciation of the districts and a withdrawal of funds, despite the fact that Ford funds never amounted to more than a fraction of the districts' budgets. (The board of education provided 98 per cent of the budgets for the three districts.) At the same time, other critics held that the foundation should have played a *more* active role, essentially to "tame" the demonstration districts. Apart from the fact that such a role would have contradicted the very self-governing basis of the project, the foundation took the position that settlement of the school strike must come directly from the parties involved. It would not intervene on either side and even declined to make pronouncements on the strike until nearly the very end, when it felt called upon to respond to UFT President Albert Shanker's insinuations that some mayoral appointees to the central board of education and Board of Regents member Dr. Kenneth Clark were pawns of the Ocean Hill governing board because nonprofit organizations with which they were associated had received Ford grants. McGeorge Bundy called the charges false and irresponsible.

Mayor Lindsay himself, as a public figure who was both wealthy and had worked hard to establish rapport with the ghetto community, was severely denounced. More than any New York mayor since Fiorello LaGuardia, he had refused to be bound by the shibboleth that education should be insulated from the governmental process (from "politics," as the defenders of the school system would put it). A successful reform candidate, he meant to include educational reform in his program for the city, despite his limited constitutional leverage for change. His first bold move was to obtain the state legislative mandate to devise a decentralization plan, and, for all practical purposes, it was his last. Like many minority-party mayors who lack a base of support in the party structure, he was willing to gamble on a quicksand issue like public education in order to build his own constituency. His failure to obtain legislative approval of a bill the legislature itself had asked him to bring in marked the beginning of the boomerang impact of the school issue.

Pro-union forces accused Lindsay of being a dupe of the black community, willing to sacrifice employment rights of white teachers, if not their personal safety, and to tolerate black racism in the interest of catering to the city's racial minorities. Ironically, the mayor was increasingly criticized by militant elements in the ghetto communities—for dispatching police to Ocean Hill–Brownsville, for not galvanizing into aggressive support of the demonstration districts a board of education that now contained a majority of his own appointees, and for making compromises in the legislative proposals for decentralization. The board of education itself came in for sustained criticism from opponents of the demonstration districts for failing to "discipline" the districts soon enough or severely enough.

Mayor Lindsay's pleas for reason did not prevail in a city ridden by propaganda, sensational rumor, and real fear. The damaging effect in terms of race relations in the city cannot be minimized; nonetheless, it is remarkable that worse did not occur. Nearly a million students out of school for eight weeks did not, as some had predicted they would, wreak havoc. Verbal abuse did grow more and more bitter on both sides as the strike progressed, and there were instances of threats and intimidation. But almost no incidents of physical violence occurred, and there were no deaths or serious injuries. Considering that urban centers all over the country had suffered five continuous years of rioting resulting in human fatalities and destruction of property, the intense school confrontation in New York was remarkably peaceful.

But the level of animosity reached during the strike was more than sufficient to make the legislature a willing target for UFT and CSA pressures. It readily agreed with the argument that the demonstration districts were forerunners of what could happen if decentralization were introduced throughout the city. The legislature accepted the contention that the districts were easily susceptible to takeover by extreme militants. Despite the fact that the union had escalated a dispute over personnel powers in one district into a citywide confrontation, defying the state law against strikes by public employees, the legislators generally held the ghetto community responsible for the strike and the ensuing disruption throughout the city.

The legislature brushed aside compromise bills. Instead, it passed a law preserving central board of education authority in virtually all functions except the appointment of district superintendents. The law divided the school system into from thirty to thirty-three districts, but, in effect, it wiped out the three demonstration districts by specifying a minimum pupil population for each new district. Ironically, this fixed pattern and other standardized and centralized features of the bill contrasted sharply with the diversity built into the Bundy Plan, which allowed for options in the size of districts, method of election, degree of autonomy, and other features.

In the area of personnel, the law seems to lock in the present procedures more effectively by preventing merged lists for principals—a device many cities have used to increase the appointment of black administrators—and by requiring that all names on the present list be assigned by April, 1970. The bill, therefore, may likely close off appointments of additional blacks for at least five years. The law also tightens the central reins on personnel transfers by community district superintendents even *within* their districts—a clear violation of the essence of decentralization, to say nothing of the concept of community control. The Board of Examiners, the frequently criticized but remarkably durable agency for qualifying teachers and controlling most promotions, remains virtually intact. The law denies community school boards discretion on budget priorities and selection of school sites (although their advisory role is expanded). Moreover, textbooks must be chosen from a centrally approved list. While the law permits districts to receive private federal and state funds, all such grants must flow through the office of the chancellor, as the new chief executive of the citywide school system is known.

The law changed the central board from an appointive system to a five-sevenths elective body—one member from each of the boroughs and two appointed by the mayor.* This system, many predict, will ensure a white, probably nonliberal majority on the board. There are no restrictions on the financing of citywide or district school board elections, an omission that provides the organized citywide groups with carte blanche to finance campaigns and influence the very people with whom they must negotiate their

---

* The courts subsequently declared this procedure unconstitutional, because it violates the one-man, one-vote principle. The legislature then extended the life of the interim board for an additional year.

contract. (An interim school board consisting of five members appointed by the five borough presidents provided what may be a foretaste of the future by negotiating a contract that acceded to the union's demands.)

Strictures on district board elections—preregistration of parents, residency requirements, and a complex system of proportional representation—are such as to minimize voting by the poor. (The initial elections under the law, held in March, 1970, produced a voter turnout of about 15 per cent, in contrast to turnouts in the earlier demonstration district elections of from 20 to 30 per cent.) Moreover, paraprofessionals (most of whom are neighborhood residents) are, as employees, ineligible as candidates for local boards; this policy deprives communities of the participation, in either school work or school policy-making, of some of their most interested and energetic residents. Teachers and principals, most of whom do not live in the districts where they work, are permitted to run for boards in their home districts.

Summing up, we can say that the legislation rolled back even those few gains the demonstration districts were able to make in their short lifetime, to say nothing of rejecting all the major reforms proposed by the Bundy Plan and even compromise adaptations of the plan. The text of the legislation need hardly have stated, as it does in several sections, that the new local districts are not to be considered local educational agencies but, rather, subdivisions of the central agency. The "decentralization" bill was a mockery of its own title.

The union, which had sought to cultivate the image of an underdog fighting for elementary rights, actually emerged as an instrument strong enough to block innumerable other power sources in a city reputed to advance through a conciliation of strong groups with overlapping and conflicting interests. Nearly everyone had underestimated the power of the professional educators to mass such force in a struggle against change of the status quo.

Whether the legislature would have defeated effective decentralization had the demonstration districts not existed is, of course, a matter of speculation. The teachers and administrators would have rallied support in any case, for major changes in the school system affect other interests as well. The school system's maintenance personnel, for example, have accumulated many prerogatives over the years, and, under community control, they too would have had to be more responsive to community needs, surrendering some of their "rights." (It is no surprise, therefore, that school custodians went so far, during the strike, as to change locks to prevent parents from reopening schools, and to shut off heating systems in schools that parents had forced to reopen.) Furthermore, the pressure of minority groups to share power on the educational front has its counterpart in the trade unions and in such other public service sectors as the police and fire departments. Each of these groups, demonstration districts or not, might have regarded a breakthrough on the school front as a forerunner to shifts in power in their own fields.

But, undoubtedly, had there been no demonstration districts, the legislative battle would have been more balanced. The legislature itself, after all, had mandated the mayor to draft a decentralization plan, which implies that it was inclined to follow through. As it turned out, the demonstration districts gave the UFT and the CSA their battle cry. Decentralization was turned, in less than a year, from a theoretical concept to the eye of a hurricane of urban strife. The raw politics of urban reform combined with the deep current of racial unrest to give New York City and the nation vivid lessons in the problems and challenges of meeting the long-suppressed needs of the deprived minorities of the large cities in the face of other established interests. In the spring of 1968, the Kerner Commission report warned America that it was still "one nation, divided." Less than six months later, New York City had become "one city, divided." The demonstration school districts provided the edge of cleavage. In retrospect, therefore, it is tempting to consider creation of the demonstration districts a major strategic error. Yet, one must temper this by asking whether calm would otherwise have prevailed in the ghetto communities.

Legislatively mandated decentralization, even if it had won approval, would have been a comparatively long process—a one-year minimum for the mayor's advisory report to be followed by legislative action, plus no less than one additional year (and, most likely, three) for implementation. Without the demonstration districts, would mounting pressure from ghetto communities for a response to worsening educational conditions have subsided? There is no certain answer, but it is quite possible that the existence of the districts merely hastened the inevitable.

In their short history, the three demonstration districts in New York City became symbols for the larger national struggle for black control of local institutions. The responses of the professional educators, the teachers' union, and public officials indicated the true dimensions of the complexities and obstacles in reallocating power—not just in the public schools but along a wider front, and not only as between depressed urban minorities and the larger society, but among other groups that are challenging prevailing institutions and arrangements of forces. During the crises in the New York City demonstration school districts, therefore, black and white people in cities throughout the country—"clients" and members of professions alike—watched as if to judge the problems with which they too might have to contend in the future.

7

Participation and Quality Education

The secret of education lies in respecting the child.—RALPH WALDO EMERSON (*Lectures and Biographical Sketches*)

The bedrock test of community voice in the education process is whether it produces quality education: Does the new system pay off for the individual child?

Participation in any constructive enterprise is, in itself, not without considerable value for the participant. It fulfills the human need for contact with fellow men. It relieves the isolation to which, in some degree, everyone is subject and which, carried to the extreme, grows into alienation. Participation tends to enhance self-esteem; the very act of involvement with others is some proof to the participant that he is accepted and that, even if his role is minor, he is not without worth. Participation is also likely to provide the individual with some intellectual stimulus through his exposure to the viewpoints of others. If only because it is a form of experience, participation is educational in the broadest sense. In interpersonal terms, it teaches—at least at the subconscious level—the dynamics of "give and take," of power relationships, and of planning and working toward goals.

In addition to fulfilling such needs, real participation in public education is also essential to the concept of public education as a political (governmental) institution as well as a pedagogical enter-

prise. Even if parent and community involvement should interfere with professionals or otherwise reduce the "efficiency" of the
school, such participation is the paramount way of preserving the
democratic process in the schools as in other public institutions.
Those who equate participation with interference are, at bottom,
hostile to participation.

Along with other advocates of community control of the
schools, we rest our case on the potential this approach has for
both preserving the democratic process and achieving quality
education. Our opponents—and a third group, the skeptics—usually focus on the test of quality education alone.

We believe that quality public education without parental
participation is a contradiction in terms. Opponents say that,
even if participation contributes to quality education, it is just
one of several components, and, moreover, if it is carried too far,
it can endanger quality education—for example, to the point
where it weakens the primacy of the professional educator.

Some critics also charge that the advocates of community control of the schools are less concerned with what is taught in the
schools than with who runs them. Simply bent on displacing the
holders of power and patronage, they are, charge the critics, just
latter-day incarnations of the school administrations of a century
ago, before civil-service reforms replaced a political spoils system
in which school jobs were given out by ward leaders and city hall.

The skeptics call for evidence, and the skepticism is thick, because the community-control concept has been born amid painful social and political struggles. Even the most sympathetic
skeptic asks, Is it really about education, or are the schools just a
ripe battleground for the latest stage of minority militancy and
turbulent, uneasy youth?

If not such skepticism, at least a restive curiosity was expressed
by Jason Epstein:

> That the [Bundy Plan] fails to show how decentralization might
> actually affect the children and their teachers . . . is perhaps under-
> standable, since [its] aim is largely political. But the pedagogical

question remains, for it would be foolish to reorganize the system only to discover that this sort of tinkering made no difference at all: that no matter how the system were organized and no matter who got the jobs the problems in the classrooms would remain; that the real difficulty had lain in a different direction all along.

The answer is rooted in the premise that basic reform of a *public* institution does not simply consist of apparent improvements in the quality of its professional functions; it depends also, and inextricably, on the strength of the political process through which the institution is governed. The improvement of professional function *without* democratic process is technocracy. The failure or short life of many purely pedagogical reform movements in public education may be traced to the absence of participation by parents and the community.

Accordingly, the following discussion of how community control opens the way to better education should be read in the context of our belief that the movement for educational reform through community control is, and needs to be, indeed political as well as educational.

We shall first look at the nature of quality education and explain why we feel it should be conceived of in broader terms than those of the prevailing common-sense definition of learning academic subjects. We shall also examine whether parents, when they acquire a truly determining voice, are capable of pursuing the goals of quality education or whether they are likely to exploit their power mainly to achieve other goals.

Furthermore, two particular aspects of curriculum-planning deserve special scrutiny. One is the extent to which school programs should reflect the background and needs of the racial and ethnic group or groups of which a particular school may be primarily composed. The other is the nature of a humanistically oriented curriculum.

Finally, we will examine the capacity of community-directed schools to break out of traditional constraints in such matters as personnel and the use of novel and productive resources.

Much that we believe community-directed schools are capable of lies in the future, simply because such schools have hardly begun. But there is enough preliminary evidence at hand, even at this early point, to suggest strongly that there is substance to the assumption and hope that community schools can help usher in an era of quality education.

The Standard Definition

Before examining the relation between participation and quality education, it is essential for us to understand—in fact, to redefine—quality education.

Quality, first of all, is relative. The performance, or level of learning of an individual child can be measured against that of fellow pupils in an individual class or against that of others either in the school or in the entire community. In highly developed countries with rapid communications, the effective bench mark is the total society into which pupils pass and in which they must live and earn a living. Thus, the straight-"A" pupil in a Negro high school in the South—at least, until the recent advent of special-admissions procedures and remedial programs, although, to a great extent, even now—could hardly compete for college admission with a "C" student from a middle-class Northern suburban high school.

The double standard of education (and grading) has been a notorious scandal in American education, not only between regions but often from school to school in the same city. Standardized national tests of achievement (at various grade levels) have served some useful purposes. (Let us put aside, for a moment, the defects of standardized tests, including the cultural bias that places a premium on verbal ability and, hence, favors middle-class students.) These tests have helped to expose vast discrepancies in educational standards. They also facilitate the work of such specialized users as college-admissions officers and recruiters for business and the armed forces. But the individual student who is receiving passing or even superior grades in an inferior school is suffering a deception and is due for a rude shock when he enters the competitive world outside.

A study at a large Midwestern state university, for example, showed that 70 per cent of Negro undergraduates had precollege test scores that ranked them below the 50th percentile of the college of their choice within the university. The finding is not, in itself, surprising; what is surprising is the uniformity of results regardless of the degree of integration of the high schools the students had attended. And, although the study was limited to one university, the research director said the findings "strongly suggest" poor high school academic training (rather than degree of integration or the students' economic status) as a source of the inadequate preparation of black students for college. High schools and school boards, he said, "would do well to dig deep into their *practices,* procedures, and *curricula* and to examine *their staffs* for factors which bring black students with high-school diplomas to colleges and universities less adequately prepared than their white counterparts in the skills and knowledge necessary to pursue college level studies." (Italics added)

In their extensive study, "The American Negro College," Christopher Jencks and David Riesman reported that College Entrance Examination Board scores in most Negro colleges seem to average in the 300's, and that some Negro colleges report *medians* in the 200's. Of *all* the students who take the SAT, those who score below 300 make up only 2%, and those who score below 400 comprise about 6%. Riesman and Jencks note, "Perhaps no more than 10 or 15 per cent of the students at most Negro colleges rank above the national undergraduate average on verbal or mathematical tests."*

And, yet, the ghetto demand for more opportunities to attend college, seen as a means of escaping the poverty cycle, is spreading, to the predominantly white colleges of the North as well as to

* Some colleges have begun to abandon SAT examinations for admissions in favor of a combination of other performance criteria and personality factors.

both black and mainly white colleges in the South. A plethora of pre-admission college programs and other measures to help Negro undergraduates after they are enrolled testifies to the inadequate preparation in the public schools. To admit such students without special aid exposes them to insurmountable academic obstacles and the likelihood of failure. The colleges and such foundation- and government-supported programs as Upward Bound bespeak recognition of this need, and, largely because of them, many Negro students' college records exceed the levels predicted by their college entrance scores. Equally important, these programs have had greater success than the public schools in relating to black students and achieving substantial gains in their self-confidence as well as their academic achievement.

Quality has a time dimension as well. What passed for a first-class undergraduate science course twenty years ago would hardly suffice for an advanced course in today's better high schools. To take another example, vocational education suffers not only from a social-status stigma but also, in most instances, from obsolescence. Its content is overladen with crafts and skills that are either outmoded by the time the student enters the world of work or relevant only to dead-end jobs. No matter how well an obsolete or irrelevant course is designed and taught, it falls outside the definition of quality education. This failing applies not only to the criterion of vocational relevance but also to that of personal relevance. Quality education must include content that revolves around what the learner perceives as a reality. The first thing schools teach children, however, is that learning is separate from living. As John Holt, one of today's most perceptive and articulate analysts of teaching and learning, describes the scenario, "You come to school to learn, we tell him, as if the child hadn't been learning before, as if living were out there and learning were in here, and there was no connection between the two."

But the most crucial element in the prevailing definition of quality education is the cognitive denominator. Despite the sea of rhetoric among educators and philosophers, the predominant definition of quality education in the American school is grade-level performance on standardized tests.

Some of the most extensive studies of the performance of American schools, Coleman's included, focus almost exclusively on the cognitive product of the education process, not on how well the schools are meeting the developmental needs of children. As Henry S. Dyer of the Educational Testing Service noted, even the three noncognitive variables that Coleman did consider—self-concept, interest in learning, and sense of control of the environment—are treated as *conditions* of learning rather than as *goals*.

For all major school subjects, there are now standardized tests that are administered across the country. In studies of educational quality, of "disadvantaged" learners, and of poverty, reading is the subject on which most interest centers. Despite disclaimers, the overwhelming emphasis of the American school curriculum is on cognitive learning and the development of academic skills. In the high schools and, increasingly, in elementary schools, the academic subjects hold sway. How a student performs on standardized tests of cognitive learning and academic skills determines the academic track on which he will be placed, whether he will go on to college, and, if so, which college he will attend.

Performance testing represents an advance over a method of measuring the quality of education by the *inputs* to schools—the funds spent per pupil, the condition of the school plant, the texts and other materials—along with such factors as class size, the number of years of training possessed by the staff, etc. The Coleman Report, of course, was not the first attempt to measure quality by the yardstick of *output* of schools—that is, in terms of pupils' performance. But, by dint of its auspices, the mass of its data, and the prestige of its investigators, it served, once and for all, to shatter the myth that, so long as the inputs were equal, the quality of education in one school was equal to that of another. As Coleman himself observed afterward, "The crucial point is that *effects* of inputs have come to constitute the basis for assessment of school quality (and, thus, equality of opportunity)."

But there are reasons to avoid using the Coleman Report as an unassailable basis for determining school policy. One does not necessarily disparage the report by pointing out that its basic measure of achievement is the standardized test, which, in the last decade, has come under sharp attack on several grounds. Especially as the testing industry has grown, as machine and other objective testing has spread to greater masses of students, and as standardized tests have become more widely used, a growing skepticism and, in some cases, a resistance to testing has developed. Reservations about the value and validity of such tests stem, in part though not at all entirely, from their use with "disadvantaged" students. A growing body of research indicates that it is not only I.Q. tests that, because of their high reliance on standard verbal ability, are culturally biased against minority-group children; standardized tests of subject matter also share this bias. Standardized testing for all children, "disadvantaged" or not, has been criticized, too, for the premium it places on rote learning, for the way many such tests discourage imagination, and for the encouragement they give to the development of test-taking acumen as an end in itself.

The latest attack on testing is by students and others who have urged the replacement of graded courses with a pass-or-fail system. Beginning on college campuses, the pass-fail reform is already on the agenda in some elementary and secondary schools, private and public. The objections center not only on the invalidity of the tests as a measure of intellectual progress, but also on their capacity to produce distorted values and practices, such as rampant competition, cramming, and cheating, all of which may result in cynicism about the school or college, if not a disdain for learning itself. Instances of misgrading tests in order to prop up the reputation of a teacher, or even of an entire school, are not uncommon.

These objections had already gained currency before "disadvantaged" learners became a focus of national attention. Nonetheless, academic achievement is measured almost entirely by student performance on tests, and, in the schools, acceptance of grade-level performance as the measure of quality education is nearly universal.* It is the standard by which both the middle-class suburban parent and the ghetto parent measure how well their children are doing in school. Indeed, reading and arithmetic achievement scores have been among the most potent ammunition that ghetto parents have used in their attack, in recent years, on the inadequacy of the public schools. That the scores were potent was evident in the resistance to their disclosure; some school systems guarded them like state secrets. The revelations (under pressure) of reading scores for the New York City public schools and of other meaningful performance data developed by Kenneth Clark for a study by HARYOU, an early antipoverty agency, were strong precipitating factors in the movement for real community participation in the education process.

An even more penetrating measure of academic achievement, cutting across racial and class lines, is under way—that is, an assessment of education that seeks to measure what Americans at various ages have actually learned, as opposed to how they perform in school and college on standardized tests or tests confined to a particular community or institution. Since 1966, private foundations together with the U.S. Office of Education, have sponsored a National Assessment of Education Progress. By 1971, when it is anticipated the project will be completed, we should have a far greater fund of knowledge than ever before about American educational standards. According to the director, Dr. Ralph W. Tyler, the purpose of the project is to provide "census-like data on educational levels of important sectors of our population, in order to furnish a dependable background of information about our educational attainments, the progress we are making and the problems that we still face in achieving our educational aspirations." Results will not be reported in terms of

* As a mark of status rather than of quality, however, inputs still weigh heavily. Many parents are impressed by the physical appearance of the school plant and by class size. Perhaps one of the unspoken but most wisely used measures of a school's status is the color of its student body. Thus, in large cities in particular, white middle-class parents speak of a "good" school as one with the fewest nonwhite children, no matter that it may have a lackluster staff and an anemic academic program.

individuals, schools, school districts, or states. Rather, findings will be treated in terms of geographical regions, age-levels, sex, socio-economic levels, and types of communities.

The project has aroused intense opposition among some of the hierarchy of the National Education Association, who fear it may be used to make comparisons between schools. The main thrust of the assessment, however, is to provide some reliable information about the actual results achieved with the nation's expenditures for education. But the national assessment will not affect the prevailing measure of quality education; it will only make it more accurate.

The Emerging Definition

There are interesting similarities, as well as significant differences, between the outcry of a decade ago against school dropouts and the current ferment over the failure of ghetto education. In essence, both alarms have been directed against the failure of urban education. But the former, stemming mainly from national agencies, was motivated largely by a concern for the aggregate costs in welfare and rehabilitation implicit in a sizable undereducated population. The latter, finding its most poignant expression in the cries of ghetto parents, is concerned with the individual human tragedy sown by undereducation. Thus, the outcries against the failure of education emerge as "death at an early age" and "educational genocide."

They resemble the earlier alarms by referring, in large part, to the fact that ghetto children are being short-changed in reading skills and those other aspects of quality education defined as grade-level achievement. But, consciously and unconsciously, a vital new element has arisen. Ten years ago, most likely, the desires of Negro parents might have been satisfied with equality of performance. But today "deprivation" has acquired other dimensions, and in the process the definition of quality education is taking a new shape.

The dominant theme in the new definition lies in the *affective* domain—the development of human beings with a sense of self-worth and an ability to function affirmatively and humanely with their fellow men. To the planners and policy-makers of the post-Sputnik era, such goals represented the "soft side" of education. They carried unpleasant overtones of the "progressive" school of education, and they were regarded as irrelevant, if not downright inimical, to cognitive learning, the mastery of skills, the stockpiling of knowledge—in short, to quality education, as then defined.

As opposed to the *talk* of the schools about respect for the child and individual differences, its *acts,* as John Holt reminds us, say to the child,

> Your experience, your concerns, your curiosities, your needs, what you know, what you want, what you wonder about, what you hope for, what you fear, what you like and dislike, what you are good at or not so good at—all this is of not the slightest importance, it counts for nothing. What counts here . . . is what we know, what we think is important, what we want you to do, think and be.

The argument over the school's responsibility for anything other than academic skills is as old as American public education itself. In the birthplace of the common school, Massachusetts, the Boston school committee, more than a century ago, said that the school's role included "forming [children] from animals into intellectual beings, and from intellectual into spiritual beings; giving to many their first appreciation of what is wise, what is true, what is lovely and what is pure." In an era characterized by new immigration and the pernicious effects of rising industrialism, the New England schoolmasters saw their goal as the shaping of the personalities of children. The goal of personality development was then stated as "control of passions," "destroying a taste for a lower pleasure," "control," and "self-discipline." Like the next generation of school reformers, the Progressives, they took responsibility for the physical, intellectual, and personality (then stated as moral) development of the "whole man."

But, as Michael B. Katz, historian of the period, has noted, the school came close to, but always stopped short of, defining the goals of education in terms of the joy and delight it brought to the individual. At present, the humanitarian aspect of education is coming out of exile, but not as a means of molding "different" children to the prevailing society, and not under the auspices of the upper and middle classes. The events and trends discussed earlier are responsible for the re-entry of affective objectives into public education. One factor is that the vast compensatory programs designed to redress the educational imbalance between the rich and the poor—programs aimed squarely at raising the grade-level achievement of the children of the poor—have largely failed.

The emergent, humanistically oriented redefinition of quality education is also a product of the new voice and new avenues of expression that thwarted minorities found in the accelerating civil rights movement. At one pole, ghetto anger—or "black rage," as two Negro psychiatrists, Price M. Cobbs and William H. Grier, have put it—and justified impatience were expressed in civil disorder. At another, a generation of skilled leaders began to emerge, creating new dialectics and calling the whole prevailing society into question. It is idle—and dangerous—to rationalize either riots or ultramilitant black power separatism as the behavior of a small minority of the black population. They are the tip of a pyramid and they should serve as a warning that danger, frustration, and questioning of the dominant order are widespread in the broad base below.

The blacks' new sense of worth has found expression in a rich variety of activity and behavior—ranging from the adoption of African dress to the formation of black student groups, first on Ivy League campuses and soon almost everywhere black students attend colleges. But the core of the attitude was expressed simply by a small group of Negro demonstrators at the 1968 Republican convention. A thirteen-year-old Mississippi boy led them in a chant:

"I am black," he shouted.

"But I am somebody," the demonstrators responded.

"I may be poor,"

"But I am somebody."

"I may be hungry,"

"But I am somebody."

Thus, the climate for challenging business-as-usual in the schools was developing strength from a widespread challenge to, if not revolt against, the conventional order in all aspects of American life as it affected racial minorities. As racial pride began to grow, the bonds of centuries of self-hatred and imposed inferiority began to loosen. As noted earlier, parents could no longer accept the dominant reasons given by the educators for educational failure—that is, the parents' own inadequacy, their children's defects, or the deadening environment of their homes. Looking at the system itself, Negro parents found massive *attitudinal* defects. They found that all aspects of the school—the staff, the curriculum, the goals—derived from a culture and socio-economic viewpoint other than their own. Furthermore, parents found that the professional educators as well as the policy-making boards of education were either unconscious of, or hostile to, the need to stimulate the pride and self-worth of disadvantaged children. They found that, all too often, teachers and administrators *expected* black children to fail, and professional evidence is being introduced to support the parents' suspicion. As two leading current scholars of the subject (Robert Rosenthal and Leonard Jacobson, in their study *Pygmalion in the Classroom*) put it, "one person's expectation for another's behavior could come to serve as a self-fulfilling prophecy." They say that extensive evidence and experimentation, with respect to ghetto school children in particular, is "compelling" in showing that teachers hold up lower standards of achievement for children of more deprived areas. In fact, in one extensive experiment, "the more intellectually competent . . . children became, the more negatively they were viewed by their teacher," a disturbing hint of vindictive attitudes by teachers, reminiscent of Jonathan Kozol's grim accusation (in the subtitle of his book) against the Boston public schools,

"The Destruction of the Hearts and Minds of Negro Children."

In any case, the ghettos' demands for educational reform now embrace both a concern for the psychological health and racial integrity of the children as well as for their achievement on grade level. The former, known to educators and psychologists as the *affective* domain, should not be external to education. It is not optional or "soft." It is intrinsic to quality education and demands a wholesale reorientation of educational goals, practices, and personnel.

Ghetto parents are not alone in shaping the new definition of quality education. As *The Wall Street Journal* observed of the community-control dispute in New York City, "the drive to bring the schools closer to the people they serve is an effort to improve education for all—to humanize a system that has grown dehumanized in the eyes of people in all parts of the city, not just its slums." The demands of the poor (and of many other parents) on this score are often more implicit than explicit. But quite explicit expressions have come from a group of articulate critics of the prevailing educational order, from middle-class sources, and, unexpectedly, from the business community.

Several humanistic critics have broken out of the traditional professional channels to spread their ideology to the public. They include John Holt, Jonathan Kozol, Herbert Kohl, Abraham Maslow, Carl Rogers, and Robert Coles. In his provocative book *Education and Ecstasy*, *Look*'s senior editor George Leonard has depicted tomorrow's education as affective. A glance at American educational history quickly discloses, of course, early roots of a humanistic, personality-centered view of education. John Dewey and George Counts, to cite two of the leading philosophers of humanistic education, said that quality education must include conscious efforts to foster a sense of individual identity and a consciousness of the social order. Counts warned in 1952, for example, that "certain of our practices of mass education tend to weaken the source of individuality and to strengthen the tendency toward the robotization of life." He said that the cultivation of individual excellence "in all of its diversity" was "a crucial and urgent responsibility of democratic education." Later, the Eight-Year Study (a comparison of progressive and traditional schools, begun in 1930 by the Public Education Association and later supported by the Carnegie Corporation and the General Education Board) elaborated on the need and composition of humanistic and student-centered curriculums.

Some humanistic ideas were put into practice widely in American schools. But they were implemented at a level removed from the students themselves. That is, students were taught *about* personal concerns, identity, and social responsibility. The curriculum did not provide for students actually *living* such situations and learning by reference to their own experience. The schools acted as if talking about empathy and "give and take" constituted learning them. The schools never embraced them so firmly as to legitimize them as educational goals accorded equal status with traditional subject matter. In short, the humanistic curriculum was not organically applied, except in such isolated instances as the New Trier, Illinois, public schools and private schools like the Dalton School. For the most part, not only was it imperfectly applied but it never had sufficient popular understanding and support to withstand the assault eventually trained on it. This attack branded progressive education in simplistic terms, as a frill, as soft-headed, as inimical to "hard," subject-centered learning.

The new reform movement is evolving from an intense process of self-development. It is organic because it has arisen from the deepest of personal concerns: in the ghetto, for survival; outside the ghetto, for purpose in life.

Many college students who have "made it" in the prevailing terms of quality education are themselves exerting pressure for new educational objectives. The student rebels from Berkeley to Columbia have, by and large, been high academic achievers. Their revolt has several roots—from the Vietnam war to the impersonality of mass education. One of their discontents is the limitation—some call it aridity—of curriculums that are purely cognitive and bear little relation to their own concerns. Aside from the genuine anarchists among the dissenting students, many seek a more humanistic academic climate, in which the traditional pursuit of knowledge for its own sake or for the sake of a political or technological order is leavened with the pursuit of ways to individual fulfillment. They, too, are fed up with paternalistic educational hierarchies, with credential-based authority that discourages true inquiry by the uncredentialized (particularly the young), and with cynical adherence to tradition-bound rules of the game.

The irrelevance of college curriculums is an issue raised not only by the most alienated students alone or by affluent white students alone. It has come to the fore at small liberal-arts colleges as well as at the multiversities. Black students have demonstrated not only on campuses where they are a small fraction of the population but also at predominantly Negro colleges. One of the earliest demonstrations took place at one of the highest-ranked predominantly Negro schools, Howard University, where, in the spring of 1968, 1,000 students occupied the university building and were supported by 3,000 other students who defied the administration less aggressively; the university trustees agreed to meet with students to resolve grievances and "deal with relevant, contemporary issues." A key issue of black consciousness in relation to Howard is whether a Negro—and, by extension, a Negro university—"can be as abrasive in pursuit of excellence as a white man," as education writer Susan Jacoby has wondered.

In fact, middle-class questioning of the traditional terms of quality education begins earlier than with campus revolt. It is close to the surface right at the site of the most "successful" schools—outside the ghettos, in well-to-do suburbs and middle-class urban neighborhoods. These schools produce not only tomorrow's college rebels but also the young men and women whose disaffection with society takes the form of extreme alienation, retreat into drugs, and other forms of deviant behavior. Their schooling alone is not responsible for such behavior, but it has contributed to it. At the very least, their education has failed to answer deep personal concerns. In the most successful schools, the price of playing the academic game is paid. Students who know they must feed back what most teachers want, that they must accumulate high grades at any cost (including cheating or droning memorization), and that they are subjected to hallway and other building regimens more befitting a prison than a center of learning are storing up resentment.

That the reaction to nonhumanistic teaching and school organization may be surfacing even earlier than college is suggested by such growing symptoms as strikes by high school students, the high school underground movement and the increasing militance of student unions.

In such unexpected quarters as the business world, too, the prevailing definition of quality education is under scrutiny. The commercial and industrial world depends, of course, on the education system to provide trained manpower. "Training" and "skills" used to be largely synonymous with knowledge of the processes of the office and factory. Business has long-standing complaints against the failure of education to produce immediately productive workers, both at the blue- and white-collar levels. Major companies conduct extensive training and retraining programs for new workers, and the training schools of some large industrial firms rival colleges in size. In addition, two strong trends in recent years in the commercial world have broadened the definition of skilled and trained manpower.

One is automation, which has eliminated many repetitive human tasks that require constant attention to machinery, precision in measurement, and voluminous processing of forms of data. Automation has also advanced standardization, so that basic differences among products and services grow smaller. Increasingly, the decisive distinctions lie in human factors—courtesy, flexibility, or reputation for reliability, for example. Furthermore, automation has combined with increased communication to expand the size of commercial industrial units. The seats of highest power, once occupied exclusively by financial or sales experts, are now shared by "pure managers," whose prime talent is the ability to manipulate other people. At lower levels, too, interpersonal skill is an increasingly sought characteristic. Since machinery and systems have been engineered nearly to infallibility, the greatest potential for inefficiency, failure, or error lies in the human factor.

Another significant trend is the vast growth of the service sector, in which the "product" is the attention and responsiveness of the seller to the buyer. The importance of morale, clarity in communication, responsibility, and motivation—all of which, as noted, are increasing in the production sector—are virtually the name of the game in the service sector. Yet, all along the line, management finds that its personnel, highly trained in technical and professional skills, are grossly inadequate in the skills of human interaction. Especially at the junior-executive and middle-management levels, but also in the executive suite, men are found wanting in awareness of the psychology and dynamics of individual and group behavior. They are also unaware of the bases of their own drives, strengths, and inadequacies. The need is further accentuated by the growth of international business, coinciding with the rise of nationalism in the former colonial countries as well as in the West. Sensitivity to other cultures and races is no longer an interesting oddity but a practical necessity for effective functioning of business abroad.

To meet these needs, a whole new field has arisen in the business world—sensitivity training. In rudimentary form, sensitivity training may be conducted on the job, through manuals or lectures. These may be supplemented by retreats away from the office where personnel can concentrate in individual study and group-dynamics exercises on problems of communications and employee-supervisor relations. At a more sophisticated level, management sends its staffs and executives to sensitivity-training schools, the most well known of which is the National Training Institute at Bethel, Maine.

Business and industry will seek still further to fill the gap in the area of human-relations training, if the schools and colleges ignore it. But society should question the wisdom of leaving such training primarily to business and industry. Their chief motive is, naturally, profitability, which is not always compatible with democratic ideals or the integrity of the individual personality. One does not have to be distrustful of business to prefer that such matters be left instead to institutions, like schools and colleges, that are dedicated to broad social purpose.

Thus, what many educators consider idealistic, "soft," and unnecessary or disruptive to the "proper" curriculum, the commercial marketplace now regards as a most practical component of quality education. The debate over whether education should have a vocational bias, therefore, takes an interesting new turn, for humanistic matter is now valuable for work as well as for individual growth and fulfillment. Resistance to, or disparagement of, a humanistically (affectively) inclusive curriculum and school climate becomes less defensible than ever. If professional resistance continues, educators may be the last to define quality education in its new terms.

On the professional level of public education, such internal reformers as Abraham Maslow, Carl Rogers, and Theodore Brameld have kept alive the basic doctrines of Dewey and his disciples. But, alone, they can be no more successful than their intellectual ancestors in fundamentally reforming education toward humanistic objectives. Experience has shown how vulnerable to ridicule ("life adjustment," "frills," etc.) are educational objectives that are grafted onto the educational structure by professional reformers alone.

Quality Education and Community Control

For educational objectives to take firm root—to be legitimatized —requires, first of all, a demand by the public. As always, the most difficult connection to achieve is that between felt needs for change and actual response by the system. The possibilities for doing this provide the main (though, by no means, exclusive) basis for linking a real community voice in education with the quality of education.

In demanding a determining voice in their own urban schools, communities consisting mainly of racial minorities seek to reverse the old system's negative, self-fulfilling prophecy toward their children. (Their children were not expected to learn, and they did not.) Decision-makers, who are supposed to represent the concerns and aspirations of the children and community, must develop a climate in which a positive self-fulfilling prophecy prevails. In establishing the theme of *accountability,* therefore, the community's aim is to have children learn. The community expects a payoff in the tender of achievement. Under an accountable system, the community's response to continued failure to produce such results would be to make further changes. The community would hold their representatives (usually elected) accountable for results.

Also, there probably is an even deeper connection—in a psychological sense—between community voice and the individual child, particularly the black child. Not only do those black children with a sense of internal control subsequently do better in their school achievement, but those who do well in school achievement undoubtedly begin to gain a sense of internal control. As sociologist Thomas Pettigrew has noted, the Coleman Report suggests that each child may face a two-stage problem:

> First, he must learn that he can, within reasonably broad limits, act effectively upon his surroundings; and, second, he must then evaluate his own relative capabilities for mastering the environment. The critical stage for white children seems to be the second stage concerning the self-concept, while the critical stage for Negro children seems realistically enough to involve the question of manipulating an often harsh and overpowering environment.

Nor is the phenomenon peculiar to the black minority. In their study of Catholic school achievement, Andrew M. Greeley and Peter H. Rossi inferred that Catholic pupils did well because of the security generated by the ghetto atmosphere of Catholic schools.

Under community-directed schools, the educational environment is far less likely to be hostile or intimidating to the minority child. He will thus have a sense of being able to function in the school environment and, in turn, a greater sense of internal control—the prime prerequisite to effective learning, according to a growing body of educational evidence as well as psychological insight.

At least at the outset, communities striving for an accountable school system are, like others, seeking for their children conventionally measured achievements. But community-controlled schools are riding—if not themselves generating—a wave of educational reform, particularly along humanistic lines.

Consider, for example, attempts to judge such schools as those in the Ocean Hill–Brownsville district or Washington's Morgan School. As one teacher in an experimental district in New York speculated:

> Our experiment will be evaluated in terms of the established conventional criteria: reading scores, discipline, standardized achievement, tests, etc., some of which measure what they are intended to measure, for *middle-class children*. We have a problem when these criteria fail to measure the extent to which a child has been educated, when they simply test rote memorization, stifling of initiative and training in sitting through standardized examinations. Unleashed creativity or a critical outlook, for example, would probably lower a child's scores on these exams, rather than raise them. If the conventional criteria measure the wrong things, their effect is harmful to our students, yet they will determine to a great extent whether or not we will ever be free to develop our own yardsticks. In effect, we must miseducate the children before we will be allowed to educate them.

In Washington's community-controlled Morgan School, the staff was ambivalent when reading scores rose, since they had been damned so long as a middle-class game. The staff is at least as impressed with lower vandalism, higher attendance, and manifestations more difficult to measure, such as better behavior and improved self-image. Evaluation could not be comparative, since, before community control, as Professor Harry Passow's exhaustive report notes, the District's school system had "no measures on the extent to which schools are helping students attain other educational objectives, for there are no data on self-concepts, ego-development, values, attitudes, aspirations, citizenship, and other 'nonacademic' but important aspects of personal growth. However," he goes on, "the inability of large numbers of children to reverse the spiral of futility and break out of the poverty-stricken ghettos suggests that the schools are no more successful in attaining these goals than they are in the more traditional academic objectives." And, as one writer put it, "The blacks, bitter that [before community control] so long as the teachers were certified and the rules followed no one cared what the school was accomplishing, ask why only when *they* run a school these things should become important."

In Search of Curriculums

The simple-minded specter that the uninformed or the malicious have conjured up about the program in community-controlled schools range from Swahili-conducted classes on black violence, in ghetto communities, to antilibertarian John Birch indoctrination, in conservative communities. Community-controlled schools may, indeed, be expected to correct certain distortions in today's "accepted" curriculum, and, in this, they have behind them the authority of eminent scholars. In American history, to take perhaps the most glaring field, the noted student of the Reconstruction period C. Vann Woodward has, along with others, extensively documented misinformation and misinterpretation that have for decades emanated from scholars and been embedded into school textbooks and curriculums. The new emphasis on Negro history, in which both black and white scholars are examining concepts and events in a wholly new framework, will have a positive effect on the curriculum for all children. However, the notion that community-controlled schools will discard or pervert academic subjects in favor of exotic, ethnically encompassing, or totalitarian programs is false. If for no other reason than fiscal necessity, community-controlled schools would be subject to the same formal curricular guidelines as other schools in a given state. That is, they will be required to teach a given number of hours and years of particular subjects.

But state requirements are not really the main deterrent to abandonment of academic subjects. Returning to our underlying assumption that parents want what is best for their children, parents will demand that community-controlled schools equip their children for survival and competition in the world beyond the schools—whether for college entrance or skilled employment.

But what lies beyond the narrow construction of "curriculum"? The humanistic view, which we believe is high on the hidden agenda of the community-control movement, holds that curriculum includes not only formal subject and course requirements but also the process of interaction between the pupil and his teacher and between the pupil and the total school environment. Thus, a true curriculum includes such intangibles as the "tone" of the school, the attitudes of the staff, and the style in which the school program is conducted.

Under community control, skill-training and academic mastery are likely to be meshed in a curriculum, mode of operation, and total school staff that will be more relevant and adapted to the learner than traditional systems. The school's curriculum and social reality will be intrinsically connected. For example, the desire for instruction in Swahili in some predominantly Negro schools has been ridiculed by opponents of community control of education. Yet, the pursuit of this language is, for large numbers of black Americans, adult and children, a legitimate means of attaining self-discovery and a cultural and historical perspective.

The skeptics of more humanistically directed schools fear the neglect of traditional cognitive learning. The British primary schools, for example, have stolen a march on American education with reforms in both middle-class and low-income areas. The reforms give children considerable leeway to choose which of several diverse activities going on in the classroom simultaneously they will engage in. Emphasis is also placed on children learning from each other as well as from teachers, and on a curriculum that responds to pupils' experiences and interests. Despite the fact that the reforms are said to have influenced about two-thirds of the primary schools in England and were endorsed in an important two-year study, opposition in some English circles continues on the assumption that the new-style schools neglect cognitive learning. The evidence is actually to the contrary.

More personality-conscious curriculums may, in fact, stem from what even some sympathetic observers see as a growing disaffection from the tradition of learning. Erich Fromm points out that, while more and more cerebral education cannot be helped in the natural sciences, "it could be helped in what used to be and still is called the humanities, where people are taught concepts, but they are not taught or confronted with the experience which corresponds to these concepts. They see, as the Zen Buddhists say, the finger which points to the moon and mistake the finger for the moon." This explains, Fromm believes, why so many of our young generation have become "fed up with . . . the living tradition on the strength of which we are here." He hopes that, if from the current movements for change, education becomes more relevant to modern youth, youth "will relate itself to the living tradition, not simply by accepting it but by digesting it, by being in touch with it, and by creatively changing it."

A few professional educators, also, affirm that there is no necessary conflict between the teaching of traditional subject matter and an active concern for the needs and feelings of pupils. Bernard J. McCormick, the superintendent of the Pittsburgh public schools, which have made one of the most sustained and intelligent (if not altogether successful) efforts to overcome educational disadvantages among low-income Negro students, has said, "Many of us who have worked for years with inner-city youth would agree that the social-personal development of such pupils may be even more important to their future fulfillment as adults than is their mastery of subject matter."

At the extreme, of course, are educators like John Holt, who

appear to believe that, as they are today, most schools do more
harm than good: "The idea of a 'body of knowledge' to be picked
up in school and used for the rest of one's life, is nonsense in a
world as complicated and rapidly changing as ours. Anyway, the
most important questions and problems of our time are not *in*
the curriculum, not even in the hot-shot universities, let alone
the schools." It is little wonder that Holt has advocated the abolition of all tests and grades, of the fixed required curriculum, and
of compulsory school attendance.

Most humanistic critics of education would settle for redressing
the imbalance that tilts teaching far in the direction of the cognitive. They do not believe it is an "either-or" proposition between skills and subject matter, on one hand, and the "socio-
personal" aspect of schooling, on the other. The latter, they say,
should make it possible for better cognitive learning to take
place. Both are required for a "relevant" curriculum. Through
relevant curriculums, children should learn both the skills *and*
the behavior needed to deal with social realities. The curriculum
should deal continuously with children's concerns—their quest
for identity, their feelings of power or powerlessness, and their
desire for personal connection with other individuals and with
external forces and institutions that will affect their lives. The
aim in such a curriculum would be to equip children with a
richer range of responses (*including* academic skills and knowledge) in dealing with their concerns.

One of the authors (Fantini, with Gerald Weinstein, in *Making Urban Schools Work*) has conceptualized a school that would
meet these objectives in terms of three tiers of responsibility:

(1) *Development of skills and knowledge.* The aim would be for
the child, first, to master the skills of absorbing and evaluating
information, and second, to learn the major concepts of disciplines that are essential building blocks for his cognitive development (including reading, computation, writing, and speaking
skills, and basic information in science and the social sciences).

(2) *Development of personal talent and identification and de-*

velopment of interests. The range here would be broad—from a student's learning a musical instrument to mastering a subject that is not a part of the first tier. It would include talents usually associated with that part of education oriented to work careers but would not be limited to "vocational educational" students.

(3) *Social action and exploration of self and others.* This category would comprise the schools' main responsibility for the affective aspects of education—power, identity, and connectedness. In this area, the school must not allude, in passing, to social realities but must skillfully impart an immediate sense of them to the learner. This would expose pupils to the concepts of personal power and power in relation to other people, and also provide clinical situations for actions related to pupil concerns, both inside and outside the classroom.

As the black and other minorities begin to legitimize affective objectives, it is likely also that objectives related to social action will also be introduced. The emergence of direct action is a legitimate expression of participatory democracy, especially an instrument necessary to achieve social change. The old system taught blacks to adjust to an unjust social system, to a negative environment that stunts or distorts human growth and development. The new objective is to introduce the learner to a kind of behavior that will foster his taking a part in *reconstructing* negative aspects of the environment so that it can affect human development positively.

It is here that cognitive knowledge must be married to pupils' concerns and feelings as they affect behavior. For knowing something cognitively does not always result in behavior based on that knowledge. On the broadest level, for example, millions of Americans have knowledge of injustice and poverty but do not act on them or, in fact, resent or oppose such action by others. Knowledge can be a basis for feeling, but only feeling generates behavior. Therefore, if the goal of education is to produce better people and a more humane society, knowledge (education) should relate to feeling, for otherwise knowledge is not likely to affect behavior. That democratic principles and ideals have been taught poorly by the nation's public schools is evident in the discrepancy between them and the behavior of individuals—as indicated in the Riot Commission Report and other grim commentaries before and since on "the dream deferred" and the dream shattered.*

The three-tiered model opens up possibilities for greater student participation and self-awareness (for example, through teaching younger pupils); for greater responsibility as a citizen (for example, through understanding social interaction and cultural diversity) as well as for social-action opportunities built into the curriculum; and for the student's future role as a parent, because he will be more aware of himself and others.

A similar vision has been suggested by Professor Frederick J. McDonald, a Stanford educational psychologist. He calls for the schools to be transformed into "learning centers" (which may be located in school buildings or in other parts of the city) in which the learner is far more active than passive. The major forms of student activity would be social interactions, and the environment would be one "in which a variety of teaching methods are used, from role-playing to group-therapy sessions, from lectures and discussions to whatever method stimulates social interaction among the individuals involved."

The primary requirement of such a school would be "that it create shared experiences—experiences that develop a communality of feeling and values and foster new forms of social organization that bring a variety of people into a closer social relationship."

It would be naïve to assume that community-controlled schools are, as their first order of business, proceeding in a formal way to

* Three hundred participants in a 1968 conference at the University of California (Berkeley) on Patterns of American Prejudice stated that no one in educational institutions was doing much about prejudice. The conferees concluded that the schools should grasp "missed opportunities" to reduce racial and ethnic prejudice: "The picture we gain from questionnaires answered by teachers," said psychologist M. Brewster Smith, director of the Institute for Human Development at Berkeley, "is one of passivity and unconcern."

establish such a framework. For one thing, if they are subjected to anything like the pressures of interests that oppose them (as in the case of the New York City demonstration districts, as imperfect as they are as analogues of what community-controlled school districts should be), much of the initial energies of community-controlled schools will be consumed in details that seem to have little to do with the curriculum—housekeeping matters, budgeting, staffing, interminable meetings with authorities at higher levels to clarify or fight out lines and limits of authority and responsibility. Considerable effort will also be spent in responding to pent-up demand by the community for action on grievances and for evidence, sooner than anyone should hope to expect, that their children's school performance is improving. Moreover, many minority parents might react no differently from most white middle-class in suspecting a formal structure that would seem to de-emphasize "hard" learning, that is, subject matter.

Such conservatism may be expected initially in matters of school discipline as well. Kenneth Haskins, the principal of Washington's Morgan School, had to resist the insistence of some parents that corporal punishment be revived when the community gained effective voice in governing the school.

But what is altogether likely—and signs are appearing already —is that such schools will, *de facto,* evolve into humanistic patterns. That assumption lies in the nature of the community-controlled schools—its proximity to the child and his family, its concern for responsiveness by the school staff to children's needs, the sensitivity of the chief administrator and the staff he employs to the climate and needs of the community, and the active engagement of parents and other community residents in the school programs in a variety of roles.

Language: An Example

As an example of how community control would function in terms of a specific subject, let us take language, a subject area that is plainly a basic academic tool and, yet, is inextricably tied to family, neighborhood, and, sometimes, racial or ethnic environment. The spoken level of language, the forerunner of the vital tool of reading, is most "culture bound." Before he sets foot in a school building, almost every child has solved the mystery of language—as John Holt has observed, "a task far more difficult, complicated, and abstract than anything he will be asked to do in school, or than any of his teachers has done for years." It is in the *manner* of speaking that the first wide gap exists when teachers and their children come from different class or ethnic backgrounds. Each child has worked out his own model of the grammar of language, a model that works for *him,* but, historically, the schools have sought to bend linguistically different children to a norm. When the difference consisted of a foreign language spoken in the homes of first-generation children, great effort was made to enforce the use of English. In some schools in the Southwest, even up to the present, Mexican-American pupils are punished for speaking Spanish on the school grounds. The more succcessful (in the school's terms) the efforts were, the more ashamed of their parents' native language children were made to feel, and generations of immigrant children were deprived of the opportunity of bilingualism. It is commonplace now to deplore the schools' stupidity in those days, and we spend millions, through the National Defense Education Act and other means, to teach second languages. Lest we feel too righteous about our modern outlook, however, let it be noted that linguistic suppression persists in many schools, although in a rather different form.

It is a truism that a goal of any school program should be the child's self-confident growth in the use of the native language. Yet, while teachers certainly agree with the statement, school practices often conspire against this goal. There is a breakdown between what is said and what actually takes place. For example, opportunities for verbal growth in the classroom are completely at variance with the criteria teachers say they use in measuring growth. Thus, although verbal fluency is supposedly valued, study after study shows that most of the time students are not permitted to talk at all, and, during the time when they may speak, it is usually to state facts and give explanations. Assumptions about grammar and correct speech inherited from the nineteenth century still dominate the curriculum, as folklore if not as prescriptions for education. As a result, instead of children growing self-confidently excited by their natural lively interest in reading, writing, and talking, expression in any other medium than "standard" or "correct" English is suppressed, if not killed, in school.

Although the school curriculum also alienates many "advantaged" children, the "disadvantaged" child whose speech sharply deviates from the school norm is most likely to be "turned off" by the school. Sitting undifferentiated in thousands of American classrooms are students from many backgrounds. They arrive with thoroughly different orientations to school and to their role as pupils, with differences in language use and learning style. How the teacher responds to these differences becomes a critical factor in shaping a child's educational career, in general, and in guiding his use of the English language, in particular. The school can suppress these differences, with consequent effects on educability, or it can capitalize on them in order to teach more effectively.*

One of the most vivid accounts of general teacher-failure in this regard and the success of one particular teacher is Herbert Kohl's *36 Children,* his story of teaching a sixth-grade class of Negro children in a Harlem school. Through an arduous process of seeking to understand the children and through parallel self-examination, Kohl, in less than a year, brought sullen, sometimes troubled, seemingly nonliterate children to write poems, essays, and short novels, with pleasure. Kohl emphasized but did not confine himself to the children's own concerns. They were deeply concerned with their own lives, families, and neighborhoods. But

---

* A mathematics coordinator in New York's Ocean Hill–Brownsville demonstration district says, "Students cannot learn math until they feel good about themselves. You can't just tell them math is beautiful. You have got to show them how it relates to the ability of a black man to run a store."

they could also be brought to grasp and write and talk about Greek myths, science fiction, and other themes. They began to publish their own class magazine, but the response of other teachers was to dampen their imagination and expressiveness. Kohl relates how one teacher told one boy who had written for the magazine, "Child, your imagination needs a rest. Children, I don't understand why you talk of so much fighting and stabbing. You can't possibly know about that. Tell me now, who knows what a junkie is? See, I told you no one knows. Newspapers and magazines aren't for that type of nonsense." Whereupon she read, as a model of what literature *was* for, a poem from another class:

> *Shop with Mom*
> I love to shop with mom
> And talk to the friendly grocer,
> And help her make the list,
> Seems to make us closer.

"The children slumped into their seats," writes Kohl, "demoralized."

Where linguistic and cultural differences are most pronounced, teachers are particularly handicapped by their own deep-seated prejudices and conscious beliefs about language behavior and by a general unfamiliarity with facts about language. They need help in sorting out their own attitudes and values about teaching the native language so that they conform more to facts and to interpreting new knowledge that is relevant to the teaching of the fundamental skills.

Some of this knowledge is contained in a relatively new branch of learning called socio-linguistics, which has received a great impetus from the Center of Applied Linguistics in Washington. A Center researcher, Joan C. Baratz, points out that school psychologists as well as teachers fail to pay respect to the fact that the syntax of low-income Negro children, while differing in many ways from standard English, has its own internal consistency:

The psychologist, not knowing the rules of Negro non-standard

English, has interpreted these differences not as the result of well-learned rules but as evidence of "linguistic underdevelopment." He has been handicapped by his assumption that to develop language is synonymous with the development of the psychologist's own form of standard English. Thus he has concluded that if black children do not speak like white children, they are deficient.

This statement seeks to explain the matter mainly in terms of a technical defect in school personnel—namely, ignorance of the rules of nonstandard English. We would underscore another set of factors—many professionals' lack of respect for the child and his culture, and their unwillingness to search for that which engages the child and draws out his native linguistic ability, gives it exercise, and develops it further.

Perhaps these defects in the professional go part of the way in explaining why new projects and programs in the language fields have affected relatively few classrooms. Compensatory education has tended to treat differences in language behavior as pathology, generally ignoring the cultural context. Training institutes and workshops, consisting mainly of lectures, expose the teacher to new information but leave him with undigested concepts and barely touch on attitudes. Texts and other new instructional materials, few of which have been tested on diverse populations, seldom illustrate how to deal with the problems encountered in classrooms.

Finally, experimentation is not encouraged. In contrast, a community-oriented system will be more likely to free teachers of distantly formulated prescriptions. A white teacher of English in the Ocean Hill–Brownsville district, for example, dropped the prescribed New York City eighth-grade curriculum in favor of full-time creative writing for her students. Her class came to the point where it was writing an essay a day on subjects like "alive," "the wind," "water," "fire," and "what it feels like to be born." "Most ghetto children have been taught English and reading for years and in fact have learned nothing," she comments. "They have only memorized a lot of words and rules. But they still don't have active fluency in the language. This can be developed only by using it creatively."

The language "handicap" is not, of course, confined to low-income black children. In the Southwest, 1½ million Spanish-speaking children of school age received an average education of 7.1 years, while neighboring white children received an average of 12.1 years. The Bilingual Education Act was passed in November, 1967, to help solve the problems of these children by granting funds to local school districts to devise their own "adequate curriculum." The belated funds being poured into bilingual education programs must, however, be accompanied by attitudinal changes that accord respect for forms of speech other than standard English. One of the most severe weeding-out instruments in the entire academic process is reading ability, and debates on the proper method of teaching children to read have raged throughout education for decades. In a massive compendium and appraisal of the various theories and experiments in reading, Professor Jeanne Chall in 1967 touched upon cultural questions usually ignored in the controversy over pedagogical tactics. The question which haunts her book, as Jason Epstein has pointed out,

> is whether a common language can be taught or learned at all, no matter what the pedagogical tactics and no matter how the schools are administered, once the children sense the hostility to their style of life and their color of an alien and overpowering environment; once they discover, in other words, that no matter how hard they try, they are unlikely ever to be accepted as genuine participants in American society.

In the community-centered school, however, the pupils' styles of life are accorded recognition and respect throughout the curriculum, and it may well develop that barriers to language and reading ability will begin to crumble.

A group of nonpublic community-centered schools, the New York Urban League Street Academy program, has already demonstrated on a widespread basis what Herbert Kohl showed in a single Harlem class: that ghetto children are capable not merely of learning language but of using it for literary and journalistic purposes. The students publish a monthly newspaper called *Forty Acres and a Mule,* which they use not only as a voice in the ghetto but also as a training ground in specific newspaper skills. The newspaper has requested and obtained technical assistance from students and faculty of the Columbia schools of journalism and business. It is militant, yet its militancy is program-oriented. As one Street Academy graduate puts it, "We are challenging the system by outperforming it."

One of the first programs established in the Ocean Hill–Brownsville schools was bilingual instruction that teaches Puerto Rican pupils to read first in Spanish. And, in one of the Ocean Hill schools that is predominantly black, Spanish-speaking children are taught all subjects in Spanish. Although the Federal Bilingual Act had been on the books for two years, it is a noteworthy coincidence that the New York City Board of Education did not introduce bilingual schools until a bilingual experimental program had been set up in one of the community-controlled experimental districts. The board of education program aims merely at teaching Spanish-speaking students English; of the demonstration district's program, an international authority in bilingualism said that, "in terms of the amount of investment, the yield is the greatest that I have ever seen."

New York's own City University was ahead of the public school system, even though the federal bilingual funds do not apply beyond the high school level. The university, giving recognition to the needs and diversity of racial minorities, established the first bilingual demonstration at the college level in 1968. Conducted at a community college and combining instruction in English with college-level instruction conducted in Spanish, the program is directed at students who are graduates of high schools in Puerto Rico. Higher education is, for all practical purposes, closed to most newly arrived Puerto Ricans because of their in-

ability to communicate in English.* They often suffer psychological and social problems adjusting to the culture and environment
of New York City and retreat into a "Spanish-only" ghetto. The
City University program is designed to help them in a framework that does not negate or downgrade their native culture and
language.

Diversity and Relevance

Because it arose mainly in racial ghettos, critics and opponents
of the community-control concept ridicule or discount its educational components as consisting mainly of overblown group
awareness or "nationalism." The most common butt of disparagement is the desire for teaching of Afro-American history and culture in some predominantly black schools. These subjects are said
to be essentially outside the definition of quality education.

Even a sympathetic observer like Peter Schrag, who acknowledges that the black experience can bring to the classroom "its
own passion, its own humanity, its own techniques for survival in
a society that threatens increasingly to make every individual in-
visible," fears that the most immediate results of black-community
power in the schools are likely to be political and not educational,
with an overemphasis on the achievement of outstanding Negroes
and a tendency to romanticize the glories of Negro survival under
brutalizing conditions. (The image of "every man a Nat Turner,"
he says, is as sentimental as the mythology of the happy slave.)

That such an emphasis may, indeed, emerge when ghetto communities gain control over their schools is not only understand-
able, it would be unnatural if it did not, in view of the extreme
neglect of such matters by conventional schools. This neglect,
painfully slow to come to general attention, is still being limned
in many parts of the country. As recently as 1968, for example,
the Michigan Department of Education issued a report on the

* It was found by New York social agencies that a fifth of some 1,800 youths
who had come in for assistance in a one-year period had a high school diploma
from Puerto Rico but did not speak English.

treatment of minorities in American history textbooks. The report concluded that the books "are very seriously deficient in their treatment of minorities in general and Negroes in particular . . . historically inaccurate, misleading, and distorted." One text, it noted, "not only ignores slavery as an economic institution, it spares its tender readers an account of what it meant to be a slave. . . . The author discusses the Civil War . . . without once mentioning slavery." The treatment of the current civil rights movement also was skimpy or misleading. While several textbooks discussed civil rights legislation and such leaders as Martin Luther King, Jr., they failed to mention poverty and discrimination.

Moreover, the evidence is strong that a student's awareness and knowledge of his cultural and ethnic identity has much to do with his capacity to gain a quality education—that is, if quality education is defined to include the personality development of the child. Another part of the proposition, as noted earlier, is that a child cannot proceed with his full powers to the more traditionally defined learning if he is uncertain or negative about his own identity and worth. Thus, community-controlled schools are often at great pains to emphasize individual personality. Every classroom in Washington's Morgan School has a full-length mirror, and next to one a poem says, "I'm tall, I'm short, I'm white, I'm black, I'm pretty, not so pretty, I'm smart, not so smart. My hair is short and curly. My hair is long and curly. Whatever I am, I'm here. I'm alive. I'm proud to be me."

Furthermore, American school systems have always pledged to respect cultural diversity as a main tenet in the ethos of our society. As the point is elucidated by Dan Dodson, Director of the Center for Human Relations at New York University and a specialist in school-integration efforts:

> No nation can maintain the distinction of being democratic if it does not make allowances for cultural diversity. Such differences cannot be "just tolerated." They must be respected and encouraged so long as they have value for any segment of the citizenry. Thus, in a real sense, this opportunity to pursue autonomous goals is a

measure of "democratic." No person can make his fullest contribution to the total society with a feeling of compromise about "who he is" because he is a minority group member.

For the most part, however, the public schools follow the credo only with token gestures—for example, with references to holidays, customs, and foods—or by fatuous, sometimes embarrassing and offensive assembly programs.* Not only has the traditional urban school failed to capitalize on diversity; worse, it has penalized it—not only in language suppression, as noted, but in other overt or subtle ways. When the school itself is staffed entirely by persons of another ethnic origin, for example, and members of the students' own race occupy only janitorial and other inferior positions, and the school board is poorly or not at all represented by the largest ethnic group, then the student has glaring evidence of the inferior status assigned him. Harold Howe II speaks of "a vast psychological distance" between the clientele of today's urban schools (the students and their parents) and the suppliers of education (teachers, administrators, and school board members)—a gap that manifests itself in the high dropout rate "stemming in large part from the inability of many students to see any connection between their studies and their lives."

That advancement of black identity on many levels is educationally important has been recognized in some parochial schools more readily than in public education. In Milwaukee, an inner-city parish school has religious statues and figures in paintings with black skins, and black power slogans are posted on bulletin boards by lay and religious teachers. The school, incidentally, is nongraded and draws assistance from student tutors and counselors from Marquette University.

Even when, at a relatively late hour, regular urban school systems have responded, they have not done so energetically. In Janu-

* For several years, for example, all the New York City public schools have closed on the Jewish High Holy Days in the fall. Yet, not until the Ocean Hill–Brownsville demonstration district distributed circulars about the origin and meaning of the holidays did any of these schools ever attempt to explain the holidays to its non-Jewish pupils.

ary, 1969, the president of the San Francisco Board of Education expressed dismay at the length of time the school administration had taken to develop courses in ethnic studies: "The 'Anglo' is illiterate in most of these cultures," he said. "It is the responsibility of the school district to make these courses accessible."

Relevance, of course, is neither confined to, nor synonymous with, ethnicity, or else we would not have had the widespread outcry for relevance—first, on college campuses, and, now, in white middle-class schools as well as in the ghetto. Many aspects of the school curriculum other than ethnic themes may profitably be reexamined in urban education with a view to what engages the interest of pupils and motivates them. We will take one example in some detail.

Geography, biology, and social studies may be given richer meaning through new patterns of conservation education. Much of what passes for conservation in urban schools is hortatory and fails to make convincing connections between wilderness, open space, clean rivers, and the deteriorating city environment. Its typical emphasis is on preservation of a kind of nature the city child knows, if at all, only from a rare day in the country. Exotic and irrelevant to urban pupils, it fails, therefore, as both propaganda and education. But some programs in American cities are beginning to experiment with environmental education attuned to the urban child's own value system and experience. By building from experiences already of deep personal concern to the child, such teaching helps him, through the traditional intellectual skills, to enlarge his sensitivity and to cope with these experiences.

Proceeding from the concrete to the abstract, studies in geography may begin in the immediate locality and move outward; and science investigation may arise in curiosity about the familiar and immediate. Well-kept old neighborhoods and run-down newer ones, imaginatively planned playgrounds, trash-filled empty lots, streets where abandoned cars accumulate and deteriorate, areas infested with rats—all of these, if approached with an inquisitive and pedagogically sensitive mind, might suggest ways to teach and encourage in children an active interest in their surroundings.

This systematic use of the child's immediate physical world as an educational resource is, by definition, a kind of environmental education. The objectives are both pedagogical and social: to capture the interest of those students who have not been reached by the more traditional subject matter or who are not culturally conditioned to learning from books; to channel these interests into constructive learning patterns; and to help each student come to recognize that he is neither wholly the helpless victim nor the complete master of his environment. The British have shown the way in the Nuffield Junior Science program, which has been under way since 1964 in the schools of Leicestershire in the English midlands. There, teachers and children are being encouraged to ask questions about their immediate environment that lead to various kinds of intellectual inquiry. For instance, classes of seven- to eleven-year-olds are taken on walks in the city streets and asked to notice physical features. One girl plucks a bit of moss from a shaded portion of a stone wall. She and one or two others observe that no moss grows where the wall is in the sun. Why? The moss is brought back to the classroom which is furnished with work tables to accommodate groups of two to four children. It is placed in the light. How much light can it survive? A boy picks up a bit of street paving and, in the classroom, begins, by increasingly sophisticated methods, to find out how it was made and then learns how to make it himself. Other children have noticed water gushing from a hydrant. Where does it come from and where does it go after disappearing down the sewer? The questions set the stage for a trip to the waterworks. Four children soon find themselves deep in investigations of "their" river, measuring depth, rates of flow, charting its course with instruments the teacher helps them devise, taking samples of polluted water, asking questions as to who manages the water system and how.

In Portland, Oregon, the Boise Elementary School, which serves a community with a large proportion of low-income and welfare families, is moving environmental science from the classroom to the neighborhood. Nearly all the school's 650 students are Negro, many with severe behavior and learning problems. Standing on the banks of the Willamette River, the school has, at its doorstep, an outdoor laboratory, familiar to all its students. The Boise School has designed an elementary science program comprising a progressive series of environmental studies from kindergarten through the eighth grade. It is clothing biology with immediate reality by using the fact that its river is polluted and that fish have more difficulty surviving in its waters than do the tame guinea pigs in their classroom cages.

Schools making the study of nature meaningful for city children can enlist other institutions in the community. For example, the Massachusetts Audubon Society had, for several years, contracted with rural and suburban communities to train teachers and provide study materials. For more than a decade since the Society established an expansive nature center, it had had no connections with the Boston schools, although the center is a five-minute walk from a stop on the Boston subway system. Now, with a director sympathetic to the environmental-education needs of urban children, the Society is developing, for the Boston schools, a guidebook to the natural and man-made features of the city. The Society will demonstrate the use of the guidebook to teachers and parent volunteers. Concurrently, Boston's educational television station is producing films on selected environmental problems that enable children and their teachers to analyze and look for solutions to the problems in their immediate area. The station will make suggestions for local projects, including the measurement of water and air pollution, for which kits, specially designed for viewers, will be provided.

In New York City, Wave Hill, a center for environmental studies, in collaboration with faculty from a municipal college, is developing an experimental urban-environmental–education program for ghetto youngsters and teachers from four predominantly

Negro and Puerto Rican schools. Environmental experiences that are readily available to the pupils and that stimulate students' interest and develop basic intellectual skills will be related to science, mathematics, social studies, art, and language. The college will evaluate how well the program attains objectives in terms of subject matter and teacher and student behavior.

Relevance may also be increased by locating learning in sites more realistic than the school itself. The classroom may not be the ideal place for learning—at least not on a day-in, day-out basis—for children who live in an age of rapid communication, fast-cut films, growing urban congestion, and a generally denser texture of existence, where turbulent events often occur at their doorsteps. Yet, urban schools fail, by and large, to take advantage of the enormous institutional riches with which they rub shoulders. The city itself is a teacher.

The best that most schools can do to break out of their rigidity is to bundle children up every few months on a "field trip" to a museum or factory—an expedition that frays the nerves of most teachers, provides most pupils with an irresistible lark and occasion for tomfoolery, and, in terms of subject learning, yields next to nothing, although as a form of recreation it may, indeed, be useful.

A few schools are beginning to tap surrounding resources more imaginatively and more soundly for educational values. The Philadelphia Board of Education, for example, in 1969 opened a "school without walls," which uses a variety of nearby business, scientific, and cultural institutions as learning laboratories. The school has no physical facilities as such, and nearly all of the students' time will be spent with the participating institutions. Among the institutions that it uses as learning laboratories are the Franklin Institute, a scientific center; the Academy of Natural Sciences; business offices and manufacturing plants. An insurance company, for example, offers a statistics upgrading course, with its own experts serving as instructors. The science academy gives a course on evolution and other fields in which it is experienced and better equipped than the wealthiest school could be. The participation and cooperation of nearly twenty such outside institutions has been enlisted, including the Greater Philadelphia Chamber of Commerce, and the *Philadelphia Bulletin* and *Philadelphia Inquirer*. Some offer work opportunities to the students.*

The school operates year round, with no fixed time schedule. The students were selected at random from each of the city's eight school districts on the assumption that it would benefit all students, those from higher as well as from lower-income neighborhoods. Students are also being sought from a number of suburban and parochial school systems. The basic units of the school are tutorial groups (of fifteen pupils) in which counseling, encouragement, and self- and group-evaluation take place. Each group is expected to acquire the basic skills of language and mathematics. Pairs of groups will form a seminar in which their experiences in the participating institutions will be discussed.

Another salient feature of the school is maximum student responsibility. Students determine which courses will be given and have a choice from some ninety that are offered. Student-staff "town meetings" decide school policies, including such matters as rules, implementation, and the extent of student and faculty authority and responsibility.

* * *

Although some of these examples are drawn from schools that are not community-controlled, they are rare, which dramatizes the shortcomings of the traditional school system as a whole. Our point is not that traditional schools are incapable of quality education but that, in the present urban crisis, they have been laggard and unresponsive. We believe—from the concept of the community-controlled school and from the limited experience such schools have had to date—that projects like those described here would be the rule rather than the exception in such schools.

* By way of contrast, in a protest as recent as 1968, students in the highly selective Bronx High School of Science listed among their demands the creation of field trips in various subject areas.

Many of the in-school supplemental programs and after-school, adult, cultural, and other programs initiated by the demonstration districts in New York and by community-controlled schools elsewhere are funded by non–board of education sources that are equally available to regular schools. Many such programs could be instituted through regular board of education procedures. That they were not under the traditional system of governance reflects the mental framework of so many school personnel who plod through days, weeks, and years without allowing anything to happen that will create unpleasant attention from one's superiors. For going out and looking for new money and new programs is, to many superiors, going out and looking for trouble.

In addition to bringing more children into the world, education needs to bring more of the world into the schools. Community-controlled schools have done more, in their short lifetimes, to bring adults into the schools than have the great majority of conventional schools. They have opened the schools to parents and other nonprofessional aides and to professionals in fields other than education. With a more free-wheeling attitude toward credentializing regulations, education courses, and other formalistic restrictions, and with a more cosmopolitan view summed up in the attitude, "We will take the help we need wherever it may be found," community-controlled schools are more likely than those professionally controlled to fill the schools not only with responsive teachers but also with nonteachers in a variety of fields— writers, scientists, etc.

The School Climate

In re-examining their wares, educators must think not only of what is being taught and, to some extent, how it is taught, but also, and with equal regard, they must think of the "climate" of the school itself, the nature and mood of the school as an institution in which young people spend some of the best hours of their lives.

Despite vast changes in the urban school population and the

style and pace of American society, including the more rapid maturation and greater sophistication of children, too many urban schools are carbon copies of their predecessors at the turn of the century.

In inner-city secondary schools, as surrounding neighborhoods have, in recent years, been the scene of increasing racial tension, and where disorders of various kinds (including the peddling of narcotics, and intrusions by nonstudents) have occurred in the school building, the mood is increasingly repressive. If not regular police, then paid private guards, are stationed in many ghetto school buildings, and the mood has infected the classroom too. In the name of making teaching and learning possible, such measures often serve merely to alienate students further and to impede if not absolutely prevent learning.

Even a modest self-concept among black children is not detrimental to academic performance, provided they can depend upon the *environment* to dispense rewards in a fair and equitable way. Psychologist Irwin Katz believes the data of the Coleman Report indicate: that "debilitating anxiety in minority-group students may be more a function of perceived isolation and exclusion from the main American opportunity structure than of awareness of one's intellectual limitations relative to classmates."

The educational system is expected to transmit society's basic political and social values to the young, through a process sometimes described as "political socialization." Designed to instill in each new generation the political attitudes and behavior patterns that the society deems useful in its adult citizens, political socialization is based on and intended to preserve stability and consensus in the adult population. Public education is the place in which the nation sets out most formally to secure the allegiance of young people to the system, and we have a long history of "citizenship" programs in the schools.

But in the United States today, stability and consensus are conspicuously lacking. There is a strong, open conflict between ethnic groups and the dominant society, between the affluent and the poor, and between generations. The conflict concerns wealth and other material resources, but the basic issue is the division of political power. At the same time, the crises of race conflict, of the impact of war on social reform and the new generation, and of a technological culture give rise to individual needs no less vital than those of the political system itself. No young person today can contemplate his career, his personal life, or his civic aspirations without considering how he will respond to the social crises that are enveloping his life. To the extent that we maintain schools that fail to show each student that he can play meaningful civic roles and that his interests and those of groups to which he belongs will be considered when public policy is being made, we run the risk that resignation and alienation, or a violent opposition to democratic process, will become the dominant response of young people in coming decades.

Schools, in general, tend to present an optimistic view of American society that glosses over or avoids controversy about basic features of our political system. Crucial social and political issues are either excluded from textbooks or discussed superficially. In addition, teachers' classroom commentary about politics and social issues is often inhibited by various community pressures. Thus, children are often left to learn about politics (as they usually are to learn about sex) from peer groups, casual conversations, and the mass media.

For schools to equip our youth with the tools for systematic, rational inquiry and analysis needed to cope with a seemingly chaotic world, will require, as Herbert Kohl suggests, a balance —"to teach honestly and not anger or alienate the children"—for which, in turn,

> one must be honest about failure and hypocrisy in American life. One cannot talk of equal chance and freedom of choice to people who have no opportunity or freedom or at best very little.
> We must allow children to recognize how subjective the notions of "strange," "savage," and "primitive" are, and how self-justifying and misleading so much of the propaganda they receive is.

The study of literature [must] be willing to admit conflict, violence, the unpleasant into the classroom.

Until recently, to suggest the admission of such candor into the public schools of most communities would have been to invite accusations of naïvete. Local school boards, even if they were so urged by the professionals, would not, either because of their own conservatism or fear of criticism by patriotic or conservative groups, permit such teaching. Witness Jonathan Kozol's own reprimand in the Boston school system a few years ago for using a socially critical work by the black poet Langston Hughes. But the groundswell of student pressure for more relevant teaching, plus the gradual introduction into the teaching ranks of college graduates of a generation that has been less willing, perhaps, than any other to suffer cant and propaganda that gloss over the unpleasant in life, may well change the climate in many school districts—by necessity, if not by conviction. It is fair to assume that community-controlled school districts may lead the way, because they may be expected to reflect more nearly the views of students that allow for greater expression of views on relevant curriculum. Although parents in these districts are, like those elsewhere, conditioned by current practices, community control is likely to expose them to other educational philosophies. The concept of community control includes the freedom to choose that which appears best for the children of a particular community. With knowledge of various alternatives, community-controlled districts should not imitate any "single best" administrative style. Furthermore, such communities, initially at least, are more likely to be in low-income areas, where one of the most glaring facts of life is the daily struggle against poverty and discrimination, two of the conditions of American society to which the curriculum has been largely oblivious.

The school's concerns with society must be part of its awareness of, and responsiveness to, the concerns individual pupils have. The range of student concerns is wide, from feelings of

inadequacy and impotence to, at the opposite pole, overweaning
aggression and superiority. The concerns relate not only to self-
image but also to future roles, in school and in the world of
work, and to relations with family and friends. Although it has
been evident, in the last few years, that deep personal concerns
are affecting youngsters at all socio-economic levels, these concerns are accentuated in racial ghettos by the depersonalization
that is aggravated by second-class citizenship. Community-controlled schools in low-income ghettos are arising out of this very
neglect by the rest of society. More than most institutions, they
are likely to recognize the individual's need for respect and dignity.

Peter Schrag has written that, if traditional schools are irrelevant to the Negro,

> it is not simply because they are missing the peculiar idiom of the
> ghetto, because they deal in white picket fences and green lawns
> while their pupils know only tenements and asphalt. It is because
> they don't deal in the fundamentals of life at all: birth, death, love,
> violence, passion; because they don't recognize the morality or the
> brevity of human existence; because, in their passion for funda-
> mentals they miss the elemental; the tragic, the heroic, the beautiful,
> the ugly. And it is in these things that the Negro and his experience
> may have far more to ask, far more to contribute.

Quality During Transition

As the grim example of New York indicates, achieving community control will be a painful process, attended by assaults from
entrenched interests, time-consuming legal struggles, and costly
legislative battles against uphill odds. Even when a community
receives grudging official sanction, as the New York City demonstration districts had, it can expect that much of its energy will be
diverted from the business of building quality education to the
necessity of self-defense.

But, even under these circumstances, changes indicative of
quality education begin to appear. For example, on the embattled
Ocean Hill experimental district, *The Wall Street Journal* was

able to report the following developments during a period in which the district's worst disruptions and attacks occurred:

> The number of parents visiting schools and attending PTA meetings has increased as much as tenfold in the past two years. . . . Children's interest in school, as evidenced by attentiveness in class and work taken home, is said by teachers to have risen considerably in the past year. . . . School administrators say that discipline has improved and that suspension (one-third the rate of the previous year),* vandalism and thefts have declined.

In its six elementary schools, the district set up a parent-child reading program, which trains parents to help children, with the aid, one hour a week, of a paraprofessional trainer who comes to the home.

In 1968, five graduates from the one intermediate school in Harlem's I.S. 201 demonstration district were admitted to the elite Bronx High School of Science, compared to just one student from *all* other junior and intermediate schools in Harlem.

But, in some situations, dramatic educational innovations and spectacular improvements in performance are not possible in short order. First, the wreckage from years of neglect and decay must be cleared away. Some basic order must be restored to schools that were either lethargic custodial institutions or chaotic madhouses. Thus, as some schools begin to come under community control, the initial emphasis is on order and imparting basic skills.

In several community-controlled schools, the basic classroom strategy is to give children as much individually tailored instruction as possible, through the use of self-teaching or programmed materials and upgraded instruction. These are designed to allow youngsters to advance at their own pace and permits the teachers to devote attention to pupils who have trouble. Grade designations also have been eliminated. In one Ocean Hill–Brownsville school, a new individualized reading program was established, as

---

* The three districts developed more equitable suspension policies.

were two-nights-a-week Spanish courses for English-speaking parents and a similar course in English for those whose native tongue is Spanish. Two hundred and forty mothers were appointed as classroom aides, to take attendance, collect homework, help with discipline and, sometimes, even teach under the supervision of regular teachers.

In some community-controlled schools, individual parents serving as representatives to the governing board or as paraprofessional employees have become "towers of strength" and leaders of the school as effectively as the most charismatic principal. An Ocean Hill intermediate school is successfully using eighth-graders from a "marginal behavior" group as student-teachers to help other students in an individualized reading program.

Washington's community-controlled Morgan School obtained a $100,000 federal grant for a Follow-Through program for 200 five- to seven-year olds. It is staffed by seven teachers and fourteen community interns, who work in two teams, each with four classrooms. As described in *City* magazine:

> The children stay within each room for set periods, but there are many different things going on. On a visit recently, children were being drilled in numbers. They were sitting casually, free to move around, but every group had specific direction and purpose. Some children were cutting out pictures from scrap magazines. Another day they would take the pictures, paste up a little book, tell a story, write it down if they wished. Another group, around a brightly dressed African teacher, was throwing out colored cubes for 10, then 13, then 17. Another was rapidly holding up fingers for called-out numbers. The kids knew their stuff. They use no readers. Says John Cawthorne, who directs the program, "People read for information and enjoyment," and he tries to get kids to use books this way too. Later in the day, the children—who go to school all day—relaxed after lunch to the tones of African rhythms and Bach. Walls were decorated with numbers in sequence, bar graphs of children's heights, letters, and words.

The children are encouraged to observe and participate in the community. One expensive outlay to be made by the local board

—the kind of expenditure that the central board would never make—is the purchase of cameras so the pupils can take pictures of the community and discuss and write about the pictures.

In some schools, the educational "innovations" are indirect, mundane, and, yet, extremely significant. In the I.S. 201 demonstration district, for example, one of the unit administrator's proudest achievements is a health program, which has traced many learning deficiencies to heretofore undetected physical problems. It was found, for example, that an additional 30 per cent of students had hearing and vision defects than had been previously diagnosed. The district initiated a program of medical referral far more thorough than conventional school health programs, especially in that it follows through to make sure that each child receives treatment.

Similarly, in one school in Ocean Hill–Brownsville, there had been no testing for mental retardation, despite the fact that state law requires children so classified to be tested every two years. When, after the demonstration district was established, tests were given, several children previously classified as retarded were found to be well above the I.Q. range for the mentally retarded. Another school in the district doubled the number of youngsters (from 300 to 600) for whom the school was providing lunches, by removing the requirement that parents sign a statement of need.

The attitudes of teachers are ranked high in priorities of community-controlled schools. For example, David Spencer, the chairman of the governing board of the I.S. 201 demonstration district in New York City and a layman, gives new teacher-orientation lectures on the nature of the neighborhood. The district has also made special efforts in sensitivity training and in regular in-service training of teachers, through cooperating universities as well as with its own resources.

Yet, teaching approaches are not monolithic. If there is any trend, it may lie in the less structured approach of young and inexperienced though highly motivated teachers, who oppose plan books, lesson plans, and other traditional procedures, in contrast to more systematic (which does not necessarily imply irrelevant) approaches by more experienced staff.

Ethnically oriented studies in community-controlled school districts go beyond narrowly conceived racial appeals. For example, the schools in Ocean Hill–Brownsville offer Afro-American and Puerto Rican history and culture to an extent heretofore unavailable in the New York City schools, but Keith Baird, director of the African–Latin American studies project says, "We aren't concerned with putting one culture over another but with supplying the missing pieces of black culture." However, some Negro parents, according to one governing board member, "are concerned that when [they] go into a classroom there are pictures of Malcolm X, of Stokely Carmichael, of Eldridge Cleaver, etc.—not that they are opposed to these people but they are not sending their children to learn about these men." The district had Leslie Campbell, self-described black nationalist revolutionary, teaching Afro-American studies, but it also had Allan Kellock, a white teacher who has studied in Ghana and Egypt and was completing a doctorate in African history at the University of Wisconsin.

Thus, while some schools have introduced Swahili, they also have expanded the availability of European languages. Most students in the intermediate schools in the district are given an opportunity to study Spanish, and top students of English are permitted two years of French study. This may not strike parents of suburban or private secondary schools as particularly revolutionary, but, for the ghetto intermediate or junior high schools of New York City, it is.

In another subject area, critical observers who scoff at the use, in mathematics courses, of African counting games where seeds are transferred from one bowl to another should note, too, that Ocean Hill–Brownsville also has experimental individualized mathematics-instruction and mathematics learning machines. Some teachers in the I.S. 201 district have, on their own, sought out, conducted research on, and used programmed instructional materials.

And, yet, a distinction must be drawn between educational improvement and "innovation." The postwar path of American education is strewn with experiment after experiment that has failed to stem educational failure. Some of the highly publicized innovations have missed the point altogether, while others never had their full day in court. Although a school's proclivity for experimentation is still a come-on for many status-minded parents, others who are quite as concerned for their children's education have grown chary of shiny new approaches, preferring instead that their children have the benefit of better prepared teachers and a more sympathetic school climate. Thus, one black teacher in one of the New York City demonstration districts, in commenting on a new programmed-instruction system, said he was "sick and tired of black children being used as guinea pigs." A similar attitude is reflected among some parents and older teachers in the Ocean Hill–Brownsville district, who have complained that some highly motivated but inexperienced young teachers in the district have moved too far ahead of supervision in their free-wheeling innovation. But the trend in the district toward experimentation and innovation seems clear. Certainly, the curiosity about educational developments is strong; in the summer of 1969, teachers, paraprofessionals, and a governing board member from Ocean Hill–Brownsville spent two weeks in England studying the reforms of the British infant schools.

Resistance to New Definitions

Opposition to more humanistically oriented curriculums and to a more democratic and liberal school climate is sure to arise. The signs have already appeared (school board candidates in various parts of the country in 1968 and 1969 were able to win victories on the "law and order" slogan). The opposition is likely, if for no other reason than that of historical precedent. We are most familiar, of course, with the national reaction against the so-called progressive-education system, which, in fact, was a warped version of what the progressive-education philosophers really espoused but to which the label nevertheless stuck. So, too, in the first great educational reform in the country, in the mid-nineteenth century, divisions arose between advocates of rote recitations and so-called "soft-liners," who, as historian Michael Katz has noted, "would reform instruction to accord with the interests of pupils." Some soft-liners even advocated replacing corporal punishment with an emulation-of-good-behavior performance along with a reward system. Horace Mann, one of the strong advocates of motivating children by appealing to their interests, was attacked by the bureaucracy of the day, represented, most eminently, by the Boston schoolmasters. Nothing was more important to the schoolmasters, says Katz, than submission to authority. They maintained that, even in a democracy, authority was necessary: "He who would command even, must first learn to obey," and "immediate obedience to rightful authority must be inculcated and enforced upon children as the very germ of all good order in future society."

Ironically, inasmuch as Mann advocated a strong state board of education, normal schools, and statewide educational statistics, the entrenched schoolmasters opposed centralization. Their strength lay in resistance to outside influences. Lest parallels to the present on this score be drawn, it is necessary to note that the hallmark of their decentralization was a professional monopoly on school decision-making.

The current echoes may already be heard. Mortimer Smith, a leading advocate of "basic education," for example, described Jonathan Kozol's *Death at an Early Age* as "sentimentality . . . what may be described as the all-Negro-children-have-beautiful-souls approach to teaching the disadvantaged." Equally unsatisfactory, he continued, is "any teaching theory based on the current romanticism about the 'culture' of poverty which some sociologists find so stimulating. They urge us not to corrupt it with middle-class values."

Smith also condemns the "social theorizing" whereby linguists maintain that schools in cultural ghettos should introduce pupils to the standard speech necessary for academic, vocational, and social purposes without making them feel that their own dialect is inferior. "I reject the idea of linguistic equality," he has written, "and suggest that teachers in city schools owe it to their Negro pupils to demonstrate that one thing is better than another in language." Putting aside whether Smith has oversimplified the product of linguistic scholarship as being a theory of "linguistic equality," research by the Center of Applied Linguistics does conclude that the dialect and linguistic system of Negro children in Washington is, indeed, as fully developed as standard English.

Another, at least implicit, avenue of opposition arises from the direct equation of quality with resources. Thus, UFT head Albert Shanker declared:

> The major difference in educational achievement between the children of Scarsdale and the children of Harlem is not due, as some have suggested, to local control of schools but rather to the creative effects of wealth and poverty on the lives of children. . . . educational advantages claimed for local control are illusory—specifically, the prediction that local control leads to creative innovation. The thousands of small districts across the country use the same textbooks, materials, and curricula.

Shanker overlooks the role of education as a means to understanding of the self, and concentrates instead on the environmental handicaps traditionally invoked to account for the academic failure of ghetto children: "We do not yet know whether even the best education can completely overcome the effects of hunger, slum housing, disease, overcrowding, and broken-up families." His prescription lies in conventional compensatory and supposedly preventive measures—small classes, preschool education (beginning at age three or even earlier)—along with "better on-job internship training for teachers."

The desire for a more humanistic style will have to face generational problems in community-controlled districts as well as in conventional ones. At a meeting of one of New York City's demonstration districts, a father demanded to know why school authorities did not encourage more of the "whupping" that, as a boy, he had had, in home and school, for misbehavior. He was answered by a young black college student who explained that learning and growth today are not helped by holding children in awe and fear of authority-figures.

But the trend seems unmistakable and irresistible, and, as the psychotherapist Bernard Steinzor has noted, the increasing emphasis on self-knowledge and self-revelation

is at the heart of the Western tradition. An open-hearted person in an open society is a revolutionary aim, and it is yet to be accepted as a condition of public life. Intimacy, in an expanding society committed to democratic relations, requires that people make a real difference to one another. The combination of isolating indifference and the lack of respect expressed by submitting to or dominating other people result in the kind of suffering we are accustomed to define as mental and psychosomatic symptoms.

8

The Community-Control Concept

> We are still called upon to give aid to the
> beggar who finds himself in misery and agony
> on life's highway. But one day we must ask
> the question of whether an edifice which pro-
> duces beggars must now be restructured and
> refurnished. That's where we are now.—MAR-
> TIN LUTHER KING, JR.

The community-control concept as a means for urban school reform has now undergone its first test in the real world. The results, while inconclusive, are not negligible. The setbacks have
been more dramatic than the advances. But the potency of the
concept has been demonstrated: From the anguish of the New
York City demonstration school districts, affirmative consequences
have emerged that may prove to be stronger than the strife that
attended the projects; and the participatory movement has developed in a range of social classes and professions, the goal being
to make human institutions recover their human purpose. How
the community-control concept fares in its next great test will
depend on how well all parties have learned the lessons of the
first.

While it can hardly be considered a full-fledged movement,
efforts for community control are having their effect in various
parts of the country. Two state legislatures (New York and Michigan) have passed decentralization bills for New York City and De-

troit that delegate some degree of power to elected local district boards. Although plans for effective local control were defeated in both instances by the opposition of the teachers' union and professional groups, it is probably significant that some kind of citywide plan was adopted. During the early phase of implementation of the plans, both cities faced demands by minority and other community groups for expansion of the legislative mandate to achieve greater community control. These were, with minor exceptions, turned down, but one can anticipate continuing conflict over the appropriate division of power between the central and local districts.

In Massachusetts, a legislative committee, at this writing, is considering a bill that provides for a limited delegation of power to local districts in cities of over 150,000 population (Boston, Worcester, and Springfield) on petition for community school district status. The teachers' union in Boston has voiced serious objection to the plan. In California, a legislative committee initiated a feasibility study for decentralization of the Los Angeles school system under legislation approved in the 1969 session. A plan for citywide decentralization is projected as an output of the committee. In addition to these state actions, several large cities are considering proposals or are engaged in studies of decentralization. Most prominent are Washington, D.C., and Milwaukee. Model Cities proposals in a number of cities (Gary, Indiana; Dayton, Ohio; and Philadelphia) include plans for community control of schools in their demonstration areas. The Model Cities program has the potential of becoming an important vehicle for community control. Impetus for an increased community role is also manifest in expanding Head Start and Follow-Through programs throughout the country.

Mounting frustration with efforts to reform the urban school structure in many of the large cities has stimulated development of an alternative or parallel system of private schools based on the community-control concept. These schools, generally located in ghetto areas, are established apart from the public system but often rely on public funding, either from state day-care or federal Head Start or Follow-Through programs; several have also received foundation support. The East Harlem Block School in New York City and the Roxbury Community School, the New School for Children, and the Highland Park School—all in Boston —are among the better-known experiments in this category.

But the stirrings for community control of the public schools is not an isolated phenomenon. A palpable reaction to giantism in government, as contrasted with long-time theoretical discussion of decentralization in modern urban society, is under way. A dominant theme among political theorists of the postwar generation was the deploring of the inefficiencies and duplication of Balkanized political units in American government—overlapping jurisdictions that prevented concerted attacks on inadequate transportation, pollution, water supply, and other problems that spill over political boundaries. Despite their strong advocacy and efforts by some thoughtful political leaders and citizen groups to institute metropolitanism through annexation, consolidation, and other techniques, few were successful. The political scientist Edward Banfield, an exception to the prevailing academic view, reflected that the existence of hundreds of independent local governments "may not be as bad as it is made to sound." Perhaps there should be even more, he said. Citizen resistance to governmental consolidation a decade or two ago often was based on parochial and sometimes exclusionary grounds, and, to some extent, still is. But now, ironically, some of the support for larger units of urban government reflects illiberal motives. Larger units tend to dilute the newly active strength of blacks and other low-income minorities who are clustered together and whose power lies not in their numbers but in their potential for acting cohesively on particular issues and in governmental units where they predominate. (The issue of minority representation arose almost immediately, for example, in connection with the 1969 New York City school decentralization law, for the designated districts are so large that blacks and Puerto Ricans have complained that they would be outvoted by the white majority and, thus, would not gain representation on the newly constituted local school boards.)

Whereas small governmental units were once defended for exclusionary and other negative reasons, there are now affirmative motivations. They include a desire for readier access to agencies charged with meeting local needs. From access to participation is the next step, and it is a giant step. But, without smaller units, effective participation is very difficult. Alongside this growing pressure for greater access to local government, we shall note, later, various movements for more responsive government at higher levels, including the federal government.

The community-control concept differs from the more glamorous reforms of the postwar era (for example, compensatory education programs), we believe, in that it is both more fundamental and more comprehensive. It can be disguised or diluted—into administrative decentralization, for example, or dependent parental participation. But, in its unadulterated form, the concept cannot merely be folded into a prevailing system and eventually smothered or discarded.

Several factors account for this indivisibility. For one thing, community control alters basic power relationships and, thereby, prevailing assumptions. The new participants in the educational process may lack backgrounds in educational theory and practice, but this does not prevent them from driving relentlessly to the core of fundamental issues in school policy. In fact, their freedom from some of the ponderous baggage with which professionals are burdened enables them to point to the emperor's nakedness more readily than many career specialists in education or child development. This observation is meant neither as a starry-eyed view of the wisdom of the untutored poor nor as an indictment of professional insight. The point is only that the entry of altogether new participants is likely to open up quite interesting new questions and approaches. If the professional participants keep an open mind, their own skills and knowledge can interact productively with the contributions of the newcomers.

The concept also is resistant to absorption because it is not confined to curriculum, personnel, or any other single function. Any part of the system that affects the well-being of their children, parents and the community will consider fair game for review and, if necessary, change. Furthermore, the concept—ideally, at least—is open-ended. It is a *framework* for change more than it is change itself. The history of too many reforms (in other fields as well as in education) is that, while they are fresh replacements for prevailing orthodoxy, after a time they tend to harden into an orthodoxy of their own. Community control, to the extent that it follows democratic procedures, carries its own seeds of renewal. Its very reason for being, it must be remembered, is as a reaction to rigidities and unresponsiveness.

The resiliency of the concept has yet to be proved, of course. Its present phase is apparently indistinguishable from one through which other innovations have passed. That is, some school systems have bounced back from the challenge of implementing community control. But, while other school officials approach community control gingerly (fearing, at all costs, upheavals like Ocean Hill–Brownsville), there is genuine interest in closing the gulf between parents and community, on the one hand, and the professionals, on the other. Thus, some significant concessions have been made—for example, initiating administrative decentralization or granting parent groups a voice in the selection of administrative personnel (though the selection is limited to a pool still regulated by the profession). How durable and meaningful the concessions are depends on continued community surveillance. Withdrawal or dilution of concessions by the dominant system may, by rubbing discontents, actually serve to intensify demands for full community control. On the other hand, it is possible that real community control might be staved off indefinitely by extremely skillful school officials who combine limited concessions with the abandonment of some old habits of inflexibility and dogma and movement in the direction of change.

Evidence of the latter tendency is already appearing. "Parental participation" is becoming a watchword in many recent pilot projects and experiments that have nothing to do with governance of the system. For example, whereas systemwide reviews of curriculum once gave only lip service to the parental role, if any part at all, parents, in some situations, are now consulted at strategic decision-making points. Other evidence consists of the heightened interest in some improvements that are more likely to occur in a community-controlled system than in professionally monopolized systems. For example, many schools were already using parents and other nonprofessionals as aides before the community-control concept emerged as a major issue. But seldom were these aides viewed as anything but subprofessionals. Community-control proponents envision that the school system will be more hospitable to the use of such people, to the point of encouraging them to advance up a ladder of professional development. Thus, some school systems are beginning to make regular provision for teacher aides to be trained and promoted to higher levels of authority and responsibility, eventually to full professional status.

Emergence of the community-control concept has also increased awareness of the exclusionary effects on minority teachers of lock-step procedures for advancement to supervisory rank. Some programs have been set in motion, therefore, to accelerate the rise of talented minority professionals to higher positions. Such programs do not require waiver of merit or standards of competence. Rather, their crucial element is a *will* to overcome deficiency, to break out of ingrown, guildlike examination and certification mazes. Thus, a school system may provide special leaves and incentives for minority personnel to take courses and otherwise qualify for advancement. But, of course, such changes do not come easily, and organized educators still usually oppose moves they construe as the relaxation of formal requirements. (New promotion procedures and the adoption of merged lists in Michigan and New Jersey were challenged by the professional staff immediately.)

Affirmative response to cultural differences of minority students has resulted in greater reliance on a multi-ethnic approach. Both in the Northern cities with large Puerto Rican populations and in the Southwest, where large numbers of Mexican-Americans live, many schools are shifting from a policy that penalized the use of Spanish by pupils whose native language it is. Some schools are even capitalizing on the situation by teaching subjects in Spanish in the early grades while pupils also take English-language instruction. Other instances of growing official sensitivity to the cultural identity of nonwhite pupils include, of course, the proliferation of black-studies programs. Six states (California, Connecticut, Illinois, Kentucky, New Jersey, and Pennsylvania) have, since 1964, either passed laws or strongly urged that the role of America's minorities be accurately depicted in school instruction. It has been reported, that, in thirty-two of the fifty states, material on the Negro's role in history is either available or in preparation for public school use. Many ethnic studies programs are, as yet, poorly formed, but what is important is that some school systems are reorienting themselves with respect to minority culture and values. Instead of consciously or implicitly suppressing them, they are beginning to accord them recognition, although tangible resources and programmatic support for them do not always follow in like measure. The community-control movement is not solely responsible for this new attitude, but we have no doubt that it has accelerated it. Demands for responsiveness to urban-community needs have made it clear that, in the last third of the twentieth century, depressed minority groups will actively oppose the use of the public schools as an instrument for downgrading their racial identity. Educators are beginning to abandon the analogy with European immigrant children of the late nineteenth and early twentieth centuries, whom the schools sought to assimilate to the dominant culture by penalizing and suppressing differences.

Nowhere is evidence of these responses plainer than in New York City. There the report of the Bundy Panel won a secure place in the history of urban education by formulating the underlying principles of community participation in setting basic school policy. There, later and independently, three demonstration districts gave the community-control concept its first major trial. In contrast to its reaction to previous reform efforts, the school system has not rebounded to the *status quo*. The sharp challenge of the decentralization plan and the three demonstration districts has given renewed confidence to parents throughout the city. They are more assertive in holding professionals accountable for performance in the schools. Moreover, the school system has found it impossible (or impolitic) to revert completely to old policies and practices. The millennium is far away, but a tightly closed system has been opened up. School officials appear readier to respond to questions and to seriously consider, if not, in many cases, to meet legitimate requests from parents and community groups. The rule book, even on such matters as the red tape involved in taking students out of their classrooms to learn from field visits and other community resources, has been relaxed. Where school officials continue to be rigid, parents have found other agencies more willing to act in their behalf in educational impasses. For example, in the fall of 1969, the City Council responded to parental pressure to expedite textbook orders; heretofore, the Council would have declined to intervene on the grounds that the matter was the province of the professional educators. In short, despite a weak decentralization bill at the state level, community control has planted a firm foot in the door of the New York City schools, and demands for a stronger parental role will increase.

Concurrently, other factors are working to end the isolation of the New York school system. Stimulated in part by the community-control dispute, demands arose for liberalized admission policies to the City University system. Demonstrations and other pressures led to announcement of a plan for an open-admissions policy in the City University, similar to the policy long obtaining in several state university systems, whereby any graduate of a public high school is admitted to some unit of the university. By implication, the debate on open admissions pointed to failure in the schools: If the mass of New York's black and Puerto Rican students could not meet the City University's normal entrance requirements, the schools had not prepared the students adequately. In subsequent years, the performance of lower-ranked high school students who enter the City University may serve as another source of demand for accountability by the public school system. If its products do not perform well, the schools will be confronted with a large part of the blame, and the higher-education system may exert pressure for improved performance by the schools, even while special remedial programs at the college level will also be necessary.

The Lesson of New York

Those who seek to carry community control forward would do well to learn from the political errors of the New York City effort. In a sense, the lesson of these errors is a microcosm of the reappraisal forced on American society after the first heavy wave of resistance—commonly called the white backlash—to the pace of social reform in general, and racial change in particular. Perhaps the most sobering lesson—particularly for those who view the matter primarily as a moral issue—is that awareness of past injustices inflicted on minorities is not sufficient to overcome the fears of a present majority that feels threatened by the uncertainties of rapid change. The sense of threat is strongest among the white near-poor and lower-middle class heads of families, who are still not secure in their jobs or in their credit-purchased possessions and feel abused by an increasing burden of taxation. A thrust for substantive reform, such as community control, must include some appeal to this group on the grounds of self- or common-interest. Furthermore, the middle class generally must be assured, to the extent possible, that there is an educational basis to community control, that while the achievement of reform is a political process, the goal is not power for power's sake alone. On this count, the fact that none of the three demonstration districts in New York was in a predominantly white neighborhood was a major shortcoming.

Another defect lay in the inflexibility of some of the leadership at various levels of the community-control effort. They failed to coordinate their efforts and to establish priorities, both crucial failings given their limited resources and energies. They did not grasp the necessity of working with one part of the prevailing system—the legislature, in particular—while at the same time contending with another. They forgot or discounted and, in either case, failed to capitalize on, the fact that the legislature had made it possible for a formal decentralization plan to be put forward in the first place. While the organized teachers and supervisors lobbied effectively in the state legislature, the community-control proponents did not mount a campaign in the legislative arena.

Granted that the community-control forces lacked resources anywhere near those of the UFT and CSA. Nonetheless, they could have maintained some effective presence. They did not, one is forced to conclude, in part because they regarded the legislature—along with the board of education, the educational bureaucracy, and the UFT—as part of an oppressive system. Indeed, when rhetoric ran high in the embattled ghetto community, leaders may have feared that attempts to bargain with any part of the system might endanger their status in their own communities. Their mood of isolation and embattlement increased during the struggle. Instead of intensifying efforts to win over public opinion, community leaders tended more and more to picture an establishment arrayed against the community-control concept and the demonstration districts.

These attitudes were, of course, grounded in justifiable suspicions based on long and bitter experience. But, in New York, they were self-defeating from the first round of the decentralization—community-control struggle. The Bundy Plan itself was viewed with almost as much suspicion by community-control advocates as it was by the majority of teachers and supervisors. Disbelief that a progressive, equitable blueprint could emanate from the establishment tended to dilute any wholehearted support the plan may have had from the strongest ghetto community leaders. In retrospect, some have acknowledged that the plan was a strong framework for effective community voice in educational decision-making. Moreover, they concede that its safeguards, which at the time they criticized as compromises, were necessary to assure teachers and others that the school system could be reorganized through a transitional period, during and after which the rights of all would be protected. There is no certainty that strong community approval would have offset opposition to the plan, but a strong coalition would certainly have been some defense. Concerted ghetto support was the minimum necessity for such a coalition, and it did not develop. Opponents gained the initiative almost before the plan was published and never lost it.

The demonstration districts themselves illustrated the danger that small factions and local political leaders may seek to exploit the desire for community control to their own advantage. For these districts spent an inordinate amount of time on dealing with "the system," and too little on broadening community support in order to assure involvement beyond a limited activist community group. While the dual nature of reform as being both political and educational must be recognized, it is clear that, when personal political motives override the interest of reform, educational goals can be destroyed. A shift in leadership without substantive change is an illusion of reform.

Such retrospective appraisals run the risk of oversimplifying the situation. No one should forget the accelerating alienation in New York's ghetto community in the mid-1960's, the years of double-dealing at the hands of educational authorities, and the assault that strong decentralization plans and the demonstration districts suffered. The advocates of community control could well feel besieged. The point is simply that not all those outside the walls were brandishing weapons and some, indeed, might well have brought relief to the besieged, if only it could have been accepted. Other potential elements in the unrealized coalition were not faultless. New York is, after all, a center—some say *the* center—of political and intellectual liberalism. Liberals, in general, did not embrace community control as a cause. Some, indeed, sympathized with its opponents, and perhaps, most simply, took no strong stand on the issue. The motives of white liberals in New York were, as noted earlier, complicated by loyalties to the union tradition and by their commitment to the ideal of school integration, despite its failure in New York even before the first strong decentralization–community control effort began. Also, the events on the New York school scene coincided with an increasingly open chilliness between the black community and white liberals. Some of the latter may have sensed intellectually that the community-control issue transcended the ghetto community, yet they opted out either because they felt they would be unwelcome or because they could not participate in a movement directed by blacks, including, by their lights, some unsophisticated ghetto residents. The latter view is, in effect, quite close to the illiberal attitude that low-income blacks lack the capability of making decisions in such complex areas as education.

Finally, there is the lesson of polarization versus accommodation. Urban affairs are, more than ever, the interplay of multiple interest groups—cooperating, contending, or compromising. In New York, those with a vested interest in the educational *status quo* showed few signs of adjusting to the pressure for necessary change, whether such impetus came from official bodies, such as the legislature and the mayor's panel on decentralization, or from the ghetto community, in the demonstration districts. This rigidity, in turn, was matched by an unwillingness by some activists to negotiate in a situation they viewed as encirclement. Experience in some of the most effective antipoverty programs has shown that, after a period of stubborn defensiveness by entrenched powers and of strident demands by the powerless, many urban issues can be negotiated, with a net gain for the poor. Daniel Bell has observed that the poverty programs are a compromise between community demands for a "final say" and the resistance of politicians against being displaced or bypassed: ". . . the more the community is drawn to the process of consultation, participation, and advocacy of its own interests, the closer it may come to demanding that it be the final authority."

In the New York City schools, the community was not drawn into "consultation, participation, and advocacy of its own interests" and its first moves to take the initiative were thrown back. The essential element of trust that is necessary in the process of urban interest groups' accommodating to one another had been weakening in the New York schools for many years. For some, the time had already come when, as John Dewey said in an earlier era, "No . . . compromise with a decaying system is possible." The fierce resistance to the initial signs of effective community participation was the final shattering of trust—not, as many have said, the opening chapter in a divisive struggle. Thereafter, only the most extraordinary mediating efforts could have averted the rupture that ensued, and no such efforts came forth.

Toward "Maximum Feasible Participation"

As we noted at the outset, the community-control concept emerged from two main tributaries—the civil rights movement and the increasingly evident failure of public education to serve the children of urban ghettos. It has since coincided with and, in some cases, affected streams of activity in other fields.

By the late 1960's, the antipoverty-program concept of "maximum feasible participation of the poor" was being widely discredited, especially inside the federal government. Significantly, its counterpart on the public school scene developed not as a mandate in a government program but as an organic grass-roots phenomenon. With the limited exception of Head Start, neither the federal poverty program nor direct aid to education ever posited a participatory role for parents in the public schools. The dramatic emergence of that concept may have kept "maximum feasible participation" alive, if not in full vigor, in its darkest hours. The concept has survived in government programs such as Model Cities legislation, and it is spreading on a broad front of private and public activities.

One important development is that greater, if not maximum, participation is no longer applied to ghetto and minority groups alone. The notion that citizens in a free society can and ought to seek redress from administrative tyranny and institutional obsolescence has been embedded in the American tradition, but has atrophied through disuse. Now, it is coming into lively play, cutting across class lines and extending to many fields besides public education. For example, the relentless sweep of the bulldozer, once deplored mainly by a few critics who were labeled incurable romantics, now encounters strong resistance from middle- and upper-class sections as well as low-income areas victimized by urban renewal. The resistance runs deeper than the traditional reflex against interference with one's backyard. People are looking beyond the bulldozers to the basic policies and the agencies responsible for them. Protections against arbitrary decisions by distant planning bodies and highway departments are being legislated and adjudicated. Similarly, policies and practices affecting the general environment are undergoing increasing scrutiny and challenge by the public. Air, water, and noise pollution are now lively issues. While industry and government have not been transformed overnight into defenders of ecological sanity, they are plainly aware that they are likely to incur resentment and resistance if they ignore environmental factors. The new and highly controversial Master Plan for New York, issued by the City Planning Commission late in 1969, makes constant reference to the need for community participation in the development of neighborhood policies.

Challenges of a new character are also confronting American industry. They are rooted not in the traditional battlegrounds of labor policy or monopolistic practice but in the quality of products and services. It is too early to tell whether industry faces a consumer revolution, but "consumerism" has emerged from distant corners and the province of small groups and has begun to stimulate action at the federal and local levels.

Despite the emergence of extreme radical movements, the main currents of student and citizen activism do not seem to us to betoken a deep desire for revolution. Aroused middle-class students, concerned adults, and angry minorities are not seeking the overturn of the American political system, but they are confronting the institutions of the system with demands for substantial reform. Moreover, the challengers are, by no means, confined to those outside particular social and economic institutions. Within professions and institutions, a spirit of active disquiet is growing, a decided unwillingness to accept tradition and the *status quo*.

The most conspicuous case, of course, is the universities. The re-examination began with student demands on a range of issues, from government-related university programs, to curricular relevance, to student participation in educational policy. The ferment spread and grew in intensity on campuses of all sizes and types, including sectarian colleges. Today, the student movement has its extremist elements, but it is characterized mainly by a kind of responsible activism whose watchword is restructuring rather than revolution. University faculty, administrations, and trustees are beginning to pay heed, and wholesale re-examinations are under way in many institutions. Governance is, by no means, the only aspect of university life being questioned, but it is certainly one of the central issues, and unprecedented changes have already begun, including student representation on decision-making bodies (even boards of trustees). The issue has spread, as we shall discuss later, to secondary schools as well (public and private), on a range of issues from curriculum to rules about student dress and publications.

Not only in education but also in such professions as medicine, architecture, and the law, both young practitioners and students are seeking a greater voice in policy determination in professional schools and in the firms, hospitals, and other institutions where they work. They have also begun to debate fundamental goals and practices—for example, asking the medical profession to assume greater responsibility for the ill health of the poor, the architectural profession to exercise a stronger voice in the social consequences of design and construction, and the legal profession to take a more affirmative and active part in civil rights, the rights of the indigent, and attacks on other social problems, instead of leaving such matters to legislators and professional reformers alone. Ralph Nader, a young lawyer who achieved national prominence as a one-man crusader for auto safety, has assembled a group of young lawyers into a Center for the Study of Responsive Law. In the summer of 1969, the Center drew 100 students, who investigated federal pesticide regulation, the Food and Drug Administration, government air- and water-control agencies, the Civil Aeronautics Board, and the Interstate Commerce Commission. Nader has probed such issues as radiation health hazards, coal-mine safety, and the dangers of artificial food ingredients—and, moreover, has stimulated governmental action on them. His work, and less well known efforts by others around the country, constitute a "people's advocate" system, aimed at inducing responsive action by government bureaucracies. Not the least of these are legal agencies supported by the Office of Economic Opportunity. Going well beyond conventional legal representation of the poor in individual consumer and tenancy cases, they have sought to break fundamental ground in such areas as welfare rights, the rights of public-housing tenants, and political representation. A measure of their effectiveness was a strong, though unsuccessful, attempt by Senator George Murphy and other conservatives to weaken their advocacy-muscle by placing the legal services programs under the direction of state governors.

In religious institutions, clergy and laymen have demanded a re-examination of practices in the light of professed ideals. In some dioceses, lay boards have been established for parochial schools, and nuns and lay teachers have organized to play a role in policy-making and to promote educational change. Gerald Grant, a Harvard teaching fellow who served with the New York Archdiocese's Committee on Catholic Education, reports that two ghetto parochial schools are among "the most thoroughgoing and successful community school experiments that I have seen anywhere." And examples abound in other areas. A movement in the library field, whose services are used by a notoriously small proportion of the population, seeks to serve the disadvantaged better—to reach the "unreached." Impatient with inflexible public library systems, some librarians have gone so far as to bring their collections outside the library building—depositing small paperback collections in bars, barber shops, and beauty parlors, combining story hours with babysitting arrangements, and setting up a sidewalk service with brochures, bookmarks, and a small collection on a book rack to encourage new people to register and take out books. But these efforts are frustrated, by a hostile or indifferent climate in the regular library building. One severe critic of the existing order, a Los Angeles librarian named Don Roberts, declared at a conference: "Shouldn't we think about . . . adaptation of the [New York school] decentralization plan for public libraries, giving over the branches to community control?"

One of the few large professions in which such ferment is not yet evident is teaching. One reason is that teachers have been a principal target in community control efforts. Teacher self-esteem is an issue, because many have the honest conviction that they have given their best efforts and should be protected from the disapproval of parents who feel these efforts have failed. They feel threatened emotionally as well as professionally and financially. Nor should it be overlooked that community-control movement followed close on the heels of the first real surge of successful teacher unionism. The largest teachers' union, and, indeed, the largest local of any American labor union, the United Federation of Teachers in New York, has been the recognized bargaining agent with the board of education for only a decade. The history of teacher unionism, dating back to World War I, had been marked by innumerable problems and inhibitions. In its earlier phase, the most persistent fear was loss of professional dignity. In the 1930's and 1940's, ideological disputes, centering on a left-wing faction, impeded the union's development. When major differences were finally resolved, the movement accelerated dramatically. It followed generally liberal lines, and one of its cherished claims was that it had supported the cause of the American Negro. Thus, union conflict with ghetto communities was a bitter and ironic development for many union members. It soured the sweet taste of success in organizing and in winning at the bargaining table not only many economic gains but the beginning (notably in New York City) of a voice in educational policy. Also, it posed a potential threat to the unity of an organization that had struggled for decades to overcome disunity.

Yet, ghetto parents could not share these sympathies. For all of unionism's common interest with the civil rights movement, too many unions continued discriminatory practices. As for the teachers' union's new gains, parents who observed the continuing educational failure of their children could well regard these gains as having done nothing for them or even as having come at their children's expense. The union, in their eyes, had assumed a place of distrust alongside such other elements of the educational power structure as boards of education.

Whatever the reason, there is little evidence of the teachers' union and organized school administrators engaging in searching examinations of their roles in this new society of swift changes and of growing awareness among those at the bottom of the ladder. As a result, black teachers in some cities have pulled out of the regular teachers' union—500 in Philadelphia, for example. The American Teachers Association, a national Negro organization, merged, in 1966, with the National Education Association, which had begun chipping away, in the 1960's, at segregation practices among local affiliates. But, paradoxically, the first militant black teachers' organization, the Afro-American Teachers Association of New York, was organized a year later, followed, in the next two years, by similar groups in Newark and Detroit. The issues among the new black teacher groups vary from ethnic identity (there is a precedent in the existence since the 1930's of Jewish and Catholic teacher associations in New York City), to active encouragement for Negroes to disaffiliate either from the NEA or from AFT local unions, to activity on particular issues.

The Newark group, for example, sought to eliminate written teachers' examinations, because most of the prospective teachers struck down by the test were Negroes.

These defections by black teachers are not, as some have charged, antiunion *per se*. They are, rather, directed against union policies that the disaffected teachers believe to be inimical to the interests of minority communities. Tension between teachers' unions and the community threaten to offset the gains of the union, and, thus, a New Caucus, led by a black union officer from Detroit, urged the 1968 national convention of the American Federation of Teachers to join the community in its drive for control as a means of uniting white and black unionists.

"Concerned teachers" groups, whites and blacks, supporting community control, have formed in some cities, but the membership is small. The few schools that have come under community control have attracted some young new teachers with the heightened social awareness that is becoming more evident in other professions. In Ocean Hill–Brownsville, a veteran teacher was quoted by *The Wall Street Journal* as saying,

> When these new teachers arrived you could feel the difference. There was much less tendency to prejudge the children. The new teachers looked upon them as a group of kids who had to be taught, not as ghetto children who probably couldn't learn much. When I taught in this school a few years ago, teachers in the lounge talked mostly about their husbands, furniture, house—that sort of thing. Now most of the talk here is about how to teach these kids.

Contrary to the prevailing pattern in most ghetto schools, some new teachers have moved into neighborhoods where they teach, and many often visit the homes of their pupils.

We believe it is by no means inevitable that teachers will continue to lag behind other professions in awareness of the need for professional change. After World War II, when union membership actually declined for a short time, the union was urging members to band together to curb the abuses of principals and superintendents. The shock of ghetto demands and militancy has drawn

organized teachers and the school system's management closer together. Right now, not many teachers, to say nothing of their
organizations, would share the belief of the Washington Teachers
Union that "teacher rights may well be more closely protected in
a community controlled school than by the downtown board."
But a continuing state of siege is untenable, and the identity of
interests between teachers and parents may well be re-established
through the community-control efforts. As teachers work more
closely with parent groups, their shared interests should become
more evident.

Even at administrative levels, some educators sense an identity
of interest with the community in the struggle to break rigid
patterns. For example, school principals with the energy, the will,
and the talent to lead creatively and flexibly can function better
when they are free to make a range of important on-the-scene
decisions without constant reference to central authorities, and
when they are free to work closely with the community.

The profession's principal institutions, too, are likely to be affected by the community-control concept. The well-known gap
between teacher training and classroom realities would become
even more pronounced if the schools were to come under community control and teacher colleges were to stay fixed in their
ways. A report of the American Association of Colleges for
Teacher Education traced failures and inadequacies in the education of disadvantaged youth to defects in the education of teachers as a whole. The judgment was accompanied by proposals for
"radical reform" of institutions that prepare future teachers. It
called for training complexes run jointly by colleges and universities, school systems, and the local community. Called *Teachers
for the Real World*, the report emphasized combining the prospective teacher's theoretical training with actual class problems.

The Student as Partner

Early theoretical constructs of community control of the public
schools gave little or no attention to the role of the student as a

partner in the process. The improvement of student performance was, of course, the ultimate objective of the concept as a whole, but it was not considered that he might himself have a part in determining the structure and program of the school. But, now, student assertiveness, beginning on university campuses, has reached into the high schools. Student activism broke out dramatically in 1968 in widespread disturbances in urban and suburban systems. According to a survey by the National Association of Secondary School Principals, two out of three principals of city and suburban high schools reported that they were experiencing some form of active student protest, as did 56 per cent of all *junior* high schools. The early protests were largely racial in character, and many still are; more recently, they have also included anti-Vietnam war themes. But underlying a good deal of the ferment is student rebellion against the schools' authoritarian mode. Students are asking for more freedom and more respect from school authorities. They are also seeking some voice on such matters as rules of personal behavior and extracurricular activities. But curriculum and personnel have also been the subject of student petitions in some instances. Aside from the small minority of students who are bent on disrupting schools for ideological, even revolutionary, motives, the majority of disaffected students are seeking constructive participation and a degree of freedom that has been absent—the more conspicuously so because the schools espouse a rhetoric of freedom. Although many schools have responded by imposing stricter discipline, students have won, in a very short time, considerable recognition by both educational and other agencies. The Supreme Court ruled that public officials may not interfere with students' rights to express political opinions in a nondisruptive way during school hours. The American Civil Liberties Union has issued a student "bill of rights" covering such matters as the right of appeal and formal hearing procedures on severe disciplinary action, such as suspension or expulsion, student editors' freedom, and expression of opinion. A member of the board of education in New York issued a policy statement supporting the general position of the ACLU on students' rights; the CSA, however, strongly disagreed with the board and the ACLU stand.

Some schools have organized, in a variety of ways, the student surge for more freedom and responsibility. These include a more meaningful role for student government, establishment of student courts and student-faculty advisory and human relations councils, less parietal behavior with respect to dress and other externals, relaxed discipline, the redesign of curriculums to permit more independent student work, freedom for selected students to take some work at universities, greater opportunities for student-to-student tutoring, occasional use of students as discussion leaders and lecturers, and even mechanisms whereby students can "evaluate" teachers by proposing improvements in methods of presentation.*

All these relate, of course, to the general question of relevance and identity. Many students were disaffected with their schools long before black power or community control surfaced. The evidence was visible in the millions of dollars' worth of broken windows and other vandalism to school buildings, in dropout rates, and in what Edgar Z. Friedenberg and others have called *ressentiment*, a chief product of the schools defined as "rationalized, covert, free-floating ill temper . . . a lasting repression of certain emotions . . . [leading] to the constant tendency to indulge in . . . revenge, hatred, malice, envy, the impulse to detract and spite."

Most authorities believe that student unrest will continue un-

---

* The experience of a regional high school in a none-too-affluent section of New Hampshire suggests that high school students are capable of using the freedom of independent work and of relaxed discipline. The Timberlane Regional High School permits its students large blocks of unscheduled time in which they are free to sit in the cafeteria, wander the halls—and do independent work or study. After a year in which students largely squandered their new freedom, they grew bored with wasting time and began to filter into the library, audiovisual rooms, laboratories, and curriculum centers, even into classes to which they were not assigned. Students are given unusually free access to teachers. They may also use the computer and complex audiovisual hardware without supervision. The school's dropout rate, 1 per cent, is sharply below that of the statewide 6 per cent.

less schools become less impersonal and more relevant institutions. One way of achieving this, of course, is to engage students directly in the affairs of the institution. Although student attitudes will sometimes be unreasonable and unrealistic, their active concern should, for the most part (since they are *de facto* agents in the education process) be welcomed for its potentially powerful contribution. It was put simply by an Oswego, New York, high school coed who defined student involvement as

> . . . the idea of getting students involved to learn about education, to come out with answers to questions just like I used to ask myself: why do I go back and forth to school every day, carry my books, get on a bus, walk through the front door, and then come back and do the same thing every day? Why do I do this so many, many days out of the year? This is an attitude that is common among students. They do want to be involved. They want to take into their own hands and their own hearts what they feel are significant issues and meanings of education—their education. Remember, this is our business too.

Reform or Rupture?

As first posed in New York City and as it is reappearing elsewhere, the community-control issue illustrates a classic political problem for established power—is the prevailing order capable of responding to pressures for social change, or does it weaken the entire social structure by failure to reform itself? In a free society, response entails an enlargement of freedom and opportunity and in certain circumstances—the civil rights and community-control issues are clear examples—a shift of some power to the formerly powerless.

The established order may be strong enough to survive one or several missed opportunities for reform. But a quick succession of such failures, especially in today's volatile and uncertain climate, carries an increasingly high price in terms of tension and polarization. We must assume that even so strong a structure as American society cannot indefinitely sustain shock and disruption without fracturing or sacrificing freedoms in return for a firm authority that forbids and represses pressures for social redress. Despite the consequences of the events in New York City, the community-control issue has, so far, been more of a stimulus to reform than a device for social rupture.

Whether the public schools will continue to be a main arena of social ferment is, by no means, certain. Despite the deep discontent of minority and other groups with public education, other issues rank higher in their priorities—employment and housing, for example. But, even if these issues take precedence, public education will not recede into insignificance—not as long as the schools are essential to social mobility and consume so many billions of dollars of the nation's treasure.

Finally, the community-control issue has posed for public education the fundamental issues addressed by Dewey, Counts, and others more than a generation ago. Will the public schools serve as the agent of a new social order, or will they continue to be reflections of whatever social order prevails? The philosophers of education framed the question in terms of the aims and content of the curriculum. The community-control movement has added a new dimension by calling for reform of the governing structure of public education. Yet, the issue of who governs is hardly separable from the question of the institution's fundamental purposes and means. We believe the community-control movement, born of human deprivation, can direct the public school to a more humanistic purpose and performance. Public education is not solely responsible for propelling American society toward a chasm of tragic divisiveness. But neither has it done very much to prevent the nation from rupturing into two societies. The great test before the public schools for the decade ahead is whether they will play an effective role in developing humane citizens or whether they will merely become more efficient machines for processing technically proficient but socially deficient men and women. Many crosscurrents have swept this question into full view. The community-control issue has underscored it in deeply graven lines.

Source Bibliography

All sources of quotations cited in the text are included in this bibliography.

Books

Aiken, Wilford Merton. *The Story of the Eight Year Study*. New York: Harper, 1942.

Berube, Maurice R., and Gittell, Marilyn, eds. *Confrontation at Ocean Hill–Brownsville*. New York: Praeger, 1969.

Cillie, Francois, S. *Centralization or Decentralization?: A Study in Educational Adaptation*. New York: Teachers College, Columbia University, 1940.

Clark, Kenneth B. *Dark Ghetto: Dilemmas of Social Power*. New York: Harper & Row, 1965.

Conant, James B. *Slums and Suburbs: A Commentary on Schools in Metropolitan Areas*. New York: McGraw-Hill, 1961.

Counts, George S. *Education and American Civilization*. New York: Teachers College, Columbia University, 1952.

Counts, George S. *The Social Foundations of Education*. New York: Charles Scribner & Sons, 1934.

Cox Commission Report. *Fact Finding Commission on Columbia Disturbances Appointed to Investigate the Disturbances at Columbia University in April and May 1968*. New York: Vintage, 1968.

Cremin, Lawrence A. *The Transformation of the School: Progressivism in American Education, 1876–1957*. New York: Knopf, 1961.

Dahl, Robert A. *Who Governs?: Democracy and Power in an American City*. New Haven, Conn.: Yale University Press, 1961.

Dennison, George. *The Lives of Children: The Story of the First Street School*. New York: Random House, 1969.

Dewey, John. *Experience and Education*. New York: Collier Books, 1963.

Fantini, Mario. *Designing Education for Tomorrow's Cities.* New York: Holt, Rinehart & Winston, 1970.

Fantini, Mario, and Weinstein, Gerald. *Making Urban Schools Work.* New York: Holt, Rinehart & Winston, 1968.

Fantini, Mario, and Weinstein, Gerald. *The Disadvantaged: Challenge to Education.* New York: Harper & Row, 1968.

Friedman, Milton. *Capitalism and Freedom.* Chicago: University of Chicago Press, 1962.

Fromm, Erich. *The Revolution of Hope: Toward a Humanized Technology.* New York: Harper & Row, 1968.

Gittell, Marilyn. *Participants and Participation: A Study of School Policy in New York City.* New York: Praeger, 1967.

Gittell, Marilyn, ed. *Educating an Urban Population.* Beverly Hills, Calif.: Sage Publications, 1967.

Gittell, Marilyn, and Hevesi, Alan G., eds. *The Politics of Urban Education.* New York: Praeger, 1969.

Gittell, Marilyn, and Hollander, T. Edward. *Six Urban School Districts: A Comparative Study of Institutional Response.* New York: Praeger, 1968.

Glazer, Nathan, and Moynihan, Daniel. *Beyond the Melting Pot.* Cambridge, Mass.: MIT Press, 1963.

Greeley, Andrew M., and Rossi, Peter H. *Education of Catholic Americans.* Chicago: Aldine, 1966.

Grier, William, and Cobbs, Price M. *Black Rage.* New York: Basic Books, 1968.

Harvard Educational Review. *Equal Educational Opportunity.* Cambridge, Mass.: Harvard University Press, 1969.

Hentoff, Nat. *Our Children Are Dying.* New York: Viking Press, 1966.

Hicks, Alvin W. *A Plan to Accelerate the Process of Adaptation in a New York City School Community.* New York: Teachers College, Columbia University, 1942.

Holt, John C. *How Children Fail.* New York: Pitman, 1964.

Katz, Michael B. *The Irony of Early School Reform: Educational Innovation in Mid-Nineteenth Century Massachusetts.* Cambridge, Mass.: Harvard University Press, 1968.

Keniston, Kenneth. *The Uncommitted: Alienated Youth in American Society.* New York: Delta Books, 1965.

Koerner, James D. *Who Controls American Education?* Boston: Beacon Press, 1968.

Kohl, Herbert R. *Thirty-six Children.* New York: New American Library, 1967.

Kozol, Jonathan. *Death at an Early Age: The Destruction of the Hearts and Minds of Negro Children in the Boston Public Schools.* Boston: Houghton Mifflin, 1967.

Leonard, George B. *Education and Ecstasy.* New York: Delacorte Press, 1968.

Levin, Henry M., ed. *Community Control of Schools.* Washington, D.C.: The Brookings Institution, 1970.

Marris, Peter, and Reim, Martin. *Dilemmas of Social Reform: Poverty and Community Action in the United States.* New York: Atherton Press, 1969.

Mayer, Martin. *The Teachers Strike: New York, 1968.* New York: Harper & Row, 1969.

Mayor's Advisory Panel on Decentralization of the New York City Schools. *Reconnection for Learning: A Community School System for New York City.* New York: Praeger, 1969.

Moynihan, Daniel P. *Maximum Feasible Misunderstanding: Community Action in the War on Poverty.* New York: Free Press, 1969.

Nordstrom, C., et al. *Society's Children: A Study of Ressentiment in the Secondary School.* New York: Random House, 1967.

Olsen, Edward G., ed. *The Modern Community School.* New York: Appleton-Century-Crofts, 1953.

Passow, A. Harry. *Towards Creating a Model Urban School System: A Study of the Washington, D.C., Public Schools.* New York: Teachers College, Columbia University, 1967.

Pois, Joseph. *The School Board Crisis: A Chicago Case Study.* Chicago: Educational Methods, 1964.

Rogers, David. *110 Livingston Street: Politics and Bureaucracy in the New York City School System.* New York: Random House, 1969.

Rosenthal, Alan, ed. *Governing Education: A Reader on Politics, Power and Public School Policy.* New York: Doubleday, 1969.

Rosenthal, Robert, and Jacobson, Leonore. *Pygmalion in the Classroom: Teacher Expectation and Pupil Intellectual Development.* New York: Holt, Rinehart & Winston, 1968.

Rossner, Robert. *The Year Without an Autumn.* New York: R. W. Baron, 1969.

Sayre, Wallace S., and Kaufman, Herbert. *Governing New York City: Politics in the Metropolis.* New York: Russell Sage Foundation, 1960.

Schrag, Peter. *Village School Downtown.* Boston: Beacon Press, 1967.

Sexton, Patricia Cayo. *Education and Income: Inequalities of Opportunity in Our Public Schools.* New York: Viking Press, 1961.

Silberman, Charles E. *Crisis in Black and White.* New York: Random House, 1964.

Simon, Herbert A. *Administrative Behavior,* 2d ed. New York: Macmillan, 1961.

Toffler, Alvin, ed. *The Schoolhouse in the City.* New York: Praeger, 1968.

United States. The Task Force on Urban Education. Wilson C. Riles, chrmn. *The Urban Education Task Force Report: Final Report of the Task Force on Urban Education to the Department of Health, Education, and Welfare, Office of Education.* New York: Praeger, forthcoming. *Congressional Record,* 91st Cong., 2d sess., 1970, CXVI, H8–15, E21–77.

Valentine, Charles A. *Culture and Poverty: Critique and Counter-Proposals.* Chicago: University of Chicago Press, 1968.

Wagner, Patricia, ed. *The Struggle for Power in the Public Schools.* Proceedings of the Sixth Annual Conference of the National Committee for Support of the Public Schools. Washington, D.C., 1968.

Weinberg, Meyer. *Desegregation Research: An Appraisal.* Bloomington, Indiana: Phi Delta Kappa, 1968.

Weinstein, Gerald, and Fantini, Mario, eds. *Toward Humanistic Education: A Curriculum of Affect* (A Ford Foundation Report). New York: Praeger, 1970.

Magazine, Journal, and Newspaper Articles

Banfield, Edward. "The Politics of Metropolitan Areas." *Midwest Journal of Political Science,* I (May, 1957), 77–90.

Baratz, Joan C. "The Language of the Ghetto Child." *Urban Crisis Monitor,* January 24, 1969, p. 18.

Baratz, Stephen S., and Baratz, Joan C. "Early Childhood Intervention: The Social Science Base of Institutional Racism." *Harvard Educational Review,* XL (Februray, 1970), 29–50.

Bell, Daniel. "Quo Warranto?: Notes on the Governance of Universities in the 1970's." *The Public Interest,* XIX (Spring, 1970), 53–68.

Bell, Daniel, and Held, Virginia. "The Community Revolution." *The Public Interest,* XVI (Summer, 1969), 142–77.

Berube, Maurice. "Problems of Teacher Unionism." *New Politics,* IV (Fall, 1965), 37–42.

Bigart, Homer. "N.Y.U. Experiment Fails to Upgrade a School in the Slum." *The New York Times,* November 26, 1967, p. 1.

Bindman, Aaron M. "Pre-College Preparation of Negro College Students." *Journal of Negro Education,* XXXV (Fall, 1966), 313–321.

Buder, Leonard. "Fifth of City Pupils Found Two Years Behind in Reading." *The New York Times,* December 23, 1966, p. 1.

"Bundy Proposals Backed by Howe." *The New York Times,* February 22, 1968, p. 28.

Clark, Kenneth. "Alternative Public School Systems." *Harvard Educational Review,* XXXVIII (Winter, 1968), 100–113.

Clark, Kenneth. "Higher Education for Negroes: Challenges and Prospects." *Journal of Negro Education,* XXXVI (Summer, 1967), 196–204.

Cleaveland, Frederic N. "Administrative Decentralization in the U.3.

Bureau of Reclamation." *Public Administration Review,* XIII (Winter, 1953), 17.

Cohen, David. "Policy for the Public Schools: Compensation and Integration." *Harvard Educational Review,* XXXVIII (Winter, 1968), 114–137.

Covello, Leonard. "Neighborhood Growth Through the Schools." *Progressive Education,* XV (February, 1938), 126–140.

Epstein, Jason. "The Politics of School Decentralization." *The New York Review of Books,* X (June 6, 1968), 26–31.

Epstein, Jason. "The Real McCoy." *The New York Review of Books,* XII (March 13, 1969), 31–40.

Fantini, Mario. "Alternatives for Urban School Reform." *Harvard Educational Review,* XXXVIII (Winter, 1968), 160–172.

Fantini, Mario. "Participation, Decentralization, Community Control, and Quality Education." *The Record,* LXXI (September, 1969), 93–107.

Fantini, Mario, and Gittell, Marilyn. "The Ocean Hill–Brownsville Experiment." *Phi Delta Kappan,* L (April, 1969), 442–445.

Featherstone, Joseph. "Community Control of Our Schools." *New Republic,* CLVIII (January 13, 1968), 16–19.

Featherstone, Richard, and Hill, Frederick. "School Decentralization: The Bundy Report—What It Really Means." *American School and University,* XLI (October, 1968), 40–48.

Ferretti, Fred. "Who's to Blame in the School Strike?" *New York Magazine,* I (November 18, 1968), 22–35.

Goodwin, Richard. "Reflections: Sources of the Public Unhappiness." *The New Yorker,* XLIV (January 4, 1969), 38–58.

Greer, Colin. "Public Schools: The Myth of the Melting Pot." *Saturday Review,* November 15, 1969, pp. 84–86.

Hare, Nathan. "The Legacy of Paternalism." *Saturday Review,* LII (July 20, 1968), 44, 57–58.

Hey, Robert. "School Tightrope," *Christian Science Monitor,* LX (November 6, 1968).

Isaacs, Charles S. "A Junior High School 271 Teacher Tells It like He Sees It." *The New York Times Magazine,* November 24, 1968, pp. 1, 52.

Jacoby, Susan L. "In Search of a Black Identity." *Saturday Review,* LI (April 20, 1968), 60–62.

Jencks, Christopher. "Private Schools for Black Children." *The New York Times Magazine,* November 3, 1968, pp. 129–133 ff.

Jencks, Christopher. "A Reappraisal of the Most Controversial Educational Document of Our Times." *The New York Times Magazine,* August 10, 1969, pp. 12–13, 34 ff.

Jencks, Christopher, and Riesman, David. "The American Negro College." *Harvard Educational Review,* XXXVII (Spring, 1967), 3–60.

Katz, Irwin. "Academic Motivation and Equal Educational Opportunity." *Harvard Educational Review,* XXXVIII (Winter, 1968), 57–65.

Kozol, Jonathan. "Hall of Darkness: In the Ghetto School." *Harvard Educational Review,* XXXVII (Summer, 1967), 379–408.

Kozol, Jonathan. "Where Ghetto Schools Fail." *Atlantic Monthly,* CCXX (October, 1967), 107–110.

"Local-Control Advocates in U.F.T. Criticize Accord." *The New York Times,* November 19, 1968, p. 38.

Mayer, Martin. "What's Wrong with Our Big-City Schools?" *Saturday Evening Post,* CCXL (September 9, 1967), 21–22, 66 ff.

Myers, Phyllis. "School: Morgan Tentative Revolution." *City Magazine,* November–December 1968, pp. 6–14.

Reeves, Richard. "City's School Strike Cuts Deeply." *The New York Times,* November 10, 1968, p. 9.

Roberts, Wallace. "The Battle for Urban Schools." *Saturday Review,* LI (November 16, 1968), 97–102.

Salisbury, Robert H. "Schools and Politics in the Big City." *Harvard Educational Review,* XXXVII (Winter, 1967), 408–424.

Schrag, Peter. "Boston: Education's Last Hurrah." *Saturday Review,* XLIX (May 21, 1966), 56–76.

Schrag, Peter. "The New Black Myths." *Harper's Magazine,* CCXXXVIII (May, 1969), 37–42.

Schrag, Peter. "Pittsburgh: The Virtues of Candor." *Saturday Review,* XLIX (November 19, 1966), 82–103 ff.

Schumach, Murray. "Allen Negotiates for End to Strike." *The New York Times,* November 3, 1968, p. 28.

Shanker, Albert. "Critique of the Bundy Report." *United Action,* I (November, 1967), 1–6.

Sizer, Theodore. "Report Analysis; Review of Reconnection for Learning." *Harvard Educational Review,* XXXVIII (Winter, 1968), 176–184.

Stretch, Bonnie. "The Bundy Report." *Saturday Review,* L (December 16, 1967), 70.

Sullivan, Neil. "Compensation and Integration: The Berkeley Experience." *Harvard Educational Review,* XXXVIII (Winter, 1968), 148–154.

"The Changing Library." *Newsweek,* LXXV (February 16, 1970), 33.

The Education Commission of the States, Annual Meeting Issue. "Teacher Militancy: Strikes, Sanctions and State Government." *Compact,* II (August, 1968), pp. 1–64.

"The High School Rebels." *New York Post,* March 2–7, 1970.

Wasserman, Miriam. "The I.S. 201 Story." *Urban Review,* II (June, 1969), 3–15.

Weiss, Robert, and Rein, Martin. "The Evaluation of Broad Aim Programs: A Cautionary Case and a Moral." *The Annals*, CCCLXXXV (September, 1969), 133–142.

Wright, Stephen. "The Promise of Equality." *Saturday Review*, LI (July 20, 1968), 45, 46, 58.

Government Publications

Great Britain. Central Advisory Council for Education (England). *Children and Their Primary Schools*. London: Her Majesty's Stationary Office, 1967.

New York City. Board of Education. Bureau of Educational Program Research and Statistics. *Special Census of School Population, October 31, 1966, Summary of Table*. Publication No. 286, February, 1967.

New York City. Board of Education. Office of Academic High Schools. *Report on Graduates (AH550)*. January, June, 1967.

New York City. Board of Education. Office of Education Information Services and Public Relations. *Facts and Figures 1966–1967*. 1967.

New York City. The City University Research Foundation with Subcontract to Teachers College, Columbia University. Marilyn Gittell, T. Edward Hollander, and William S. Vincent. *Investigation of Fiscally Independent and Dependent City School Districts*. Cooperative Research Project No. 3237, 1967.

New York State. State Education Commission. Advisory Committee on Human Relations and Community Tensions. *Desegregating the Public Schools of New York City*. Albany, May 12, 1964. A Report for the Board of Education of the City of New York.

United States. Bureau of the Census. *Statistical Abstract of the United States: 1969*, 90th edition. Washington, D.C.: Government Printing Office, 1969.

United States. Commission on Civil Rights. *Racial Isolation in the Public Schools*, 2 vols. Washington, D.C.: Government Printing Office, 1967.

United States. Department of Health, Education, and Welfare. Office of Education. *Digest of Educational Statistics*. Washington, D.C.: Government Printing Office, 1968.

United States. Department of Health, Education, and Welfare. Office of Education. James Coleman *et al. Equality of Educational Opportunity*. Washington, D.C.: Government Printing Office, 1966.

United States. Department of Health, Education, and Welfare. Office of Education. *Local School Boards—Organization and Practices*. Washington, D.C.: Government Printing Office, 1962.

United States. National Advisory Commission on Civil Disorders. *Report*. Washington, D.C.: Government Printing Office, 1968.

Miscellaneous

Allen, James E., Jr. (Commissioner of Education). "Racial Imbalance in the Schools." A memorandum to all chief local school administrators and presidents of boards of education, June 14, 1963.

ASPIRA *et al.* "Preserving the Right to an Education for All Children: Recommendation to the New York City Board of Education Regarding School Suspensions." April 5, 1967. (Developed by ASPIRA, Inc., Citizens' Committee for Children of New York, Inc., Congress of Racial Equality, Inc.—Brooklyn Chapter, EQUAL, HARYOU—Act., Mobilization for Youth, Inc., New York Civil Liberties Union, Public Education Association, Puerto Rican Association for Community Affairs, Inc., United Neighborhood Houses of New York, Inc., United Parents Association, Urban League of Greater New York.)

Berube, Maurice R. "Educational Achievement and Community Control." *Community Issues,* vol. 1, no. 1. New York: Queens College, November, 1968.

Board of Education of the City of New York. Resolution dated December 23, 1954.

Board of Education of the City of New York. Statement adopted in public session, April 19, 1967.

Brager, George. "Influencing Institutional Change through a Demonstration Project: The Case of the Schools." Paper prepared for the Columbia University and Mobilization for Youth Training Institute Program, April, 1964. Mimeographed.

Council of Supervisory Associations of the Public Schools of New York City. "Response to Lindsay-Bundy Proposals; Interim Report No. 2." New York, January, 1968.

Covello, Leonard. "The Sound Background of the Italo-American School." Thesis abstract, New York University, 1944.

Dodson, Dan W. "How Realistic Is the Goal of Desegregated Education in the North?" Lecture delivered at the New School for Social Research, New York City, February 20, 1964.

"Final Report by the Advisory and Evaluation Committee on Decentralization to the Board of Education of the City of New York: An Evaluation Study of the Process of School Decentralization in New York City." July, 1968.

Five State Organizing Committee for Community Control to the Office of Metropolitan Educational Subsystems. "Position Paper." January 25, 1968.

Gittell, Marilyn. "The Community School in the Nation." *Community Issues,* vol. 2, no. 1. New York: Queens College, February, 1970.

Goodrick, M. George. "Integration vs. Decentralization." In Donald C. Rowat, ed. *Basic Issues in Public Administration.* New York: Macmillan, 1961.

Griffiths, Daniel E., *et al.* "Teacher Mobility in New York City: A Study of Recruitment, Selection, Appointment, and Promotion of Teachers in New York City Public Schools." New York, New York University, School of Education, Center for School Services and Off-Campus Courses, 1968.

Howe, Harold, II. Testimony before a New York State legislative committee on school decentralization. New York, February, 1968.

Lindsay, John V. "The Mayor and the Classroom." Address delivered to the Public Education Association, New York City, on April 27, 1967.

McCoy, Rhody. "The Year of the Dragon." Paper presented at the Conference on Educational Subsystems, Harvard University Graduate School of Education, January 24–26, 1969.

Morgan Community School Board Proposal to the Ford Foundation for the Period September, 1968, Through June, 1971. Morgan Community School Board, 1773 California Street, N.W., Washington, D.C. 20009.

National Education Association. "Fiscal Dependence and Independence of Local School Systems." Washington, D.C., August, 1966.

New York City Board of Higher Education Master Plan 1968.

New York Civil Liberties Union. "The Burden of Blame: A Report on the Ocean Hill–Brownsville School Controversy." New York City, October 9, 1968.

Public Education Association. "Community Control." New York City, January, 1969. Mimeographed.

Spier, Adele. "The Two Bridges Model School District." *Community Issues,* vol. 1, no. 3. New York: Queens College, February, 1969.

Washington, D.C., Teachers' Union. "Position Paper on Community Control." Teachers' Union Executive Board, Washington, D.C., September 24, 1968.

Wielk, Carol A. "The Ocean Hill–Brownsville School Project." *Community Issues,* vol. 1, no. 2. New York: Queens College, February, 1969.

Index

DATE DUE

MAY 2 1990			
GAYLORD			PRINTED IN U.S.A.